ALBERTO SALAZAR'S GUIDE TO ROAD RACING

ALBERTO SALAZAR'S

GUIDE TO

ROAD RACING

CHAMPIONSHIP ADVICE FOR

FASTER TIMES FROM 5K TO MARATHON

ALBERTO SALAZAR

with **Richard A. Lovett**

RAGGED MOUNTAIN PRESS / McGRAW-HILL

Camden, Maine • New York • Chicago • San Francisco • Lisbon • London • Madrid • Mexico City •
Milan • New Delhi • San Juan • Seoul • Singapore • Sydney • Toronto

The **McGraw-Hill** Companies

1234567890DOCDOC01098765432

Copyright © 2003 Ragged Mountain Press
All rights reserved. The name "Ragged Mountain Press" and the Ragged Mountain Press and McGraw-Hill logos are trademarks of The McGraw-Hill Companies. Printed in the United States of America.

Library of Congress Cataloging-in-Publication Data
Salazar, Alberto, 1958–
   [Guide to road racing]
   Alberto Salazar's guide to road racing : championship advice for faster times from 5K to marathon / Alberto Salazar with Richard A. Lovett.
      p.   cm.
   Includes index.
   ISBN 0-07-138308-5
   1. Running. 2. Marathon running. I. Title: Guide to road racing. II. Lovett, Richard A. III. Title.
   GV1062 .S25 2002
   796.42—dc21   2002008625

Questions regarding the content of this book should be addressed to
Ragged Mountain Press
P.O. Box 220
Camden, ME 04843
www.raggedmountainpress.com

Questions regarding the ordering of this book should be addressed to
The McGraw-Hill Companies
Customer Service Department
P.O. Box 547
Blacklick, OH 43004
Retail customers: 1-800-262-4729
Bookstores: 1-800-722-4726

Illustrations by Chris Dowling unless otherwise credited
Photographs by Steve Dipaolo unless otherwise credited

To Don Benedetti, Bill Squires, and Bill Dellinger for coaching, inspiration, and planting the seeds of this book.

—Alberto Salazar

To the Cook Hall Track Club, the Linda Decker running group, and a lifetime of other racing buddies who've enlivened many seasons on the roads.

—Rick Lovett

CONTENTS

ACKNOWLEDGMENTS

No BOOK ARISES in a vacuum, nor does a successful racing career. I've been collecting running lore since I was a child herding my friends into "Ready, Set, Go!" dashes down the block. But I'm particularly grateful to the coaches who so willingly shared their knowledge, thereby inspiring me to continue my own quest for learning ever-better training methods. In high school, this wisdom came from Don Benedetti and Bill Squires; in college, my mentor was Bill Dellinger. I'd also like to thank Nike for its years of generous backing, not only in the form of financial sponsorship, but moral support as well.

For technical assistance in many areas of writing this book, thanks are due to many people, most notably to Kelly Scott, physician and runner, for helping to maximize medical accuracy. Thanks also to David Costill (former director of the Human Performance Laboratory at Ball State University), his successor Scott Trappe, Tim Noakes of the University of Cape Town Medical School, and to all the other scientists who assisted with this book through their research and willingness to share their knowledge with a couple of runners. Similarly, my gratitude goes to Wyatt Brown for his advice on orthotics, to Ted Forcum and Brad Donahoe for sports medicine wisdom, to Erin Russell for advice on the finer points of stretching and weight lifting, to Faulder Colby for concrete insights into sports psychology, to Lilli Shoen for checking the numbers, and to Paula Harkin, Linda Decker, David Harding, Karen Meier, the Red Lizards, the Oregon Road Runners Club, the members of the Portland NikeTown Running Club, Jack Wallace, and the numerous other runners whose stories, shared with Rick or myself, found their way into this book. I also want to thank Vera Jagendorf and the other photographers and illustrators whose work appears in this book. Thanks for helping us look good!

Finally, I am indebted to Rick Lovett not only for the nuts and bolts of writing this book, but also for much of the background research, particularly for chapter 16 on masters running. I retired from racing before I turned 40, but Rick has found that as a masters runner, he consistently places higher in his age group than he ever did in his 20s and 30s. The book also benefits from his experience as a travel writer and his interest in a diverse array of adventure races to offer suggestions for spicing up the longtime runner's career. In addition, as a freelance writer with wide-ranging interests, he has a scientific background in nutrition, weight control, sports medicine, and the effects of age on athletic performance. This book draws heavily on the hundreds of articles he's written on these and related subjects, the numerous scientific conferences he's attended as a reporter, and the latest news releases (and magazine assignments) coming his way, even as we were putting the finishing touches on the manuscript.

INTRODUCTION

COMPETITIVE RUNNING IS one of North America's most popular sports. Unlike many other outdoor activities, it takes almost no specialized equipment—just a good pair of shoes, some comfortable clothing, and a few dollars for a race entry fee. You don't even have to join a team or find a league: most racers set their own goals and pursue them entirely on their own. Best yet, nobody is going to care whether you're fast or slow, tall or short, thick or thin.

Each year, millions of people await starting horns in communities ranging from Anchorage to Amarillo, Ottawa to Orlando. Some have been racing for years; others are first-timers, drawn to the thousands of 5-kilometer, 8-kilometer, or 5-mile fun runs that celebrate the Western world's continuing health boom. Once they've tried it, many of these people become hooked on racing. There is a collective adrenaline, an almost palpable sense of expectancy and challenge, that pervades even the smallest, most low-key races. Even those who never thought of themselves as athletes can be caught up by it—discovering to their amazement that they can do more than they'd ever imagined possible, whether it's running faster than expected or simply covering a long distance.

Once you've tasted your first racing success, the next question often is: *How can I do even better?* That's often followed by: *How good could I be?* The ideal way to answer such questions is by working with a coach, but most people have no opportunity to do that. That's where this book comes in. It's designed to serve as a substitute coach. It will teach you how to run farther, faster, and with greater competitive zeal, at distances ranging from 5 kilometers (3.1 miles) to the marathon (26.2 miles).

Coaching is one of my favorite jobs. These Oregon Project runners are tuning up for the national championships. (Fredrick D. Joe/*The Oregonian*)

This book assumes that you are already a runner, logging at least 20 miles per week. But it doesn't matter whether you're already a racer or instead a fitness runner thinking about testing yourself in competition for the first time. Similarly, it doesn't matter how fast you're currently running, so long as you're running, not walking; the strategies in this book will work equally well whether you do 12-minute miles, 8-minute miles, or faster. Only the speediest people (faster than, say, 5:30 per mile for men or 6:30 per mile for women, at distances of 3 miles or longer) might not benefit from this book. They have the potential to be among the top runners in their states, if not the nation, and need individual coaching.

Such individuals are a very limited group. The rest of you can hope to move up substantially without individual assistance. How substantially is a more difficult question, because it depends on the amount of training and experience you already have. I discuss this in more depth in chapter 5, on speed training, but most beginning racers (those who've run only one or two races and have done no prior speed training) can probably hope to speed up by a minute a mile, possibly more. That's unlikely to move you into the ranks of the elite, but it can help you reduce a 50:00 time in a 10-kilometer (6.2-mile) race to 44:00—enough to shift you from the middle of the pack to the front 20 or 25 percent. People who've already done substantial training won't improve so dramatically, but may still have room for significant advances. I've coached high school runners who've knocked two minutes (40 seconds per mile) off of their 5-kilometer times in a single season.

To help you reach these goals, this book is divided into four parts. Part 1 deals with training for distances between 5 and 30 kilometers (3.1 to 18.6 miles). Rather than presenting endless training tables, it will teach you principles that you can use to design your own training program—although there will be plenty of examples for racers of all abilities. One of this section's basic philosophies is that the best way to train is by understanding *why* your training works. That way, you'll be more confident in the result. You can also fine-tune your program to meet your own needs—and (better yet) you don't have to memorize lists of numbers or tote this book with you to the start of each training session.

Another guiding philosophy of this section is that it's preferable to set modest, achievable goals than to aim so high that you're always getting hurt or skipping workouts because of lack of time or energy. Long ago, I came to the conclusion that it's better to sneak up on your goals in easy stages than to disappoint yourself by always trying for too much and falling short. That's particularly important for recreational racers. Presumably you're racing because it's fun, fulfilling, and healthy. What's the point, if being too ambitious in the initial stages robs you of the fun?

At the same time, this book will have you using training principles employed by world-class runners. I retired from competition in 1994, but I have remained in contact with many of the world's top runners and exercise researchers, partly as a coach and partly from representing Nike's running department at world-class races. Most recently, I have been coaching the Oregon Project, a Nike-sponsored endeavor to bring world-class distance running back to the United States. Twenty years ago, there was an entire cadre of Americans who could compete at the international level. Now, the rest of the world has sped up and Americans have slowed down. As of mid-2002, only one U.S. marathoner runs at the world-class level—and he is a Moroccan immigrant whose citizenship was granted when he was already at the peak of his form.

The Oregon Project uses an arsenal of high-tech methods not available to the average runner. My racers live in an "altitude house" where the atmosphere mimics an elevation of 7,000 feet—similar to the conditions that helped build a generation of world-beating Kenyans. They have their progress monitored via frequent blood tests, plus detailed examinations of their cardiac rhythms. But these tools only give the extra edge needed for the big wins. The core of the program is training, based on principles that can be applied equally well by recreational racers.

These principles may not be revolutionary, but cumulatively, they contain a lot of elite-level information, covering topics that range from when and what to eat after a race to the best ways to design interval programs or to race through hills. Much of this has yet to filter down to the average runner, and many recreational racers are still receiving—and passing on—outdated advice. I can't promise that this book will make you two minutes faster on a 10-kilometer race than would another coaching program—but it might.

The degree to which you'll use this advice will vary. Racing is *my* career, not yours, and your training and racing program has to fit your own goals not only for running but also for other aspects of your life. For some people, that might mean doing no more than 20 miles a week, minimal speed work, and no races longer than 5K or 10K. Others may be seeking to find out just how good they can become at these and longer distances. There's no right or wrong goal. The purpose of this book is simply to help you get the most you can from whatever level of training you choose to pursue.

Part of your training is taking care of yourself off the running paths, as well as on them. That means learning what to eat for optimal performance, keeping limber, supplementing your running with strength training, and recognizing and dealing with incipient injuries. Part 2 of this book addresses all of these topics, as well as the psychological aspects of running, which range from how to keep motivated for those days you'd really rather not train (everyone has them) to avoiding self-destructive mind-sets that can ruin your performance before you take a single step.

Once you've picked a race distance and trained for it, it's time for the race. Part 3 of this book guides you through the race, stage by stage, beginning the night before and continuing with breakfast, warm-up, and such challenges as how to get your best performance in the face of hills or headwinds. If you've never raced before, this section will help you face the starting line with confidence; if you're an old hand at racing, it will still present many tips overlooked by most of your peers.

Part 4 carries you to advanced challenges, such as marathons and longer distances, and tells how to add diversity to your racing with trail runs, relay races, and other events—some rather exotic. In keeping with my belief that racing is a sport for people of all ages, this section also discusses how to adjust your training as you age, so that your career can span 20, 30, 40, or even 50 years.

FROM THE 100-YARD DASH TO THE ULTRAMARATHON

One of my early racing memories stems from sixth grade, when I participated in a track meet in my childhood home of Manchester, Connecticut. I was entered in three events—the 60-yard dash, the long jump, and the 100-yard dash—and had already won my age group for the first two when I lined up for the start of the 100. I was supremely confident of a third victory. *I'm going to win this for sure*, I thought, *because it's the longest.*

As it turned out, I got caught looking over my shoulder at the finish (a major no-no) and had to settle for second place. But what I remember most strongly was the confidence I felt at the start. Even at age 12, I knew that distance was my forte, and that longer meant better.

Eventually that knowledge would lead me to several years as one of the world's top-ranked road racers. I would set a world record in the marathon at 2:08:13 (a mark that stood for nearly two decades as the fastest ever posted by an American), make two appearances on the U.S. Olympic team, win the Boston Marathon, and score three consecutive victories in the New York City Marathon. But like any beginner, I knew nothing about the sport before I started running seriously.

When an activity you love generates positive feedback, you tend to do more of it, always seeking ways to get better. The difference between world-class competitors and other racers isn't that we're more dedicated or more willing to put in the training. Recreational racers can be very dedicated. The difference is that elite runners receive years of positive reinforcement that encourages us to delve ever more deeply in search of those iotas of speed and endurance that spell the difference between a good performance and the best your body's capable of giving. It's that positive feedback loop that ultimately allows a few of us to make running into our careers.

For me, this process began in high school, where as a freshman I was the best on the cross-country team and league champion in the 2-mile. After winning several state championships, I went to college at the University of Oregon, which has long boasted one of the nation's finest track programs. As a junior I set a 5-mile world record (22:07) in a New Year's Eve road race sponsored by *Runner's World* magazine. The same year, I qualified for the 1980 Olympics in the 10,000-meter, but was unable to compete due to a U.S. boycott of that year's games. Instead, I entered the 1980 New York City Marathon.

I created an unintended stir simply by filling out the entry form for the race. That form asked me to predict my finishing time—a statistic used by the race organizers to determine your seeding in the pack. In consultation with my coach I wrote down 2:10—exactly what he'd spent the last several months training me to run.

When I got to New York, I found that runners' predicted finishing times had been made available to the press. Having made the Olympic team and previously set a world record, I wasn't exactly an unknown, but my best performances were at much shorter distances. Also, at age 22 I was young for a marathoner. I was branded as cocky because of the time I predicted for myself, and I'm sure that many people were quietly rooting for me to embarrass myself.

Happily, I not only beat my predicted time (I finished in 2:09:41), but I also won the race. That silenced the critics. The next year, I came back to New York and broke the world record by 21 seconds, running 2:08:13. In 1982 I won again at New York, and that same year survived a marathoner's worst nightmare—a sprint finish—against Minnesotan Dick Beardsley to win the Boston Marathon by 1.5 seconds—at the time, the closest Boston Marathon finish in history.

Those were the glory years. In 1984, I qualified for the marathon in the Los Angeles Olympics, where I was favored to win. But I'd exhausted myself by training too hard, and it was hot—never my strong suit. I finished poorly, in fifteenth place.

The next few years were even more disappointing. I was in a downward spiral of declining performance during which I exhausted myself even more by trying to gut my way through it with ever-harder training. I eventually learned that my problem was asthma, but not before that condition and my efforts to power through it had made substantial inroads into my lung function. Today, I have only 60 percent of the lung function I had in my prime—an impossible deficit to overcome as a marathoner.

But length was still my forte. Some races are so long that lung capacity isn't the most important factor. One of these is the Comrades Marathon in South Africa, a 54-mile, 15,000-runner race conducted ever since the end of World War I. At that distance, you can't run fast enough to get particularly out of breath, even with diminished lung function. Rather, such races are tests of how long you can sustain a more modest pace.

That ultramarathon was my farewell to world-class racing. In 1994, I won it—the first American ever to do so—in 5 hours, 38 minutes, about 8 minutes shy of the course record. I still run 30 miles a week, but mostly, I coach. In addition to my work with the Oregon Project, I've trained top athletes such as Mary Slaney (four-time Olympian and multiple world-record setter at distances ranging from 1,000 meters to 10K) and Marc Davis (one-time American record holder at the 2-mile), as well as devoting attention to younger runners. I've also been having fun coaching cross-country and track at a local high school.

High school coaching, in fact, may have done more than anything else to prepare me for writing this book. Not only does it make me more familiar with the problems of people who've taken up running relatively recently in life, but it's also been an experiment in applying the training principles of world-class runners to more ordinary athletes. This book uses the same approach.

This book is also informed by my continued reading of the racing literature and by friendships with numerous world-class runners who, over the years, have freely shared their experiences. Rick Lovett, with whom I've written the book, brings his own experience, plus a background much closer to the average reader's. He tells me that he's never won a race with more than 10 entrants—and never expects to. But he is a serious recreational racer who has completed 11 marathons and scores of shorter races.

Unlike me, Rick didn't take up running until he was in his mid-20s, and even then, he was initially interested in it only as a way to condition himself for mountaineering and backpacking. Then he ran his first race—and was startled to finish in the top quarter of the pack. Over the next few years, he moved up from that beginning to run lifetime personal records of 29:30 for the 5-mile, 1:31:29 for the half-marathon, and 3:02 for the marathon—all of which put him solidly in the top 10 percent of the pack. After a decade-long hiatus when he pursued other sports (most notably bicycling, about which he's written two books), he returned to running to find that in his mid-40s, he's about 30 seconds per mile slower than he once was, but can beat most of his age-group peers. He now competes in local races, frequently winning age-group awards.

From the moment we met, Rick and I discovered that we think remarkably alike, partly because we share a common joy in a sport that has given much to each of us. Throughout this book, I've drawn on his viewpoint to complement my own. You'll also find occasional sidebar advice from him.

PART 1

PREPARING TO RACE

THE FIRST STEP in training is to pick the distance you want to race. Important as that is, however, it is the topic on which I can give you the least advice—merely the obvious suggestion that you want to start with short distances and move up only when you've gained some racing experience. Other than that, pick any distance that sounds like fun or a challenge. World-class runners tend to specialize, but there's no reason for you not to be a generalist. Racing a variety of distances keeps you from going stale and gives you fresh challenges whenever you want them.

It's best to keep your goals modest, proceeding by incremental steps rather than attempting one huge leap that may net little but disappointment. That doesn't mean that you can't aim high—merely that you shouldn't try to achieve your aim all at once.

To help you get the most from your training, this section will cover three basic topics: weekly mileage for base training (chapter 3), improving your running form (chapter 4), and speed training (chapter 5). But first, chapters 1 and 2 will lay some groundwork and explain the theory behind your training. You can skip that background if you want, but the better you understand the why's of a training regime, the better you'll be at fine-tuning a schedule to suit your individual needs.

ON THE ROAD TO RACING

I N T H E O R Y, the only distinction between a racer and a fitness runner is an entry form. If you're already running 4 or 5 miles a day, you could easily hop into next weekend's 5K (3.1-mile) road race and jog around the course as if it were a training run. Many people do exactly this—and have great fun doing it. There is absolutely no reason why you shouldn't do the same if you want to.

But this book is about a more challenging form of racing: the type in which you set a goal that will take some preparation to achieve. Part of that preparation is the training program discussed in upcoming chapters. But the planning begins before that, as you choose your goals, buy a few pieces of equipment, and make the mental transition to *racer.* There aren't many of these preliminaries, and they're not burdensome, but it pays to think about them before you start training.

WHY RACE?

It is customary for discussions of racing to offer a slate of reasons why you might want to take up the sport. But the very fact you're looking at a book about racing demonstrates that if the bug hasn't already bitten you, it's definitely hovering nearby. You don't need me trying to tell you why. If you'd like help in articulating your reasons—or simply want to hear from a kindred spirit—pick up a copy of *Running and Being* by cardiologist-philosopher George Sheehan. Written in 1978, it's still the best discussion ever penned on the allure of racing as play, sport, and personal fulfillment. I'll only add that for me, racing was both livelihood and lifestyle, something I'd probably have done even if I'd been only modestly successful.

Your goals are relevant, of course, to how you'll use this book. There are two basic categories of racers; which you fall into will dictate which portions of this book will be most valuable to you. Some runners are drawn to racing simply for the challenge of going the distance—whether it's 5K, a marathon, or something in between. For this type of racing, you simply have to log enough training mileage, do a few long runs, and learn the basics of pacing yourself to go the distance. It also helps to know how to handle hills, headwinds, and other course conditions.

> **Racing speed is a combination of talent, quantity of training, quality of training, and running form. All but the first can be improved by training.**

The other type of racing involves running against the clock. The moment you say "I want to do the race in less than . . . ," you've put yourself in this category, regardless of how slow your intended time might be. A variant on this is racing to beat specific people, whether they be age-group competitors or friendly rivals from home, the workplace, or a running club. The best way to beat them, however, is by running as fast as you can, so other than at the elite level, where race strategy comes into play, there's not much difference between racing the clock and racing your rivals.

Racing for time means training not only to go the distance (obviously important), but doing some *speed training* at a pace faster than you will be racing. A surprising

RUNNING THE DISTANCES

Road races can be any distance, and a few are very odd lengths indeed. But the vast majority fit one of the following 12 conventional categories. (To convert kilometers to miles, multiply by 0.621. To convert miles to kilometers, multiply by 1.61.)

- 5 kilometers (5K) = about 3.1 miles
- 8 kilometers (8K) = about 50 yards short of 5 miles
- 5 miles = about 8.05 kilometers
- 10 kilometers (10K) = about 6.2 miles (6.21, to carry it to a third digit)
- 12 kilometers (12K) = about 7.4 miles
- 15 kilometers (15K) = about 9.3 miles
- 10 miles = about 16.1 kilometers
- 20 kilometers (20K) = about 12.4 miles
- half-marathon = about 13.1 miles, or 21.1 kilometers
- 25 kilometers (25K) = about 15.5 miles
- 30 kilometers (30K) = about 18.6 miles
- marathon = about 26.2 miles, or 42.2 kilometers

number of racers don't understand this need; they think that if their goal is to break 8 minutes per mile in a 5K (about 24:52), all they have to do is run enough miles in training, without much concern about pace. But unless 8-minute miles are your normal training speed, you can't train this way and expect to magically make that goal on race day. Your body simply won't be prepared to run at the faster pace.

COACHING WHAT NATURE GAVE YOU

Racing speed is a combination of at least four factors: talent, quantity of training, quality of training, and running mechanics. Coaching—including this book—can address any of these except the first.

Talent, of course, is your native speed. Just as some people are gifted singers and others have voices like gravel in a cement truck, you are endowed with abilities that set the maximum performances you can achieve, no matter how hard you train. For most people, that's well below world class. But one of the wonderful things about running is that this really doesn't matter. Your goal should be to become the best runner you can become (constrained, of course, by the time available for training), and to measure your progress by your own standards, not by comparison to other runners. To facilitate that, this book will always phrase goals in terms of setting *personal records* (PRs)—with the emphasis on *personal*. In the world of PRs, a 10-minute miler who advances to 8:30s has accomplished as much as an 8:00-miler who eventually reaches 6:30s.

Coaching, therefore, is designed to help you achieve the best you can with what nature gave you. You'll do that by focusing on quantity, quality, and mechanics.

- **Quantity of training**, or **volume**, is simply the number of miles logged. To a point, the more you run, the faster you are, although there comes a level at which your body (and your social life) can't handle the strain. We discuss this in more detail in chapter 3; for the moment, all that you need to know is that most recreational racers log somewhere between 20 and 30 miles per week, except perhaps during brief interludes when they are training for long events such as marathons or half-marathons. Running more than 35 miles a week moves you into the ranks of serious racers.
- **Quality of training** has to do with the way you invest your training mileage. Some coaches speak in terms of "junk miles" or "junk training" when referring to low-quality training. I avoid those terms, but in this book I note the difference between workouts that achieve maximum benefits and those that tire you out without producing much in the way of results. At the same time, I'll hammer in the value of rest. Too many runners, in an effort to avoid junk training, do all of their workouts too fast, never giving themselves enough time to recover. Rather than making you stronger, that makes you progressively weaker and more tired until eventually you hang up your running shoes in disgust, or your body does the job for you by giving you an injury. True quality-training involves finding the optimum mix of speed work, days

off, and slower-paced training volume. Chapter 5 deals with speed training, but remember that these workouts are only one portion of a high-quality training program.

- **Running mechanics** has to do with details of stride, running posture, and arm swing. Some of these number among the limitations that dictate your native talent; if something odd about your bone structure gives you a less-than-efficient stride, then nothing short of corrective surgery (and quite possibly not even that) will rectify it. But within these constraints, there's a lot you can do to improve—and every alteration made in this arena is "free" speed that doesn't make you work any harder in training or in the race. We discuss these issues in chapter 4.

SPEAKING OF PACE

There are two basic ways to describe your running pace per mile. The formal way is to say, for instance, "I ran 8:32 per mile," of course meaning 8 minutes, 32 seconds per mile. That's too cumbersome for colloquial use, however, so runners often say instead: "I ran 8:32s," with the "per mile" implicitly understood. This book will usually use the colloquial form.

BEFORE YOU START

To become a racer, you must first be a runner.

Stated this way, that seems self-evident, but it's amazing how many people try to shortcut this vital first step. They're encouraged by well-intentioned but overly aggressive programs that take nonrunners and put them in training to run a 10K within as little as 3 months or a marathon in less than a year. I can't stop you from taking that approach, but I can advise caution. Dropout and injury rates in such programs tend to be high unless you're already involved in a sport that involves a lot of running or leaping, such as soccer or full-court basketball. If you're new to running, feel free to read this book for inspiration, but consult *Alberto Salazar's Guide to Running* for advice on how best to make that initial transition.

Equipping Yourself

Because it assumes that you're already a runner, this book also assumes that you're familiar with how to select running shoes, what to wear for different weather conditions, how to acclimate to heat and cold (important if you're planning to race in such conditions), and how to deal with road obstacles such as cars, dogs, and bicycles.

One of the basics, however—shoes—deserves a few extra words. When you start spending time at races, you'll begin to hear about some specialized types of shoes: flats, spikes, racing shoes, training shoes, trail shoes, and a few others. But you do not need special shoes for racing. The shoes you're already using should be perfectly adequate.

This presumes, of course, that you've been running your 20 miles per week in good shoes. When it comes to clothing, the number one place to spend money is on your feet. Yes, good shoes are expensive, but they greatly reduce the risk of injury, and as you move into racing, you'll be putting additional stresses on your body. Why take the chance? Find a running store you trust, and talk to the clerks about what shoes will serve you best. You can also find more advice in my *Guide to Running*. Good shoes typically cost about $80 to $95.

In addition to buying good shoes, you need to replace them when they wear out. Unfortunately, for some people that happens fairly quickly. No matter how fresh and new your shoes look, they're shot when the sole cushion starts to compress. Retire them to walking, and buy new ones.

As for the specialty terminology, here's a brief lexicon:

- **Training shoes** are what you train in—basically good running shoes, such as you probably already own. They're the only shoes that most racers ever need, because you can also run your races in them.
- **Racing shoes** are lightweight and designed specifically for racing. We'll discuss them in more detail later in the book (see pages 74 and 214), but the only real reason to buy them is if you've reached a plateau and are looking for a way to shave a few more seconds off your time.
- **Trail shoes** are sturdy training shoes, built to protect your toes from collisions with rocks and sticks. They may also have aggressive treads, like knobby bicycle tires. People who do a lot of trail running may find them worthwhile.
- **Spikes** are shoes with metal or plastic protrusions for extra traction, and are available as track spikes or cross-country spikes. You have no need for either, and shouldn't experiment with them without knowledgeable advice because they change your foot motion in ways that can get you injured if your running form isn't perfect.
- **Flats** is just another name for any of the nonspiked shoes discussed above. You'll sometimes also hear the terms "training flats" and "racing flats."

Once you've made sure your shoes are adequate, there are three types of equipment you need for racing that you may not already be using as a runner: a training diary, a good watch, and a pace calculator.

LEARNING THE HARD WAY

Here's Rick on the subject of overly accelerated training programs:

One of my friends entered a program designed to take nonrunners and train them for a marathon in less than a year. When I asked him about injuries, he admitted that he'd had more than one. "But I had great support," he said. "There were weeks when virtually everyone was having to deal with injuries. I learned a lot."

If that's the way you want to learn about injury treatment, go ahead and try one of these accelerated training programs. But if you'd rather minimize your risk of having to deal with injuries in the first place, it's better to proceed more slowly.

TRAINING DIARY

A training diary, or training log, is merely a calendar on which you jot down a few notes about each day's workout. You can buy cute little books designed for this purpose, but all that you need is an ordinary desk or wall calendar, so long as it gives you room to write (see pages 16–17). At a minimum, record each day's mileage plus a brief note about the course, your pace, and anything notable about the weather. A fairly thorough description of a summer outing might read: "Four miles, slow (about 8:45s), *hot!* River Road." Some runners, of course, might not view 8:45s as slow, but it's useful to record both the pace and your qualitative assessment of it, so that—looking back on the diary years later—you can remember how it felt.

> **Racing requires no expensive equipment that you're not already using as a fitness runner. But three items distinguish a racer from a fitness runner: a training diary, a running watch, and a pace calculator (or a good head for figures).**

The goal isn't to record numbers obsessively, but rather to chart your progress and to help you figure out which training regimens work and which don't. If something goes wrong, such as an injury or a sudden decline in performance, your training diary is the first place to turn in search of an explanation. In addition to basic distance and pace information, therefore, you might want at least occasionally to record the following.

- Your weight.
- Twinges, discomforts, or other signs of incipient injury.
- Notes about your general health, such as "cold coming on" or "had the flu last week." Even more important are notes about how you feel following the previous day's workout. "Stiff; sore muscles," for example, is important information that may mean that you've been overdoing it.
- Your resting heart rate (taken before you get out of bed in the morning).
- Changes in equipment, such as a new pair of shoes.
- Notes about bicycling, hiking, weight lifting, or other physical activities you pursued that day.
- Details of speed workouts (as described in chapter 5). If you ran six fast-paced 400-meter laps of a track, for example, you might write "6 × 400—1:53, 1:52, 1:54, 1:53, 1:55, 1:53," where the times are for each of the laps.
- Race results. Mark them in colored ink to make them easy to find; you're apt to look back at them many times in upcoming years.
- Any other factors such as dietary changes or experiments with preworkout meals that might affect your performance.

Whatever you do, don't make the training diary into a major chore. If you do, you'll procrastinate writing in it and not get meaningful information. You should be able to jot down all of your notes in a few seconds, as soon after completing your workout as possible. Keep your training diary in a convenient location, minimizing the chance of forgetting it.

RUNNING WATCH

Watches serve several important functions. First of all, most racers use them to keep track of their finishing times in races, so they don't have to wait for results to be mailed or posted on the Internet. During the race, a watch is also useful to keep yourself on pace by allowing you to track your progress, mile by mile.

In training, a watch can be used to help you estimate the length of training runs. If you normally train at about 9:20 per mile, for example, you can quickly figure out that a 31-minute outing covered a little more than 3 miles (3.32 miles, if you want to be precise!). Where the watch really comes into its own, however, is for speed workouts on a track, as described in chapter 5. Doing such workouts, you'll be timing each lap to the nearest second. That requires a stopwatch feature that displays large enough numerals for you to read them on the fly.

You may also want a watch that records and remembers *lap times*. Such watches allow you to momentarily freeze the display by pushing a button—for instance, after each lap of a track or each mile of a race. The timer continues to run while the display is frozen, allowing you to obtain not only your per-lap time for each circuit of the track (or each mile of the race) but also your cumulative time for the entire event. Most watches will store all of these numbers for later review and copying into your training diary.

Some watches store up to 100 lap times—far more than most people have any use for. Pick a watch based on your expected needs. If you're planning to run marathons, you want at least 27 memory registers (one for each mile, plus the finish). If the longest race you ever plan to attempt is a half-marathon, you only need 15 memory registers. Take some time to play with the watch before you use it;

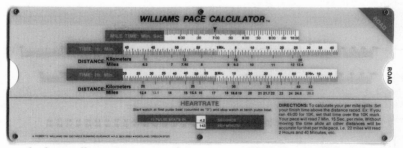

A *pace calculator allows you to match up pace and finishing time for a wide range of races. More distances and paces are on the opposite side of this device.*
(WWW.PACETHYSELF.COM)

TRAINING DIARY

SUNDAY	MONDAY	TUESDAY	WEDNESDAY
			1. Run 4 mi. Treadmill at Hearts 'R Us Health Club. Watched TV. 9:05s.
5. Long run, 8 mi. Forest Park. Cool (50°). Perfect! 9:10s	**6.** Rest. Weight 157#	**7.** Run 4 mi. 8:55s, felt easy; 2 @ 8:10s; still felt good. Racing season looms . . .	**8.** 4 mi. Treadmill Slow . . . 9:00s
12. Long run with Paul & Franci 9 mi., slow Wildwood Trail	**13.** Rest. Weight 158#	**14.** 6 mi. Felt sluggish. Went really slow all the way. Cold, rainy, all-around yuck!	**15.** 4 mi. Treadmill Slow, very sluggish
19. Bailed on long run, to baby the knee. Ran 5 on waterfront @ 9:30s. Got twinges anyway.	**20.** Rest. Weight: 159# Could shoes be getting old??	**21.** Bought new pair of Air Gust trainers. Canary yellow . . . make me feel fast. Ran 3 mi. Knee better or just wishful thinking?	**22.** 4 mi. Treadmill. Felt much better. Held back to 9:15s.
26. Long run with Paul & Franci. 8 mi., Forest Park, usual route. 9:05s	**27.** No running. Weight 158# Biked 3 mi. . . . slowly! Knee OK.	**28.** Ran 6 mi. Picked up pace to 8:05s in middle. Felt good. 65° and sunny!	**29.** 4½ mi. Treadmill, 9:00s. Knee still OK!!!

Sample training log for a fictitious 26-mile-per-week runner. The precision of some of the pace estimates indicates that this person often trains on well-measured courses and pays considerable attention to the time; you needn't be so precise. This diary shows, though, that the runner is speeding up slightly as the month progresses—very

THURSDAY	FRIDAY	SATURDAY
2. *Run 6 mi. Heavy rain. Forgot the time— too afraid of drowning*	**3.** *Rest.* *Weight 158#*	**4.** *Run 4 mi. with Pam & Mike. Caught up on old times; kept it slow* **Weekly total (includes last 3 days of previous month) = 26 miles**
9. *6 mi. River route. Great day!!! Had to hold back to avoid going too fast. Still did 8:45s.*	**10.** *No running. Biked 10 miles with kids, after work. First family outing of the spring.* *Weight 156#*	**11.** *4 mi. Stayed in neighborhood, approx. 9:00s* **Weekly total = 26 miles**
16. *3 mi. Right knee slightly sore along outside edge*	**17.** *Rest.* *Weight 157#*	**18.** *Ran 4 mi. Knee still twinges, doesn't like slanted roads. But it's my usual Sat. route . . . ??* **Weekly total = 26 miles**
23. *Knee seems OK. Ran 6 on waterfront with Frank. 8:50s. Faster than I should go, but gee, it's finally SPRING!!*	**24.** *No running. Biked again with kids. Knee said "hello" at mile 5, so I quit. Maybe I went too far that first bike outing?*	**25.** *Run 4 mi. Knee fine. 8:55s in light drizzle. Damp but OK. About 55°.* **Weekly total = 22 miles**
30. *6 mi. on waterfront with Pacific Frog Stompers. Good group, all paces, does speed workouts starting next month.*		

reassuring. Even more importantly, note how this person uses the log to diagnose, respond to, and nip in the bud an incipient problem. After you've read the rest of this book, you might think of other things that could have been added to the log, but this is far better than the record kept by most recreational racers.

some are absurdly complex, and you don't want to find yourself accidentally clearing the display midway through a race, when you merely intended to record a lap time.

PACE CALCULATOR

If running is your career, your head fills with pace-related numbers. I'm unlikely ever to forget, for example, that running 10,000 meters in 27:30 corresponds to 66 seconds per 400-meter lap, or about 4:24 per mile. But initially you have to calculate paces, rather than remember benchmarks. One way is with a *pace calculator*, a sliding converter that costs about $20. It's a simple mechanical device, with a sliding cursor that matches finishing times against paces. Lining up the cursor on 43:50 for the 10K, for example, shows that this is equivalent to a 7:04 pace for the mile. Conversely, setting the cursor at 8:10 on the pace scale reveals that this pace for the mile corresponds to a 5K finishing time of 25:21. Actually, the answers you'll get won't be quite this precise; it's hard to read the scales this closely. But you can come within a few seconds per mile of the right answer.

You can use a pace calculator not only for comparing paces and race results, but also to equate mile paces to lap times on a track—useful for the speed workouts described in chapter 5. You can also consult the Pace Chart of Common Workout and Racing Distances, which has carried out all of the necessary calculations for many common racing and training distances (see appendix).

SPEED AND DISTANCE MONITOR

Do you like electronic toys? Consider investing in a speed-distance monitor, which attaches to your shoe to monitor both the distance you cover and the speed at which you're running. More complex than a simple pedometer (a low-tech device that simply counts your steps) it measures the acceleration and deceleration of your foot with each stride to determine how far you've moved. It then beams the results via a low-powered radio signal to a special watch that tabulates the data in almost any imaginable manner. Price: about $235—but like any electronic toy, future models will become smaller, cheaper, and ever more sophisticated.

PACE MATHEMATICS

If you don't own a pace calculator, you can compute paces in your head or on a conventional calculator. Here's Rick:

Computing your pace on a conventional calculator is tedious, because you have to convert back and forth to minutes and seconds. But it's not all that hard. Suppose, for example, you've run a 46:28 10K and want to know your average pace. Begin by converting the finishing time to seconds (multiply the 46 by 60, then add the 28). That gets you a figure of 2,788. Divide this by 6.2 miles (or 6.21 miles if you want to be super-precise). That gives you your pace in seconds per mile: about 449. Dividing by 60 tells you that this is equivalent to 7.48 minutes per mile, which is *not* the same as 7:48. To calculate the seconds, get rid of the 7, then multiply the remaining 0.48 by 60. The result: 7:29. That calculation has a lot of steps, but with practice you can run through it in a matter of seconds.

Going the opposite direction is similar. If you want to know what time corresponds to an 8:30 pace on a half-marathon, convert 8:30 to seconds (the answer is 510), then multiply by the race distance (13.1) to get your target time in seconds (6,681). To convert all these seconds to a usable form, divide by 60 to get fractional minutes (111.35), then multiply that 0.35 by 60 to put it back into seconds. The answer: 111:21, or 1:51:21.

If you're good with numbers, you can calculate paces in your head. The easiest way is by a process of successive estimation that helps you zero in on the answer in a series of approximations. A friend recently asked me to do this after she'd run 1:23:14 in a 15K (9.315 miles). After walking around muttering to myself for a couple minutes, I was able to tell her that she'd done approximately 8:57s.

Here's how: First, I did a quick-and-dirty calculation. In a 9-mile race, 8:00s would be 72 minutes—too fast. Ten-minute miles would be 90 minutes—too slow. Obviously, she was in the vicinity of 9:00s. Then I got more precise. If she'd run at exactly 9:00s, she would have covered the first 9 miles in 81 minutes. Rounding off the remaining distance to 0.3 miles, I noted that 9:00 per mile is the same as 540 seconds per mile, or 54 seconds per tenth of a mile. Therefore, 0.3 miles should take 54 seconds times 3, or 162 seconds (2:42). Adding that to 81 minutes and converting to hours gave me 1:23:42.

My friend had therefore beaten 9:00s by 28 seconds. After dividing those 28 seconds by approximately 9 miles, I concluded that she was about 3 seconds per mile faster than 9:00s—or 8:57s. A calculator gives an actual answer of 8:56. The difference is due to the 0.015 miles dropped in my round-off.

STAGES OF LIFE

There is no such thing as a typical racer. Some have been running since grade school; others started in their 20s, in middle age, or even after retirement. Racing can become an important part of your life no matter what your stage of life.

Running and Pregnancy

Late in pregnancy would not be a convenient time to begin racing, but most women can probably keep at least partially trained until the last month or two before giving birth. It's important, though, to consult your doctor first. Some specialists have expressed concern about oxygen deprivation to the fetus if you run

---

Before taking up racing, you should have been jogging for at least a year and have built up to 20 miles per week.

too hard, although there are women who've run at world-class levels for the first 3 or 4 months of pregnancy with no harm to their babies. Others have run recreationally right up to the last moment, with no ill effects to themselves or their children.

The main problem is your own comfort. If running becomes unpleasant, shift to a non-weight-bearing activity, such as swimming. You'll be able to return to racing more quickly if you get in at least 20 minutes of aerobic exercise three times a week.

Children and Teens

Children are generally more fit than adults, in part because they haven't yet learned to drive. That means they can definitely accommodate the training program presented in this book—at least so long as they're not severely overweight. In Africa, children as young as ten run 5 miles each way, to and from school. Some grow up to be world-class marathoners. There are a few limitations, however: No child under 14 should run farther than 10 to 12 miles in any given day, and no growing child, even an older teenager, should run a marathon.

The program in this book is actually very conservative for children. High school cross-country runners generally progress in a matter of months from nothing to 3 to 5 miles of running a day. Kids' joints are simply more resilient than those of adults, and aerobically, children progress much more quickly than their parents do. The training of budding track stars and cross-country athletes, however, is beyond the scope of this book.

Seniors

Many people have successfully taken up running during their retirement—occasionally with inspirational success. The late Mavis Lindgren, of Portland, Oregon, for example, began running in her early 60s, ran her first marathon at age 72, and by age 93 had run 76 marathons! Racing at middle age and beyond does involve a few special considerations, however. These will be addressed in chapter 16, on masters running.

MEDICAL ISSUES

Athletics books of all kinds advise beginners to check with their doctors before setting forth on any program of vigorous exercise, particularly if you're over age 40. Consider yourself so advised. People rarely follow this advice, but you absolutely should talk to your doctor if you know you have a physical condition that might preclude racing or at least require monitoring.

Such conditions include any of the following.

- *A known heart condition, chest pain, or a family history of heart disease.* You may be able to race, but the stress of racing can trigger an attack. Find out where you stand before you begin.

Racing is for all ages. (Douglas Steakley)

- *A history of amenorrhea.* If you are a woman who at any time in your life missed six or more menstrual periods (when not pregnant) due to illness or an eating disorder, you shouldn't race without first determining if you need a bone-density scan. Hormonally, your medical history mimics early menopause, and it may not have been dealt with properly at the time. Without the right treatment now, you are at risk of an endless succession of the hairline bone cracks called stress fractures (see pages 140–42). Once the condition is stabilized, however, you may indeed be able to race.
- *Asthma.* This is a topic at which life has chosen to make me an expert. It doesn't necessarily preclude racing, but it can put a cap on your speed. A person with asthma may, for example, be able to run endless distances in training at a 7:00 pace, but trigger an attack the moment he or she tries to go below 6:45 in a race. Make sure your asthma is under control before you start racing, and adjust your training and racing goals within the constraints imposed by your condition.
- *High blood pressure.* Running can help you control your blood pressure, but you need medical advice before you start. You should have your blood pressure checked twice a year. You can get an adequate reading from one of the automated machines sometimes found in drugstores or other public places.
- *Any other medical condition that raises questions in your own mind.* Ignorance is not bliss. It's better to ask your doctor unnecessary questions than to endanger your health by not asking the questions you should. Most doctors are well aware of the benefits of exercise, and aren't apt to discourage you unnecessarily.

Even these problems, with proper treatment, are unlikely to prevent you from racing. A great case in point is masters runner John Keston, who took up running at age 55 as an alternative to having to take medication for high blood pressure. Not only did John solve his blood-pressure problem, but he also became one of the best masters runners of our era. Now in his late 70s, he continues to race (see page 245), and has rewritten innumerable age records.

So, whatever your stage in life, the odds are that racing is a sport you can enjoy. The next chapter will tell you how your body adjusts to training, after which we'll turn to a discussion of how to apply that knowledge to maximize your speed with realistic amounts of training.

Basic Principles of Running Faster

ONE OF THE GREATEST athletes of all time was the Greek wrestler Milo of Kroton who reputedly gained amazing strength by carrying a calf with him wherever he went. At first, it wasn't that hard, but day by day the calf grew . . . until eventually Milo was toting a full-grown bull on his morning constitutionals.

Milo really existed, although the bull was probably myth (a more reasonable version of the story has him starting out carrying a lamb around). But like all good legends, the story has an important reality at its core: the ancient Greeks had discovered what modern sports physiologists call the *training effect*, a simple principle that applies to all athletic endeavors. To achieve your potential you must always push slightly beyond your comfort zone. That encourages your body to make adjustments that raise your comfort zone to include the new workload—which you then raise again to start the process anew. This, in a nutshell, is what athletic training is all about. Even if your goal is simply to hold your own, you can't rest on your laurels. Otherwise, you'll gradually backslide—like Milo carrying an ever-*smaller* bull until eventually he could only manage a calf.

Since Greek times, coaches and exercise physiologists have learned a lot about harnessing the training effect. We understand, for example, that you can't push yourself harder every day, day after day, without breaking down. (Even the ancient Greeks may have suspected that something nasty, such as a ruptured disk, might have happened to Milo if he'd really attempted that trick with a calf.) We've also learned the value of mixing up hard workouts, easy ones, and rest days—and we've learned the difference between *quantity* and *quality* of training.

The details of these will be addressed in upcoming chapters. For the moment, let's look at some of the physiological factors that limit your speed and at how the training effect can be harnessed to overcome them on the cellular level. You don't have to understand this to apply this book's training methods, but most people find it easier to follow a program if they know why they're doing it.

Knowing why your training program works will also help during races. Everyone, myself included, has encountered moments of intense uncertainty, often at critical points in a race. When the going gets tough, there can be a nagging voice that says: *I'm not ready for this.* But if you understand the theory, it's easier to be confident. *Yes, I am ready,* you can reply to those ugly doubts. *I'm ready because I did x, y, and z in training and that's exactly what I should have been doing.*

I myself improved markedly in college when I learned truly to believe in my training. I'd run well in my freshman year, but as a sophomore I was disappointed, finishing sixth in the NCAA track finals at 10,000 meters. That summer, a teammate gave me that critical advice, and the next year I quit listening to the doubts. I gained confidence, won the NCAA cross-country championship, set a world record in a 5-mile road race, placed third in the NCAA 10,000-meter finals, and made the Olympic team at that same distance. It was a very good year, and part of my success came from believing that my training was doing its job.

At least as importantly, understanding the reasons for your training helps you adjust your schedule on days when it just isn't working. Suppose, for instance, that you're planning to run several half-mile repeats at 10 seconds per mile faster than your 10K race pace. But when you get on the track, you discover that you just don't have the energy. For some reason—lack of sleep, poor weather, lingering fatigue from last weekend's race, an incipient cold—you're just feeling too sluggish to run that fast. At this point, you have two choices: run as fast as you can, even if it's not the target pace, or shift your schedule and do something else.

Many runners would just power through the workout, figuring that pushing at a pace that feels hard is good for them, even if they can't hit their speed targets. If mental toughness and self-discipline are your only goals, this might be correct. But as we discuss in chapter 5, those repeat halves are designed to achieve very specific physiological goals. You won't achieve them at the wrong pace, so why beat yourself up trying to run through the sluggishness when doing so won't even do you any good? When I had days like that—and everyone occasionally has them— I rearranged my schedule to do the repeats when I was feeling more spry. Then, I'd use the sluggish day for something that took less energy. But you can only make such decisions if you understand what your workouts are intended to achieve.

MUSCLE POWER, FUEL, AND OXYGEN

Muscles have two main sources of energy: anaerobic metabolism and aerobic metabolism. They also keep a little bit of stored energy on hand in the form of a high-energy compound called *adenosine triphosphate* (ATP), which is used to facilitate muscular contractions. The ATP (and a closely related precursor called *phosphocreatine*) is enough to get you through a few seconds of intense activity—a sprinter

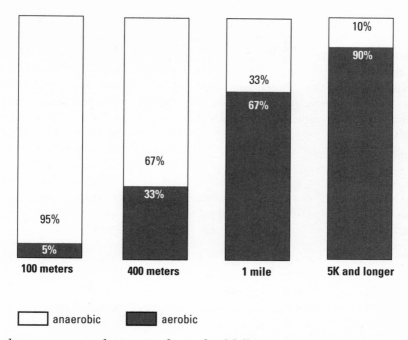

			10%
		33%	90%
	67%	67%	
95%	33%		
5%			
100 meters	**400 meters**	**1 mile**	**5K and longer**

□ anaerobic　　■ aerobic

Aerobic versus anaerobic energy demands of different race distances. Sprint races draw predominantly on the anaerobic energy-generating system, whereas longer events draw mostly on the aerobic process. The transition between the two energy systems occurs very quickly during middle distance events ranging from 200 meters to one mile.

exploding off the blocks or a football lineman struggling to reach the quarterback. After that, you need to make more ATP, quickly.

The body does this by the two fuel-burning mechanisms: anaerobic and aerobic metabolism. *Anaerobic* means "without oxygen," a term that's not quite accurate but which has become a fixture of sports-training jargon. Anaerobic metabolism actually functions perfectly well in the presence of oxygen—it just doesn't bother to use it. Aerobic metabolism, on the other hand, requires oxygen.

Anaerobic metabolism will carry you at maximum pace through a 200-meter sprint and can give you a substantial boost for about 2 minutes—an 800-meter distance if you're world class, less for the average athlete. It's a high-octane process, but you can't maintain it for long. For distance running, the body relies mostly on aerobic metabolism.

One of the most important things that sports researchers have learned is that training occurs at the cellular and even the subcellular level. Using a biochemical pathway activates the pathway that encourages biochemical changes that make it easier to use in the future. If you're a power athlete, therefore, you're going to be interested in training your muscles to store a little bit more ATP and phosphocreatine. Sprinters try to get the maximum out of that and the anaerobic pathway: for this reason, 100-meter runners seldom venture beyond 100 meters in practice; longer distances do them little good.

Distance runners don't have much need for brief spurts of all-out speed, except possibly to outkick an opponent in a close finish. Our training is designed to boost the aerobic process to its maximum efficiency so we can run our fastest at distances measured in miles, not hundreds of meters.

BASE TRAINING

Before we can go fast, of course, we need to be able to go the distance. Coaches have long known that you must train for endurance first, speed later. There's no sense pushing for speed in a 10K, for example, if you've never before run more than 2 or 3 miles.

> **Understanding how your body adapts to training will help you train more scientifically. That, in turn, will help you believe that your training will work, increasing your chances of running a great race.**

Base training, also known as *endurance training*, works by building up a training *base*, usually measured as the number of miles you log per week. Base training works at low intensities, so there's no reason to burn yourself out (and risk injury) by doing it at a fast pace. In fact, your body simply can't handle the stress of running at full pace, day in and day out. Furthermore, the goal is to train your aerobic energy system, not to push yourself into the zone where you're starting to draw heavily on the anaerobic system as well. To be effective, base training shouldn't be more than about 85 percent of race pace—well more than a minute per mile below race pace even for elite competitors. Elite athletes on base-training runs may zip along at 6 minutes per mile, but that's because they're already so well trained—and have developed so much speed—that this pace actually feels easy.

Lots of important things happen during base training, but some of the most significant affect subcellular structures called *mitochondria*. These tiny structures are the subcellular power plants at which aerobic metabolism occurs, and endurance training encourages you to make more of them. They also become larger, pack in more of the enzymes that do their work, and adapt to using multiple energy sources.

The standard energy source for untrained muscles is a substance called *glycogen*, which is made from a long chain of *glucose* sugar molecules. When used as fuel, the glycogen is broken back into its component glucose molecules. Your liver stores about 400 calories worth of glycogen; muscles can house several times that amount. Your body can also burn fat (in the mitochondria) and, in a pinch, protein (by first converting it to glucose).

PASS THE DRUMSTICK, PLEASE

Muscle cells come in two basic types: *fast-twitch* and *slow-twitch*. There is also a hybrid type with characteristics of both, but it comprises only a small part of the total.

Fast-twitch muscles contract quickly, and give you power for sprinting, leaping, and other explosive activities. But that power doesn't last long. Slow-twitch muscles have more mitochondria and are able to sustain longer but lower-intensity exertions. Another distinction is that fast-twitch cells are white, whereas slow-twitch cells are red. In humans, the two types are mixed up randomly throughout our muscles. In birds, the wings and legs are largely slow-twitch, whereas the breast is fast-twitch—explaining why chickens have both "white meat" and "dark meat."

Genetics appears to have endowed everyone with their own percentages of each type of muscle, and there doesn't appear to be much you can do about it. Sprinters tend to be mostly fast-twitch (some are higher than 75 percent). The best distance runners are the reverse. I myself have been measured as 92 percent slow-twitch. (The test involves taking a sample of muscle and looking at it under a microscope.)

Nobody has found a training method to change your muscle composition from one to the other. But you *can* train what you have for maximum performance. There's also a self-selection process that tends to send people into the sports for which their bodies are designed. If you're mostly fast-twitch, you're likely to gravitate to sprinting or weight lifting. But sprinters and football players have completed marathons, so don't let genetics keep you from your dreams. And don't set your expectations too low. Thanks presumably to my low level of fast-twitch, I was never going to be a great miler—but I could run multiple mile-repeats at paces that were only 20 to 30 seconds slower than world-class miles.

Training encourages the muscles to store more glycogen, giving them more ready fuel on hand for future running needs. But training also encourages mitochondria to look elsewhere for additional energy, and the place they turn to is fat.

There's a myth in the running literature that fat is a lower-grade energy source than glycogen. Like so many running myths, this one is based on half-truth. Glycogen is indeed a higher-grade fuel because it can power anaerobic metabolism as well as aerobic metabolism. But fat burns just fine in your mitochondria. If you're using both fat and glycogen, you have two energy sources, not just one.

The overall effect of base training is that your mitochondria become much more efficient at producing ATP. This, combined with increased glycogen storage, allows you to go farther without tiring. A pleasant side effect is that your comfortable pace will speed up, almost magically. If you're a beginning racer looking to get the biggest bang from your training, increasing your base training is definitely the place to begin (see chapter 3).

SPEED TRAINING

A few generations ago, distance runners believed that base training was the only thing they needed. But then, it wasn't until the 1930s that the first runner broke

2:30 in the Olympic marathon. Today, a 2:30 won't even get you into the U.S. men's Olympic trials, let alone onto the team.

At shorter distances, the need for speed is even more intense. Today's world record mile is 3:43:4. The world record 10K is 26:22—only 32 seconds per mile slower. Nobody can compete today at the elite level on base training alone—and you too will do better if you supplement your base with speed work (see chapter 5).

Once you've built up to a reasonable level of base training, your potential speed is dominated by three factors related to aerobic metabolism: *VO_2max*, *submaximal VO_2*, and *lactic acid*. All are affected to at least some extent by the type of training you choose to pursue (see the accompanying table and the drawing on pages 34–35).

VO_2max

You can't read much of the sports physiology literature without encountering the term *VO_2max*. Despite the odd-looking nomenclature, it's not all that mysterious a concept; VO_2max is merely the maximum amount of oxygen (O_2) that your body is capable of burning per minute. The V means it's a measure of volume (as opposed to, for instance, a weight), and in scientific contexts you would see a dot over the V, which would indicate that it's a rate of flow (per minute in this case).

VO_2max is measured by the simple expedient of putting you on a treadmill and running you up ever-steeper grades until you're about to drop in your tracks. It's a lot like a cardiac stress test except that instead of monitoring your heart, the researchers measure how much oxygen you're extracting from the air you breathe. That goes up steadily with effort until you reach the point at which you simply can't work any harder. Most people have to stop a few seconds after hitting that level. For psychological reasons that aren't as clear to me now as they were at the time, when I volunteered for this test back in 1982, I hung in at my max for nearly 2 minutes—setting some kind of lab record while doing what felt like one of the more grueling hill workouts of my life.

VO_2max measures your potential aerobic horsepower. For that reason, it's sometimes been called *aerobic capacity*, but we'll stick with the shorter scientific term. Some people confuse VO_2max with lung capacity, but it's not the same thing— VO_2max measures not only how much oxygen gets into your lungs but how much is actually used by your muscles. Theoretically, the higher your VO_2max, the more work you're able to do without drawing so heavily on anaerobic metabolism that exhaustion quickly follows.

VO_2max is generally expressed as milliliters of oxygen per kilogram of body weight per minute (mL/kg/min). Mine was 78. The highest well-conducted measurements I've ever heard of were in the range of 85 to 90. By comparison, the typical healthy young man or woman will test at about 45 to 55.

To a large extent, VO_2max is genetically determined. It's also set by years of lifestyle choices. By the time you reach maturity, it's hard to make huge changes in it, although sedentary individuals may have more room for improvement than people who've always been active. Even sedentary people, however, are unlikely

FOUR TYPES OF TRAINING

Type of Training	Description	Target Pace	Physiological Effects
Base training[1]	gently paced distance runs	no faster than 85 percent of race pace	long-term improvement in VO_2max; enhanced glycogen storage
VO_2max training[2]	fast-paced intervals lasting about 3 to 10 minutes each	slightly faster than race pace	intensity of effort improves mitochondrial efficiency beyond levels obtainable from base training
Running efficiency training[2]	numerous, very fast intervals, lasting about 1 to 3 minutes each	substantially faster than race pace	builds muscle strength and efficiency, thereby boosting submaximal VO_2
Tempo runs[2]	"comfortably" fast runs typically lasting at least 20 min.	moderately slower than race pace	shifts lactic acid curve to the right, reducing lactic acid accumulation at any given speed

[1] See chapter 3.
[2] See chapter 5.

to be able to improve by more than 25 percent. By the time you've put in enough running to be racing, you probably can manage no more than an additional 5 to 15 percent.

Even small changes in VO_2max, though, translate into significant gains in speed. All other things being equal, a 5 percent gain in VO_2max is equivalent to a 5 percent speedup, the difference between a 50-minute 10K and a 47:30. Fifteen percent, if you can achieve it, could cut that 50:00 to 42:30—an enormous improvement.

Not surprisingly, you boost VO_2max by taxing your aerobic system. Initially, that happens simply by taking up running. You can supplement this by adding other sports but these won't help as much. VO_2max training requires more than simply making yourself breathe hard; you have to use the *right* muscle cells—the ones you'll be using to run.

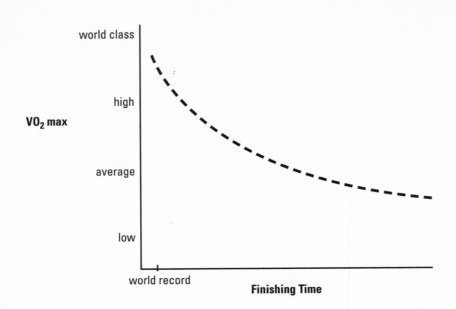

Approximate effect of VO₂max on race performance (all other factors equal).
Improving your VO₂max can speed you up—substantially. Slower runners have
more room to improve than faster ones, but VO₂max training is important for
runners of all abilities.

You can continue to improve your VO_2max by adding mileage. Some coaches, in fact, believe this is the best approach at mileages below 40 or 50 miles per week. Once you've reached that level, however, additional mileage gives diminishing returns. Also, all that running eats up a lot of time—and many people's bodies don't handle all those hours on the road any better than do their social lives. Once you've hit 40 or 50 miles a week, therefore, what it takes to move up further are workouts that entail exercise at levels higher than you normally attain in training. This type of VO_2max training will also help if time simply doesn't permit you to run more than 20 or 30 miles per week.

VO_2max training is best done via *interval* workouts that mix relatively short, fast runs and intervening *recovery* breaks. Typically, such workouts are done on a track, but they can also be done on the road or by uphill surges that mimic the intensity of track workouts. Details on this training will be explained in chapter 5; right now we're only interested in the theory. The key is to realize that you need to be moving at a pace significantly faster than you normally run. Runners who don't understand this often squander their workouts on interval sessions that feel tiring but are the wrong speed or distance to have the desired impact. How many intervals you do, and how long and fast each one is, will depend on the distance you're preparing to race.

Submaximal VO₂ (Running Efficiency)

Just as VO₂max is the maximum rate at which your muscles can process oxygen, your *submaximal VO₂* is the rate at which your body uses oxygen when working at less than maximum effort. Sitting around reading this book, you're probably using something on the order of 10 mL/kg/min; running a 10K race, you're going at a goodly percentage of your VO₂max.

To be meaningful, submaximal VO₂ must be linked to a specific pace and must be compared to VO₂max. If your VO₂max is 60, for example, and you're burning 52 mL/kg/min at a 6:00 pace, then we can think of that 6:00 pace as an 87 percent effort. If you lower your oxygen consumption at that pace to 50 mL/kg/min, you've cut the level of effort to 83 percent—a very noticeable improvement in the perceived ease of running. To put this in context, a properly prepared athlete can run a 10K at about 95 percent of VO₂max—or a marathon at about 85 to 90 percent of VO₂max. Thus, even slight changes in submaximal VO₂ translate to significantly increased racing speed.

Submaximal VO₂ is a measure of your running efficiency. Your VO₂max sets a cap on your total ability to expend energy, but you can finesse that constraint by training to become more efficient at ever-higher speeds.

At the elite level, this is generally more important than VO₂max. That's partly because nobody can reach the elite level without being blessed with a high VO₂max. But even so, there is considerable variation in VO₂max among elite runners. The great Australian runner Derek Clayton, for example, set a 2:08:34 marathon world record in 1969 with a VO₂max of only 70, besting the top marks of marathoners with VO₂max measurements above 80. Running efficiency was clearly his specialty. I myself didn't have a VO₂max that was all that high by elite standards, but I had lower oxygen consumption at a 5:00 pace than anyone previously tested. That gave me an edge in efficiency that outweighed my competitors' higher VO₂max, allowing me to be the one who finally broke Clayton's record.

Modest gains in submaximal VO₂ can be achieved very quickly. It's like tuning up a car that's burning too much gasoline. Adjust the timing, clean the fuel pump, check the tire pressure, realign the wheels, and presto—you've perked up the fuel economy by several percentage points. In running, the engine to be tuned up is your muscles, the shop is the track (or hills), and the auto mechanics are the natural processes of your own body. While you're at it, you can also learn some fuel-conserving tactics for using your tuned-up muscles at maximum efficiency. We'll discuss these in chapter 4, on running form.

Even more than with VO₂max, the way to improve your muscles' efficiency is by running intervals. Their speed requires your muscles to exert extra force to move you at the faster pace. They also extend this exertion through a wider range of motion, making your muscles more limber. Muscles taxed in this manner become stronger, and stronger muscles are more efficient—it's as simple as that. Intervals designed to improve running economy should be shorter than VO₂max repeats, and run at a substantially faster pace. Again, details will be explained in chapter 5.

Lactic Acid Threshold

Lactic acid, sometimes called *lactate*, is a molecule that's gotten a bad rap. Many people label it as the cause of sore muscles or brand it as a metabolic poison whose presence grinds your aerobic metabolism to a halt. The truth is more complex.

Lactic acid is a by-product of the metabolism of glucose to produce energy for production of ATP. Anaerobic metabolism makes lots of it, but it's also produced by aerobic metabolism, particularly when the aerobic system is pushed close to its limits. People often refer to lactic acid accumulation as meaning that your body has "gone anaerobic," but that's another oversimplification. You're actually using more oxygen than ever, but you're also relying heavily on the anaerobic system. Lactic acid accumulation means that the combined systems are having trouble keeping pace with your demands.

Lactate is itself a fuel which, at low exercise levels, is used nearly as quickly as it is formed. But it accumulates rapidly in your blood as you approach your VO_2max. Lactate levels can be measured with a quick finger-prick blood test that gives the results in units called millimoles per liter (mmol/L). When you're at rest, your blood contains less than 1 mmol/L lactate. Running, the level increases with speed—slowly at first, and then faster and faster. On a base-training run, for example, your lactic acid level is probably about 1.5 mmol/L. At the pace you could sustain for an hour-long race—probably only 75 to 90 seconds per mile faster—it

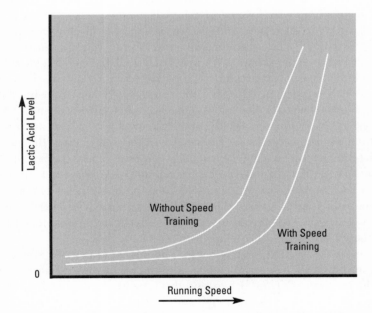

Lactic acid levels rise slowly with running speed (and distance) until you reach the lactic acid threshold point, after which they rise abruptly. Lactic acid training shifts the threshold point so that it occurs at faster speeds or longer distances, allowing you to run more comfortably at any given pace.

mounts to about 4 mmol/L. Above this pace you quickly overload your body's lactate processing systems. The level in your blood begins to snowball, rising to maybe 11 or 12 mmol/L by the time you hit VO_2max. The running speed at which lactate levels begin this rapid rise is the *lactic acid threshold*.

Many people blame postrace exhaustion on the accumulation of lactic acid, but there's no scientific evidence for this. In studies in which runners allowed themselves to be injected with the substance, they felt no exhaustion or other ill effects. Some experts believe that lactic acid is itself benign and its accumulation in your bloodstream is merely a symptom of tiredness, not its cause.

From a practical standpoint, it doesn't matter much which is the cause and which is the effect. Blood tests show that mounting lactic acid levels correlate to that "running-out-of-gas" feeling you get when you've pushed close to your limits. And the bottom line is that you can train your body to be more efficient in its use of lactic acid. This shifts the lactic acid threshold to higher speeds—preparing you to race that much more quickly. Because this shift in lactic acid threshold is a separate effect from changes in VO_2max or improvements in running efficiency, it gives you a third variable on which to target your training.

Intervals designed for improving VO_2max or running efficiency will be of some benefit to your lactic acid threshold, but if lactic acid is your primary goal you'll do better with a longer, slower *tempo run*. Picking the right pace involves hitting a fairly narrow window. Too fast, and you burn out before you've elevated your lactic acid level for long enough to teach your body to handle it. Too slow, and you don't generate much lactic acid in the first place. If you were monitoring your lactic acid level, what you'd be striving for would be to push it to just a little above that 4 mmol/L level most athletes can sustain for an hour, then hold it there for a few minutes. As with VO_2max training and running efficiency training, this will be discussed in more detail in chapter 5.

LAB TESTS AND TRAINING THEORY

People who like being research guinea pigs could monitor their VO_2max, submaximal VO_2, and lactic acid thresholds on a regular basis. The latter is relatively easy; there are home-use blood tests that will give you quick lactic acid readings. To use them, you have to get on a treadmill or track, do a workout, and draw a prick of blood immediately afterward. There have been times when I did this often enough in a single workout that by the time I was finished, I was running out of unpricked fingers.

But you can leave the lab tests to the research scientists. They've tested enough other athletes to verify that the theory works. The secret of interval training is to demand slightly more of your body than you'll be calling on it to do in the race. It won't completely adapt, but it will adjust enough to make the race pace more comfortable and therefore more sustainable.

Similarly, the secrets of other types of training also lie in finding the right pace. Once you understand this, you'll realize that many of your friends' training patterns aren't particularly useful. For example, there is no reason for running at paces faster than your comfortable base-training pace but slower than a lactic acid tempo

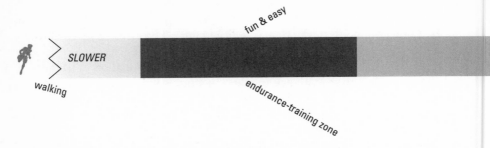

Different running paces accomplish different forms of training. Paces that are faster than necessary for one goal but not fast enough for another are dead zones. *That doesn't mean you're accomplishing nothing by running at these paces, merely that you're working harder than you need to, with no added benefit. Spend your energy more wisely. Chapters 3 and 5 tell you what pace to run for each of the four main training zones.*

run, even though lots of people work out at these speeds. You should either be doing base training for overall endurance and strength, or speed workouts targeted on one of the variables discussed in this chapter.

Rest is a crucial element of training. It's while you're resting that your muscles make the changes that build strength and speed.

CALLUSING THE MIND

Racing is both mental and physical, so there's no reason your speed training shouldn't also help prepare you psychologically. If there's a big hill in the race, for example, you'll probably gain confidence by including a similar one in training.

In college, my coach used to give us a speed workout that mimicked three stages of our 10K cross-country races. We called it the 30th Avenue Drill, because the toughest part followed 30th Avenue in Eugene, Oregon.

After a warm-up, the drill started with a three-quarter-mile interval run at a gradually decreasing pace. We'd do the first quarter-mile in about 60 seconds, the next in 65, and the third in 70 seconds. (By comparison, my cross-country race pace was about 4:50, equivalent to 72.5-second quarters.) We'd then recover for a bit at a pace that was fast but somewhat below race pace—perhaps a 5:10 or 5:15 pace. Next would come another three-quarter-mile repeat, but this one would be at a steady pace, perhaps 65 seconds per quarter (4:20 per mile). Another pseudo-recovery would follow, then we'd end with the reverse of the first interval, three quarters at a steadily speeding-up pace: 70 seconds, 65 seconds, and 60 seconds.

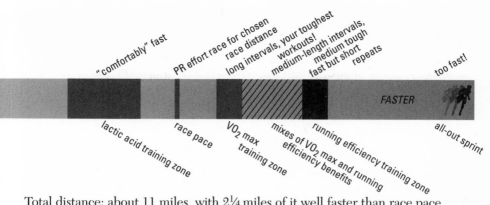

"comfortably" fast

PR effort race for chosen race distance

long intervals, your toughest workouts!

medium-length intervals, medium tough fast but short repeats

too fast!

FASTER

lactic acid training zone

race pace

VO₂ max training zone

mixes of VO₂ max and running efficiency benefits

running efficiency training zone

all-out sprint

Total distance: about 11 miles, with 2¼ miles of it well faster than race pace.

Today, I know that this was a really good workout for improving my VO_2 max. But in college, I didn't know that much about the physiology. What I knew was that the workout mimicked three key stages in a collegiate cross-country race. These races tended to start fast, as everyone jockeyed for position for the tight corners that would come later on. The first part of the drill taught me that I could go out fast and still settle into race pace without immediate burnout. The second interval mimicked the type of midrace in which a rival seeks to break you with sustained, fast surges. The final interval simulated the long drive to the finish. These were tough workouts—some would say brutal—but they taught me that I could indeed handle the punishment I'd be taking during the race, building confidence that I could indeed triumph over it. Coach Dellinger called it "callusing" your mind.

REST

Exercise strengthens the body by alternately stressing it and letting it recover. For this reason, weight lifters often speak in terms of "tearing down" and "building up."

PSYCHOLOGY IN ACTION

Mental callusing isn't solely for elite athletes. Rick tells this story about one of his training pals:

Paula is a serious racer who can hold a 6:40 pace for quite a few miles. That's good enough to place in the top three in the women's division of many local races, something she does fairly often. Once, she was running second in the women's field of a half-marathon on a hot day when, at mile 10, another woman surged from behind to challenge her. Some runners might have given up at that point. But Paula knew two things: she was well prepared to run in heat; and she'd done a lot of training at distances similar to the remaining 3.1 miles. *Oh no you don't,* she thought to her challenger. *Three-mile time trial: I've done lots of those.* She dug into her mental and physical reserves and beat her rival handily.

The moral: being able to relate race-day challenges to your training is the best way to address them. Even if you have no hope of being the fastest on the course, you know what's needed to rise to whatever challenges the race throws your way.

The "tearing down" is an actual physical process in which damage occurs to fibers in your muscle cells. Between workouts, the body patches up the damaged fibers by adding new protein to them. It does this so well that the repaired fibers are stronger than before. (The same process causes weight lifters to bulk up, as the strengthening muscles become progressively larger.) But it's important to understand that the actual strengthening—and any tweaking of your aerobic metabolism—occurs not while you're exercising but during the rebuilding process afterward.

I suspect that the same applies to other physiological aspects of training. The exercise makes your muscle cells unhappy by working them harder than they were prepared to work, running them low on glycogen, or running down their oxygen supplies. During rest, your body seeks to stave off future discomfort by making adjustments that allow it to handle a bit more of what you've chosen to dish out. But these adjustments take time, and that means rest. The bottom line: it's great to train hard, but if you don't take adequate time for recovery you won't grow stronger.

Even at the subcellular level you have to give your energy systems time to rebound. There are indications that repeated overwork can cause a long-term burnout in your mitochondria. Instead of boosting your aerobic processes, too much work gradually tears them down—possibly one of the causes of "overtraining" (see pages 48–49).

BUILDING A WORKOUT SCHEDULE

This chapter has identified four types of workouts:

- Base-training runs, for overall running strength and endurance.
- VO_2max interval runs, to boost VO_2max.
- Shorter, faster interval runs, to increase running efficiency (submax VO_2).
- Tempo runs, to reduce lactic acid accumulation.

You'll probably be happy to hear that you're not going to be asked to cram all four into any given week. Remember the need for rest? Only world-class athletes can manage a schedule that includes all of these activities each week. Most other people would exhaust themselves before they ever got to a race.

Instead, we'll break these workouts into two categories: volume and speed. The former is simply the total amount of training you'll do each week, regardless of whether you choose to do speed workouts. We'll discuss that first, in the next chapter. Then, after a discussion in chapter 4 of good running form (which is important for fast, injury-free running), we'll examine how to add speed work to your schedule—with the pleasant constraint that you won't be asked to do all three types of speed workouts each week.

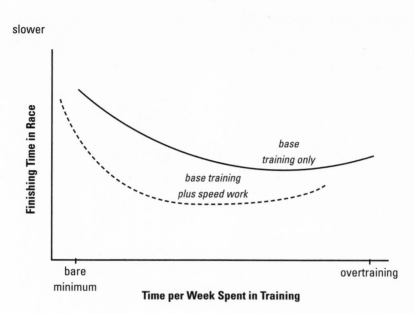

slower

Finishing Time in Race

base training only

base training plus speed work

bare
minimum

overtraining

Time per Week Spent in Training

Effect of race and speed training on race performance. Increasing your base training can speed you up, but by itself base training won't allow you to reach your full potential. For that, you need to add speed training. Speed training is also a more efficient use of your time, allowing you to reach any given goal more easily. More training is not always better, however. Too much training leaves you fatigued, sluggish, and easily injured.

BASE TRAINING

BASE TRAINING IS a bit like basic training if you're in the military. Everyone has to do it. Base training is sometimes called *endurance training*, and this book will use the terms interchangeably. These are your everyday runs, the bread-and-butter of your training program, and it is these that build long-run aerobic conditioning. The number one way to become a stronger, faster runner is by putting in the miles, year after year. All the speed work in the world isn't going to help you much if you don't consistently put in the volume.

Consistency is important, even from one week to the next. This means that you shouldn't run 5 days one week, 2 the next, and 4 the week after that. Constantly changing your routine will limit what you can achieve, so find a schedule that fits the rest of your life and stick with it. You're better off to recognize that you only have the time or motivation to run 4 days a week and to actually *do* that than to attempt to run 5 days a week and end up being erratic. If one day's schedule is unexpectedly pinched, do your best to salvage at least part of the planned workout. If you're supposed to run 8 miles and don't have time, for example, try to get in at least 2 or 3 miles. Running even a small fraction of what you intended will help disproportionately.

That said, you don't have to be a slave to your schedule. The statistic that most matters is the amount of running you do per week, not the amount on any given day. This gives you some flexibility to shift around mileage throughout the week. If you know you're going to be on an airplane during your normal Monday evening workout, for example, you don't need to abandon the planned mileage—you may simply need to do the workout on some other day. Keep the disruption to a minimum, though, by changing your schedule as little as possible.

Fitness runners can get away with running only 3 days per week, but racers need to run more frequently—at least 4 times a week, and preferably 5—unless you're old enough that your body simply can't run that frequently (see chapter 16).

Base training is the racer's equivalent to jogging: fun and easy. Good scenery and good company always help.
(VERA JAGENDORF)

The total mileage depends on your goals. Elite racers and many collegians log 70 to 130 miles per week, pretty much regardless of the distance for which they're training. My own goal was to put in as much volume as my body would tolerate—about 120 miles per week. For a recreational racer, that's an absurd amount, and unless you're blessed with a body that can handle world-class training regimens, you'd break down if you attempted it.

The table on the next page shows the minimum training volume (that is, mileage) that you need for common racing distances. You could probably get through some of the races on lower mileage, but you won't be comfortable in them, and you won't be able to truly *race* a distance whose length is too high a fraction of your weekly total.

Base training—endurance training—is the foundation of your entire running program. It builds the mileage base that supports both speed work and racing.

TRAINING VOLUME (MILEAGE) NEEDED FOR COMMON RACES

RACE DISTANCE	MINIMUM RECOMMENDED WEEKLY TRAINING VOLUME (MILES)
5K	20[1]
5 miles	20
10K	25
12K	25
15K	25
10 miles	25
half-marathon	30
marathon[2]	40

[1] You could run a 5K on less mileage, but this book assumes that you're doing at least this much weekly mileage.
[2] See chapter 15.

Increases in volume should be done very gradually. Many books permit a 10 percent increase per week, but that's far too much to sustain, week after week after week. If you were to increase at that rate for an entire year, you'd double your workload every 7 weeks—expanding it by a factor of nearly 200 by year's end. Obviously that's insane; programs that advocate a 10 percent per week increase are attempting to jump you quickly from, say, 20 miles to 25 miles, then hold you there for a few months, hoping you won't break down from the sudden change.

I prefer a slower buildup of no more than 10 percent per month. That way, you would go from 20 to 25 miles in a little longer than 2 months: running 22 miles a week in the first month and 24 miles a week in the second. The third month you'd take the final, easy step to 25 miles. At that point, however, even this slow program requires a plateau: it's unwise to increase your weekly mileage by more than about 25 percent in any given 6-month period. Even at that rate, you could go from 20 to 50 miles per week in two years—an enormous change.

If you're tempted to accelerate the process, the risk you run is a succession of nagging injuries. There are several parts of the body that have to adapt to the stress of increased mileage, and they do so at different rates. Aerobic conditioning comes first, with muscle strength following closely behind. That's why so many people try to proceed too quickly: once your muscles and cardiovascular system have adapted, workouts *feel* deceptively easy. What you need to remember is that tendons, ligaments, and bones also need to adapt—something they do fairly slowly. Bones are the slowest, and the potential injury, a *stress fracture* (see pages 140–42), is the one I most fear in beginning racers.

Stress fractures don't come from a single wrong step; the culprit is repeated jarring. I could give you one with a doctor's reflex hammer by tapping a bone over and over, never hard enough to hurt. *Tap-tap-tap* for tens of thousands of repetitions until suddenly, the bone can take no more. In running, stress fractures come on similarly, virtually overnight. One day you feel as though you could run forever—the next, *wham* you have a hairline crack in your foot, shin, or hip. The best analogy is to flexing a coat hanger back and forth. Do it enough times and the metal will fatigue and eventually snap. The chief difference is that given a chance, bones will protect themselves by getting stronger before anything goes wrong.

For the same reasons, you should never increase your base mileage while simultaneously adding speed workouts, hill running, or anything else that increases

BASE TRAINING BASICS

1. Be consistent.

2. Put in at least 4 days of training per week, up to age 45 or 50. After that, try for 3 or 4 days per week.

3. Take at least 1, and preferably 2, rest days per week. Only elite runners should train daily.

4. Increase mileage by no more than 10 percent per month for a total of no more than 25 percent every 6 months.

5. Alternate hard and easy workouts.

6. Do extra-long runs once per week, to build endurance for longer races.

7. Run at a pace that feels comfortable.

the difficulty of your training. Increase the base mileage, *then* add the other workouts once you've attained your mileage goal.

HARD-EASY PATTERN

Some people always run the same distance, day after day. But you'll get more bang for your buck—as well as more variety—by varying the distance. Rather than doing a succession of workouts of equal difficulty, you should alternate between harder ones and easier ones.

This hard-easy pattern is a core element of all aspects of training. In chapter 5 on speed training we come back to it again, treating speed workouts as "hard" days regardless of mileage. For the moment, however, we focus purely on base training, in which the difficulty of the day is determined principally by the number of miles logged.

Within the constraint of alternating hard and easy days, you have considerable freedom to design your own schedule. Just don't make the disparity between hard and easy days too great. If you're going to average 5 miles a day, for example, alternating between 4-mile and 6-mile runs is perfect. Trying to do the same with 8-milers and 2-milers makes the long days too tough to be run that frequently.

Rest Days

Your easiest days, of course, are ones on which you don't run at all.

Some runners boast that they've not taken a day off in years. At the world-class level, almost everyone runs 7 days a week, but at the recreational level this is foolish. Always take at least one day's break each week, and preferably two. World-class runners can get away without rest days because they're so well conditioned that a 15-mile, slow-paced day can actually be fairly easy. Even then, world-class training is an exercise in finding the brink between optimum training and injury. It takes a great deal of experience to feel exactly where that edge is, and it's very easy for even the best runners to slip across it. At the recreational level, there's no reason to take the risk. And, as we discuss in chapter 5, taking 2 full days of rest also allows you to pack a higher fraction of quality mileage into a low-volume schedule.

Long Runs

Another feature of your hard-easy pattern can be a weekly "long" run. By giving you one particularly hard day, these runs build overall strength and endurance even more efficiently than a simpler hard-easy pattern. They also help prepare you for longer races, such as 10-milers or half-marathons, and they add a bit of quality mileage to your training even if you're not doing speed work.

These long runs can be anywhere from 150 percent to 200 percent of your average daily distance (excluding rest days). Thus, if you're running 30 miles a week, with 2 rest days, you're averaging 6 miles on your running days. You will benefit from long runs of 9 to 12 miles.

Like any other change in your training schedule, long runs need to be built up gradually. Start at no more than 150 percent of your average daily distance, and add a mile a week until you reach your target. If you're already doing a hard-easy pattern, this won't be much of a stretch. In a 5-day, 30-mile week, for example, your hard days may already be close to 8 miles. Extending one of them to 9 miles isn't a big change.

Most people will want to do their long runs on weekends, and to take one of their rest days on the day afterward, but you can run an easy day if you feel like it. (Sample workouts that include weekly long runs are presented on page 81.)

LSD PACING

Runners frequently refer to base training as *LSD*. That's not because it has anything in common with mind-altering drugs; in running, LSD is *long, slow distance*.

Even when they're not all that long, base-training runs need to be slow and easy. Most people go too fast—often considerably so. If you do that, however, you'll be perpetually run down, frequently hurt, and likely to race poorly. Save the fast running for your speed workouts, if any, and make sure that your base training is paced so comfortably that you may wonder if you're working hard enough. If you feel like you're working hard, you're almost certainly working *too* hard.

Keeping your endurance runs slowly enough paced is particularly important if you're also doing speed workouts, because the LSD days are your recovery days. If you run them too fast, you won't be ready for your next speed workout. If you're not doing speed workouts, you can push the pace a bit a couple days a week— perhaps during part of your long run and on one of the other "hard" days. That's not as scientific as the speed training discussed in chapter 5, but it may get you some higher-quality training. Mostly, the benefit will be psychological "callusing of the mind." But even though you're probably running in the "dead zone" (too fast for one purpose, too slow for another) between LSD training and lactic-acid tempo runs, you'll probably gain a modicum of speed if this is your only speed work. But it's not a very efficient approach. View it as a stepping-stone to the "real" speed training of chapter 5.

RUNNING AT YOUR LSD PACE

There are several suitable methods for finding and maintaining the LSD (long, slow distance) training pace that best suits you:

- Run at an easy "conversational" pace.
- Test your pace occasionally to make sure it's about 1:30 per mile slower than your 10K race pace.
- Use a heart-rate monitor or a speed-distance monitor for comparing with a desired level.

How do you know if you're running the right speed? The simplest test is to see if you could carry on a reasonably normal conversation. If you're running with friends, you should be able to chatter away without being overly aware of the fact that you're on the move. A little breathlessness is OK, but . . . if . . . you . . . find . . . yourself . . . talking . . . like . . . this . . . you're overdoing it. And if you can't talk at all, you're going way too fast.

Another approach is by timing yourself on a measured distance—if you can do this without it becoming a time trial. A good, conversational pace is probably about 1:30 per mile slower than your 10K pace or 1:45 per mile slower than your 5K pace.

Yet another method of testing your pace is by counting your pulse for 10 or 15 seconds at strategic times in the run, or by using a heart-rate monitor for a continuous readout. You then compare your heart rate to a benchmark level to determine if you're going the right pace.

If you like gadgets, an electronic speed-distance monitor can also help you get a feel for your proper LSD pace (see page 18).

Counting Heartbeats

Heart-rate monitors are popular because they avoid the awkwardness of counting your pulse on the run. They work via a chest band that detects electrical impulses from your heart and converts them to a low-energy radio wave, beamed to a specially designed wristwatch. (If you and a training partner use the same brand of monitor, you may need to keep a few feet apart to keep the signals from interfering.) Costing $50 to $150, heart-rate monitors are particularly useful as tools to let you know if you're going too fast. Some even have beepers to inform you if your pulse strays above the desired range—although you may be persona non grata if you turn that feature on in the presence of other runners.

Some coaches structure entire training programs around heart-rate goals. When you're going all out, for example, your heart is beating at its maximum rate—a figure that is typically somewhere around 200 beats per minute for young runners, and gradually declines as you age. In theory, LSD running should be done at an exertion level corresponding to no more than 70 percent of your maximum.

> **Base-training runs need to be slow. Very few people run them too slowly. Many people run them too quickly. If in doubt, slow down.**

A much-cited formula states that your maximum heart rate can be calculated by starting with the number 220 and subtracting your age. I was tempted to include a table of such numbers in this book, showing the 70 percent LSD training level corresponding to each age. I chose not to because such tables give this method an aura of scientific accuracy that it simply does not possess. First of all, not everyone's heart has heard of the 220-minus-your-age formula. Cardiologists have found that one person in three has a maximal heart rate that differs from the prediction by at least 12 to 14 beats per minute—some higher, some lower. Rick is one of these people. The formula says he "should" have a maximum heart rate of 173, but in speed workouts he can hit nearly 190. Clearly, the formula understates his maximum, and at 70 percent of 173, he's barely working.

Also, factors other than exertion level affect your heart rate. On hot days, your heart must supply blood not only to the muscles, but also to the skin, to facilitate cooling. That double duty requires it to beat harder than it would in cooler weather, and your heart rate may exceed the 70 percent figure even if you're just loafing along. Other conditions can also affect your heart rate, including your state of hydration, the clothing you're wearing, and whether you're running indoors or outdoors.

Nevertheless, heart-rate monitors can be useful tools for keeping yourself on pace. Establish benchmarks by wearing one while running at an easy conversational pace, or at various slow paces on a track or other measured course. Do this several times, in case one day's outing is somehow unusual, and consider establishing separate benchmarks for cool days and hot ones. You can also compare the results to 70 percent of your personal maximum, measured by running as hard as possible for a couple minutes. Once you've determined a benchmark for your LSD runs, you can then make it your goal not to exceed that level.

I've used this approach with Mary Slaney, a four-time Olympian who returned to serious training at age 43. Concerned that she might be going too fast on her LSD runs, I gave her a heart-rate monitor and established a not-to-exceed benchmark of 140 beats per minute. That forced her to slow down considerably, from 6:35s to about 7:00s. Doing so gave her extra energy for her speed workouts, in which her performance quickly improved. The resulting better conditioning then spilled back over into her LSD runs, which she can now do at 6:50s or even 6:45s without exceeding that 140 beats per minute. Slowing down on her easy days and working hard only on the days that matter has obviously made her stronger—but it's an approach that overeager racers tend to resist.

OTHER MONITOR USES

Heart-rate monitors are valuable for purposes unrelated to LSD training. They can do any of the following:

- Teach you to run at a constant exertion rate, uphill and down. This is the best way to race through hills.
- Help you find the right pace for doing speed workouts on the roads, when a track is unavailable.
- Alert you to incipient illness or overtraining by telling you that your heart rate is unexpectedly high for a particular workout. An elevated resting heart rate is also an indicator that something may be wrong.

WARM-UP AND COOLDOWN

Training runs should start with some degree of warm-up and end with at least a minimal cooldown. Stretching should be part of the process, as described in chapter 6. But you should also run slower than normal for a few minutes, until your body feels loose, limber, and ready to go.

The purpose of the warm-up is to raise the temperature of your muscles slightly above their resting norm, without taxing them until they're ready. Warm muscles are more pliable, reducing the risk of muscle or tendon pulls when you start to lengthen your stride. The warm-up also gives time for the body to increase the muscles' blood flow, supplying them with ample fuel before they need it. Most people do about a mile of warm-up; others figure that they're warmed up when they start to sweat.

Cooldown (sometimes called "warm-down") is more controversial. It's based on the theory that ending a workout with a few minutes of light exercise will flush metabolic wastes out of the muscles, speeding recovery. But there's little if any scientific evidence that this actually works, especially on LSD runs. Nevertheless, a brief cooldown is probably a good idea after any outing. Whether the science has proven it or not, an instant halt certainly seems like a good recipe for stiffening up. In speed training, you probably want to end with at least a mile of slow jogging.

Base training should be fun, relaxed, and not too taxing. (VERA JAGENDORF)

DON'T LEAVE YOUR RACE ON THE TRAINING COURSE

As chapter 5 will discuss, speed work needs to disciplined, carefully tailored to achieve its desired ends. If you turn LSD endurance runs into speed workouts, you'll go the way Rick describes here for one of his friends:

I once trained with a group that included two fairly intense rivals. Fred was faster, but Dave was extremely competitive, prone to beating himself up in training whenever he performed poorly in a race. Fred loved to tease Dave, trying to egg him into these self-de-structive runs. He often succeeded, and there was many a day in training when Fred and Dave would go blazing out at paces I couldn't have matched if I'd wanted to.

Then, in the next race, not only would Fred beat Dave, but I would as well, even though Dave's PRs were considerably better than my own. The reason for Dave's trouncing: he had "left his race on the training course." Save the race for race day, and make sure your training is paced to achieve its goals. Be particularly careful not to become too competitive with your training partners. LSD running is for *fun*, not for head-butting.

After an LSD workout, 3 to 5 minutes of walking should be adequate—less if you're getting chilled. You're adequately cooled down when your breathing has returned to normal and your pulse fallen to 90 or so beats per minute.

HYDRATION

Even in cool weather, running generates enough body heat to work up a pretty good sweat. The lost liquid needs to be replaced as quickly as possible. Get into the habit of drinking a full 8-ounce glass of water 15 minutes before you run and immediately afterward, regardless of the weather.

There are two reasons for being fanatical about this. First, the average American drinks far too little water even for a sedentary life. If you're typical, you're likely to be beginning your runs slightly dehydrated. Also, scientific studies have shown that blood flow is better and exercise feels easier if you're fully hydrated.

Rehydrating immediately after you're finished is important because maintaining good blood flow spurs quicker recovery—translating to reduced stiffness and more energy for your next run. The sooner you can drink after each outing, the better off you'll probably be. (And, of course, stopping for a good drink occasionally during your workout is also beneficial.) It's also valuable to eat shortly after a workout.

MAINTAINING CONSISTENCY

We've already discussed the value of training consistently. If your training is hit-and-miss, your racing will be the same—probably with more "miss" than "hit."

This means you'll have to find ways to deal with the realities of running in less than ideal weather, as well as finding ways to keep vacations, business trips, and the like from interrupting your training. Here are a few tips, but they're only suggestions. Be creative.

- Dodge summer heat by running in mornings or evenings. If you're planning a hot-weather race, though, do some of your training in the expected conditions. Acclimate slowly, rather than suddenly shifting your training into the worst of the midafternoon heat.
- Use a treadmill.
- If you have no indoor place to run in winter, try to avoid running on snow, whose slippery lumps can produce injury-provoking alterations in your stride. Plowed roads or trails are good, but if these are in short supply, snow is one condition that may give you no option but to cut back your mileage.
- If you have no choice but to cut back, try to get in at least 20 minutes of running, 3 times a week. That will do a lot to preserve your conditioning.
- On vacations, you'll often have ample time to run and may find yourself energized by the opportunity to explore new routes. Business trips or really lazy vacations such as cruises, on the other hand, can wreak havoc on training schedules. It's a rare trip, though, that doesn't allow time for at least a

20-minute workout. If nothing else, your hotel may have a treadmill-equipped exercise room, open well before breakfast. Hotel clerks and concierges can also recommend running routes, or at least tell you where it's safe to go, if you're stuck downtown in a big city.

- One or two missed workouts really won't matter all that much. Don't try to "make up" for them the following week. That carries too much risk of getting hurt.

OVERTRAINING

Overtraining occurs when you run yourself down with too much mileage, too much speed, and too little rest.

Grete Waitz, a Norwegian marathoner who won nine New York City Marathons, three times breaking the world record, refers to this as burnout, distinguishing between mini-burnouts from which you can recover in a few days and maxi-burnouts for which the only cure is several months of reduced training and perhaps total rest. I prefer the British "plods," which describes how an overtrained runner feels because burnout raises the specter of permanent damage, even though I've never heard of a case of simple overtraining from which there couldn't be a full recovery. (There are some indications, though, that repeated overtraining can, over the course of years or decades, permanently affect your muscles. It's one of those situations where a little bit of rest now can pay big dividends later.)

Nevertheless, overtraining is a serious concern. It leaves you prone to other injuries, and sends you into a downward spiral of declining performances. You're not overtrained simply because you feel tired for a day or two after a tough workout. That's normal. Lingering tiredness is what you need to be wary of—particularly when it starts to affect your performance.

Overtraining can be insidious. It's a simple trap: with a big race looming, you feel run down and sluggish, so you try to power through by gritting your teeth and training harder. That makes you more sluggish, so you train even harder . . . and become slower yet. Or perhaps you've simply become a slave to your training schedule. That schedule calls on you to run 6 miles today, *and by golly*, you tell yourself, *I'm going to run 6 miles today, whether I feel like it or not.*

Suspect overtraining if you have any of the following:

- An increase in resting heart rate of 10 percent or more, measured when you first wake up in the morning. It's a good idea to measure your resting heart rate occasionally and write it in your training diary, to help you spot a change. In addition to being a sign of excess tiredness, increased heart rate can also signal an incipient cold or other illness.
- Unexplained weight loss.
- A tired or draggy feeling when running, especially one that you can't shake off in a mile or so of warm-up.
- Persistent muscle soreness and tightness after workouts.

- Increased thirst, particularly at night.
- Listlessness, waning interest in workouts, or increasing difficulty in hitting your target pace during speed work.

> **Ward off overtraining by avoiding the temptation to power through sluggishness that might be incipient overtraining. For people with the drive that makes them good racers, that's harder than it sounds!**

If you catch the problem before you're too far down the spiral, you may be able to solve it simply by cutting back on your mileage for a week and taking a break from any form of hard running (including long runs). Doing this can call for a great deal of self-discipline to override the fear that missed training will set you back. Tell yourself that overtraining is worse, and that continuing to push when you're only slightly overtrained is the way to turn one of Grete's mini-burnouts into a maxi that will cost you a lot more than a week's training.

Not that I'm the poster child for practicing what I'm now preaching. There was a time when I measured fitness by the number of miles I logged per week, and felt unfit if it wasn't in the triple digits. To some degree, that's necessary to perform at the elite level. But my career, good as it was, might have lasted longer if I'd been a little less driven about logging mileage. I'd certainly have fared better in the 1984 Olympics, when under the pressure of being the favorite, I let overtraining become one of the factors that did me in. Nor do I know many other elite athletes who wish they'd trained more intensely before major races; most admit that, like me, they'd have done better with slightly less training. So, when I preach the benefits of gradual training, view me as the reformed alcoholic warning of the dangers of overindulgence. Unfortunately, as they used to say: "Been there, done that."

RUNNING FORM

CHILDREN INSTINCTIVELY know how to run. They do it with simple abandon, often with nearly flawless form. But as we age, most of us lose that ability.
Perhaps it's from reduced flexibility, or perhaps we accumulate bad habits by forcing ourselves, for whatever reason, to move unnaturally.

Part of learning to run quickly is curbing as many bad habits as possible. It takes
time, concentration, and practice. But watch the runners in the front of the pack

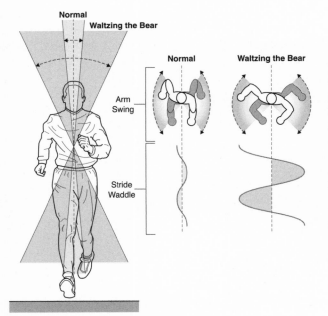

*Holding your arms
like this will make
your hips swivel,
converting your
stride to an energy-
wasting waddle.
Good running form
is designed in part
to minimize your
body's tendency to
zigzag and to keep
you moving straight
down the road.*

Don't do this! Many runners hold their arms too low, as in the exaggerated form above. Proper arm swing comes higher (below), terminating at the centerline of the body, breastbone height. Watch for errors in arm motion when you're tiring; it's easy to start getting lazy by letting your arms drop (even if not by this much).

in a big race and compare them to those in the back. The front-runners seem to flow across the pavement, with no bouncing or other wasted motion. Removing inefficiencies from your stride won't necessarily carry you to the front, but it will speed you up. And it's the perfect form of speed work: increased speed with no extra training and reduced effort. What more could you ask?

UPPER-BODY FORM

Proper stride is a mix of upper-body and lower-body motions. The two are connected: errors in the upper body translate to inefficient leg motion.

Arm Swing

The most obvious aspect of upper-body motion is your arm swing. Many middle-of-the-pack racers make one of two mistakes: either they hold their arms limply down near their hips, or they wag them in an unnatural sideways motion with each swing.

Pause for a moment to consider the mechanics of running. Your arms and legs move in cross-body tandem: as your right arm swings forward, your left leg draws forward and upward, ready for the next foot plant. You've known this since you learned to walk. If the arm and leg swing weren't properly synchronized, you'd stagger around with each stride, trying not to fall over sideways. But just as the timing of the arm swing maintains your balance, the degree of swing governs important aspects of your foot motion. If you hold your hands nearly immobile down near your hips, you'll be forced into tiny, choppy strides—inefficient, slow, and not very comfortable. If you pump them all the way up to shoulder height, you'll be able to lift your knees into an exaggerated high step—also inefficient and energy wasting.

Obviously, what you want is something in the middle. The optimum arm swing brings your hands up to chest height. If you have access to a treadmill, set up a mirror and watch yourself; otherwise, recruit a friend to help. Even on your own, you ought to be able to tell within a couple of inches where your hands are at the peak of their trajectory. Then, it's just a matter of practice.

> **The ideal arm swing brings the hands to chest height,
> angling inward about to the breastbone.**

Arm swing also has a sideways component. Many beginning runners wave their arms out to the side with each forward swing, in an exaggerated motion as though they're trying to waltz with a bear. That forces your legs to waddle inefficiently from side to side. Instead, you want your feet to move as straight ahead with each stride as possible, so that each step carries you toward your goal rather than bouncing even slightly back and forth.

In theory, you'd run your fastest if your arms drove forward and back in exactly the direction you're moving. That, in fact, is exactly how the best sprinters run. But it's tiring, and you can't keep it up for long. In distance running, your arms should swing inward as they come forward, with your hands coming approximately to your breastbone. If they swing substantially farther than midway across your body, you'll find yourself moving down the road with an odd, energy-wasting hip twist as your body overrotates with each stride. Slightly too little inward motion is less of a problem, but you'll move more smoothly if you can get that arm swing to terminate naturally at your breastbone, at approximately chest height.

> **In distance running, your torso should be upright
> or leaning very slightly forward.**

The Lean

You'll also benefit from controlling the lean of your upper body. Many uncoached runners lean backward. Other runners have been told to lean forward, but substantially overdo it. Your natural running motion has the torso close to vertical or leaning slightly forward (no more than 2 degrees). Leaning substantially forward is the way to run quickly downhill (see pages 194–95). If you do it on the flats, it's as though you're trying to plant your feet slightly below road surface with each stride. That's impossible, of course, so you land uncomfortably, with an inefficient, shorter-than-normal stride.

If you lean backward, you have an even worse problem. Now, your feet are trying to land in midair. Obviously, this won't happen either, so they'll continue swinging for-

Here you see exaggerated illustrations of a backward lean (above left) and too much forward lean (above right). What you want to do is more like I'm doing at right.

ward before hitting the pavement, too far out in front of you and too far back on your heels—a motion known as reaching out. We discuss this problem in the Leg Motion section, coming up; for now, remember that leaning backward makes it worse.

The Clench

A minor but easy-to-cure upper-body error is to clench your hands or tense up the muscles of your upper arms and shoulders—both likely at the end of a long race. You may also find yourself clenching your jaw or tightening the muscles of your neck and shoulders. Check periodically to see if you're doing this,

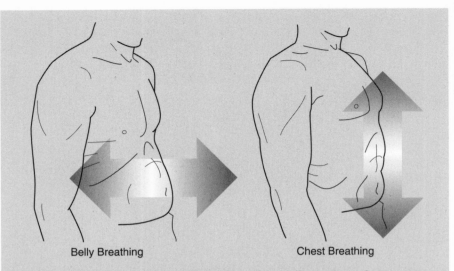

Belly Breathing   Chest Breathing

Belly breathing allows you to run faster by making full use of your lung capacity.

THE BEAUTY OF BELLY BREATHING

Good running form includes proper breathing. I learned this naturally, but Rick had to teach himself, with the help of friends in drama and music, who face similar problems:

Many adults don't know how to breathe the way nature intended. Put your hand on your stomach and watch what happens when you draw a breath. If you're breathing properly, your hand should move outward with each breath, as your belly expands. This happens because the diaphragm fills the lungs by pulling downward on them, creating suction that draws the air inward. The diaphragm's downward shift compresses the organs that lie beneath it, causing your belly to bulge outward.

That's normal breathing, called *belly breathing* by voice teachers and actors. Many people, however, have taught themselves to suck in their stomachs and throw out their chests with each breath—presumably in an effort to look thin or sexy. This *chest breathing* will cause your hand to move inward and upward with each indrawn breath. Whatever it might do for swimsuit models and bodybuilders, chest breathing restricts the amount of air you can draw with each breath, putting a cap on your running speed. (It can also give you painful side stitches; see pages 150–51.)

Learning to belly breathe may come naturally as you become more athletic, but you can speed the process with some simple drills. Bend over deeply at the waist, much as though you were planning to touch your toes. In this position, most people have no choice but to belly breathe. Now, stand up, trying not to shift back to chest breathing. It'll take practice, but eventually it will feel more natural. Lying on your back will achieve the same result. Put your hand on your stomach to ensure that it is indeed expanding with each breath, then stand up, without altering your breathing. Practice this enough times and your body will gradually relearn to breathe the way it should.

making this self-check an automatic part of both racing and training. Muscle clench-ing isn't going to ruin your stride, but it wastes energy and can leave the affected mus-cles feeling unnecessarily tired and beat up afterward. Pay particular attention to your hands; they should be in a relaxed, neutral curl, not balled into fists.

> **Concentrate on relaxing your arms, hands, and shoulders to keep from wasting energy by clenching up.**

LEG MOTION

Now let's turn to the lower body and leg motion. Here, there are three principal stride abnormalities—one correctable with practice, another with shoe inserts called *orthotics*, and another that may simply be a biomechanical cap on your native speed.

Reaching Out (Overstriding)

The major, correctable lower-body error is a problem that coaches call *overstriding*, but that might better be called *reaching out*. This occurs when your leg swings too far forward with each stride. Your foot comes down in front of your body, gen-erally far back on the heel, where the shock of impact "puts on the brakes" with each stride—an inefficient, potentially injurious practice. Also, reaching out forces you to use your hamstrings (the muscles at the back of your thighs) to pull your-self forward at the start of each stride, rather than immediately pushing off with the stronger quadriceps muscles (located at the front of your thighs). Overstriders are "pullers," while people with normal strides are "pushers."

Reaching out is an extremely common error. In part, it comes from an attempt to speed up by lengthening your stride. But the type of stride lengthening that

HOW REACHING OUT CAN SLOW YOU DOWN

I once coached a talented high school runner who had a problem with reaching out (over-striding). One day on the track, after he'd done a series of 220-yard repeats at a respectable 30-second pace, I got tough. "You're still overstriding," I told him. "I don't care what time you run, but I want the next 220 to be different. What I don't want is to see you overstriding on an-other of those 30-second repeats."

This time, his form was better. "What do you think the time was?" I asked.

He shrugged. "Thirty-one seconds? Thirty-two?"

I showed him the watch: 28 seconds. He'd sped up 6 percent while running what felt like an easier pace. That's how much overstriding hurts you, as your body accelerates and brakes with each step.

Overstride

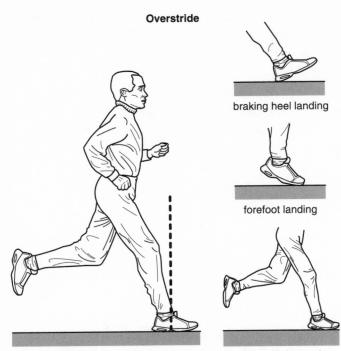

braking heel landing

forefoot landing

foot plant far in front of hips and body

pulling with hamstring

will speed you up comes not from reaching out but from a rearward extension at the end of each stride, increasing the time you spend airborne. Reaching out may feel like the obvious way to lengthen your stride, but it actually shortens it by forcing you to work inefficiently at the beginning, when your foot is too far forward. When I'm coaching people to lengthen their strides, I discourage them from thinking about stride length at all. Instead, I tell them to think about increasing the force of their stride and its *turnover rate*—the number of strides they make per minute. Initially, this feels like it shortens your stride, but it actually lengthens it by increasing the extension of your leg behind you—and therefore the amount of time you spend airborne between strides.

Ideally your foot should strike so that it's directly beneath your hips at the time your weight first comes fully on it (that is, when your shoe is fully on the ground), moving straight down at the moment it hits the pavement. But it's OK if your foot lands a few inches forward from this ideal position. A good distance-running stride also lands with the foot slightly back on the heel or up on the forefoot, not far back on the heel or way up on the toes. When trying to improve this aspect of your stride, though, don't make sudden, drastic changes; try to improve in small increments that give your body time to adjust.

Rather than worrying too much about what part of your foot hits first, concen-

Optimum "push" stride

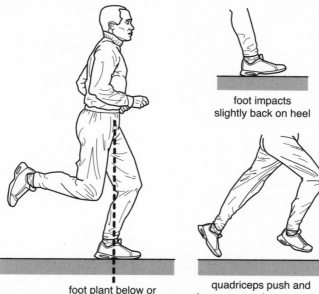

foot impacts
slightly back on heel

foot plant below or
slightly in front of hips

quadriceps push and
increase rear leg extension

trate on getting it to land directly beneath your hips. Glance down occasionally to see where your feet are landing. If they're striking far out in front of your body, it should be obvious. Smaller errors are harder to spot, but with practice, you'll learn to notice the alignment of your hip and foot at the moment of impact. If you decide you're overstriding, make a deliberate effort not to do so, even if it feels as if you're mincing your stride by taking tiny steps. Not only will the increased efficiency eventually speed you up, but proper stride will also reduce impact shock on your knees.

> **You're overstriding if your foot reaches out significantly in front of your hip at the time it hits the ground. It should come down vertically, directly beneath you at the time it makes full contact with the ground.**

I was a "puller" myself—a problem I didn't fully understand for many years. Other racers actually tried to imitate me, assuming that if I could win marathons with that overextended, reaching-ahead gait, then it must be the best way to move.

Actually, successful as I was, I would have run even better if my stride had been closer to optimal. When I did correct it, in my mid-30s, running felt more natural than ever. And other than a mishap from stepping in a hole, I never had another injury.

Toe-Off

Your toes are as important to efficient running as are your legs. As you leave the ground with each stride, you rise up on your toes, stiffening them to provide a firm platform from which to launch yourself forward.

Much of this occurs unconsciously, but it's good to think about it occasionally. Ideally, the toe-off will come evenly from your first three toes. If it comes from somewhere else—such as the little toes or the inside edge of the big toe—you're launching yourself sideways, in an energy-wasting zigzag.

Toe-off is largely controlled by your foot structure and your shoes. Some shoes cant the forefoot outward too much for some runners, forcing the toe-off onto the little toes. This isn't a problem you can correct by conscious effort; basically you're fighting a shoe designed for runners with feet different from yours. Buy a different shoe. If that doesn't work, you may suffer from *excess supination*, a relatively uncommon foot problem that may require orthotics.

Toeing off from the inside of the big toe, on the other hand, is a sign that your foot is rolling too far inward with each stride. This common problem, called *excess pronation* (or *overpronation*), requires either orthotics or shoes designed for greater motion control. (See pages 144–46 for a discussion of excess pronation and excess supination.)

Foot Alignment

Another stride problem can be identified by first running through a puddle or across a patch of firm sand. Go back and examine your footprints. They should fall in a fairly straight line, with your left footprint and the right footprint no more than a few inches off center. If you were to run down the white stripe at the side of a soccer field, you should be able to run comfortably with both feet consistently hitting the line, rather than straddling back and forth from one side to the other. In addition, the inside edges of your footprints should point pretty close to straight ahead.

If you tend to run duck-toed (toes pointing outward) or pigeon-toed (toes pointing inward), you have a potential problem. Worse is if one foot angles inward or outward more sharply than the other. Any of these patterns may indicate that something's not quite right in your legs, probably in your hips.

Friends may point out this alignment pattern and encourage you to correct it. It's yet another of those things that slow you down by making you toe-off sideways with each stride. But the solution may not be easy. With conscious effort, you may be able to force your feet to line up in the ideal straight-ahead orientation, but your body has a reason for running this way, and forcing it to do something unnatural will probably get you hurt. Most likely, you'll just have to live with it. But first, check out your arm swing, as described earlier in this chapter; if you're lucky, that's the cause. You can also turn to chapter 6 and concentrate on buttocks stretches. Your problem may be exacerbated by lack of flexibility.

Women with wide hips may have a similar problem with a less-than-ideally-efficient alignment of their thighs. If this is you, the natural flare of your pelvic bones will rotate your thighs so that your knees move inward with each stride. Although many women equate hips with weight, it really doesn't matter what you weigh; the issue is bone structure. Again, your body wants to zigzag as it runs. The lower leg compensates by flipping the foot out to the side, but the foot strike still comes at an angle that causes the arch to collapse inward, as in overpronation.

The only way to address this problem is by correcting the overpronation with motion-control shoes or orthotics, but that's seldom more than a partial solution. This is why you don't see many elite women distance runners with wide hips; more often the best have hips like teenage boys. But if you have a more feminine build, don't despair: a few women with your body type have made it to the top. They may have slightly unorthodox gaits, but they've won Olympic gold.

PRACTICING THE BAD TO LEARN THE GOOD

Rick has a good exercise for understanding the differences in running form. Try the following.

A great way to increase your understanding of the principles of good running form is to run a few yards with wildly wrong form. Try running with your torso leaning as far backward as possible. You'll find that you're reaching your legs far out in front of you and landing far back on your heels. When I tried this, my shins hurt, too; if I did it all the time, I'd probably get shin splints. Now reverse what you're doing and lean as far forward as possible without falling on your nose. You'll immediately find out what's wrong with this, too.

You can use similar drills to highlight the reasons for proper arm swing. Try running with your thumbs hooked into your waistband so you can't swing them at all. Awkward, isn't it? Now try swinging them way out to the side, much too far across your body, or far out in front of you at eye level. You'll immediately see why these motions, too, aren't exactly optimal.

Most of us, of course, don't have such radical stride abnormalities. But testing out these severe errors in running form can help convince you that smaller errors may have similar effects, even if they're less obvious.

ONE IDEAL FORM

I firmly believe there is only one ideal running form and that our bodies are all made to the same basic design, which functions best when used the way it's made to work. That doesn't mean good runners don't have idiosyncrasies; it just means that these idiosyncrasies detract, however slightly, from optimum pace.

Perhaps the greatest distance runner of all time is Haile Gebresailesse, from Ethiopia. Watching him in slow motion is an eye-opening experience. His feet come straight down at the end of each stride, with almost no braking impact, and his extension at the end of each stride is superb. Yet even he has a slight oddity: his left arm doesn't swing as much as his right arm does with each stride. This might actually help him round the corners on a track, but that isn't the reason he developed the habit. It comes from childhood, when he used to run to school 5 miles every day. His left arm was the one in which he carried his books, causing it to swing less than the right arm. It's a habit he's never quite shaken.

The lessons for the average racer? First, good form pays off. But even the best runners have quirks. While these may cause them to deviate a bit from ideal, it's not enough to keep them from winning races. So, strive to improve your stride, but realize that nobody ever quite reaches perfection.

Speed Training

5

THE TERM *speed training* is a bit of a misnomer because it implies that this is the only type of training that will make you faster. Increased volume will also help, as will correcting abnormalities in your stride, as described in chapters 3 and 4. But these methods will only take you so far. Eventually there comes a plateau that you can best break through with workouts specifically designed to boost speed. Even if you've not yet reached that plateau, speed workouts can help you improve without the time commitment that comes with increased training volume.

There are two basic types of speed workouts: intervals and tempo runs.

Intervals are comprised of alternating fast-paced *repeats*, and slow *recovery breaks*. Repeats can be as short as 200 meters (one-eighth of a mile) or as long as 2 miles (although this book won't recommend anything longer than 1-mile repeats). The number that you'll do will vary with their length, your training goals, and your overall level of conditioning.

Tempo runs are longer and slower. They're generally run as continuous sessions, although it's possible to split them in half with an intervening recovery break. All speed workouts begin and end with warm-up and cooldown jogs of at least a mile.

Most likely, you'll do these workouts on a track. Try to find one with a smooth, cushy surface; a well-maintained track is a joy to run on. Some runner-friendly towns have public tracks in city parks. Otherwise, some high school tracks are open to the public after school hours. Colleges tend to be more proprietary about their facilities, but you may be able to get access at a community college. Health clubs generally don't have full-length outdoor tracks, although a few have short indoor ones.

You're ready to take on speed training if you've been consistently running 20 or more miles a week for at least 2 months. Training for international competition, I did three speed workouts per week but I supported that with a total of 110 to 130 miles of running per week. At nonelite training levels, you should never do more than two speed workouts per week. Starting out, you might be wise to hold back to about one every 5 days—particularly if you're running less than 30 miles a week. If that's hard to schedule in a world where everything else works on a 7-day cycle, try alternating weeks: one week has two speed workouts, the next has only one. Many recreational racers do only one speed workout per week, but that's too infrequent. You need to average at least one every 5 days to allow them to build on each other to maximum effect. Otherwise, they'll always be more tiring than they need to be.

Other important tips for starting speed workouts:

- Follow the hard-easy pattern. When possible, allow at least 2 easy days between speed workouts, and don't do a speed workout on the day after your long run. One pattern that works for twice-weekly workouts is to do speed work on Mondays and Thursdays, with long runs on Saturdays.
- Races figure into this schedule as speed workouts. In other words, you should cut down on speed work before and after a race. Never do a speed session closer than 4 days before a 5K, and avoid the entire week before a half-marathon. The last workout before the race should be paced about 5 percent slower than normal, just to make sure you're fully recovered for the race. You're better off to skip a session than to wear yourself out too soon before the race. (See the discussion of *tapering* in chapter 11.)
- After a race, take time to recover, as described in chapter 14. When you resume speed training, your first workout should be something relatively easy, such as short intervals.
- Start with relatively easy workouts, adding tougher ones later. "Easier," however, doesn't mean "slower." Stick to the target paces recommended in this chapter, and adjust the difficulty of your workouts via the number of repeats or the length of a tempo run.
- How much speed work you can do varies with your weekly base mileage. Elite athletes' speed sessions, with warm-up and cooldown, can include as much as 12 miles of running. Obviously, two of these won't fit a 20-mile-a-week schedule. With that training volume, even 5-mile speed workouts would be excessive. Some coaches advise restricting speed work (not counting warm-ups, recovery breaks, and cooldowns) to no more than 10 or 15 percent of your total weekly distance, but that rule is more applicable to elite runners than to recreational runners. Elite runners train 7 days a week, while you're getting more real rest by taking the 2 rest days that are recommended. That allows speed work to be a higher proportion of your overall training. My approach, therefore, is simply to recommend that you make sure that no individual speed workout, counting warm-up and recovery, exceeds 20 percent of your total weekly distance. Otherwise, it becomes both a speed session *and* a relatively long day, an unwise (and unpleasant) combination. Only about half of that distance will be run at speed (as opposed to warm-up, cooldown, and recovery breaks), but you get to do two of these per week. At 20 miles per week, this is a bit limiting (after a mile of warm-up and a mile of

cooldown, you're only left with 2 miles for everything else). At 30 miles per week, the speed distance goes up to 3 miles per workout (6 miles per week), which is about what most serious recreational racers actually do.

- Don't do speed work year-round. Even elite racers don't do that. Each year you need at least one multimonth break from intense training.
- Avoid starting up speed work or increasing its intensity while also increasing your weekly volume. Doing so risks getting hurt, and changing only one variable at a time also makes it easier to figure out what's working—and what isn't.

It's possible to speed train indefinitely without ever testing your progress in a race. But most people want to see results fairly quickly—and periodic racing feedback lets you fine-tune your speed work. Therefore, the program in this chapter is designed with the expectation that you'll undertake it in 4- to 6-week blocks, each culminating in a race. That can be followed by another training block targeted on another race (of the same or a different length), until eventually you reach a plateau beyond which it's difficult to improve. When that happens, continued speed work will be necessary to keep from backsliding.

FINDING YOUR WAY AROUND THE TRACK

Outdoor tracks come in two flavors: quarter-mile and 400-meter. The difference is about 3 to 4 yards—not enough to matter. In colloquial speech, runners often treat the two distances as identical. A runner who's been doing 400-meter repeats, for example, will often refer to them as quarters. "Halves" and "800s" are also frequently used interchangeably. Because a quarter-mile is 440 yards, you'll sometimes hear eighths, quarters, and halves referred to in yards as 220s, 440s, and 880s, but these terms appear to be on the wane. On today's tracks, a "mile" is more apt to be 1,600 meters. The difference between 1,600 meters and a mile is trivial: about 10 yards.

Indoor tracks, on the other hand, come in a variety of lengths, often nonstandard. They're generally short, with tight bends. Running quickly on such tracks puts odd stresses on your body (not to mention the risk of colliding with a wall). Don't do speed work on indoor tracks measuring less than an eighth of a mile in length, and avoid those whose corners aren't well-enough banked to keep you from flying off at a tangent when you try to round them at speed.

EYEING THE PRIZE

For people who've never run speed workouts before, the results can be fairly dramatic. A single workout won't produce a noticeable effect, but a month of training twice a week has a reasonable chance of knocking several seconds per mile off your race pace. Repeated cycles of racing and speed work might allow you to ratchet your speed up by as much as a minute a mile over the course of a year. After that, more modest advances may still be possible.

The workouts in this chapter are designed on the basis of your current racing speed, rather than for specific targets in your next races. That keeps the speed program flexible and easy to apply, but you'll need a goal around which to plan your race-day strategy.

> **Once-per-week isn't often enough for speed workouts.**
> **Train for speed at least three times every two weeks.**

What is a reasonable target? To some extent that will depend on how much race experience you have. Beginning racers often go through a heady period, lasting up to a year or two, where it seems that everything they run is a PR. Partly, such improvements come from learning to push yourself harder than you'd previously believed possible; partly it's the cumulative effect of consistent endurance training.

Adding speed work to the mix accelerates the rate of progress. The table lists reasonable goals for performance improvements from your first training blocks. How many times you'll be able to duplicate these achievements depends partly on your natural ability: slower runners typically have more room for improvement than faster ones. Thus, if you're a man racing at slower than 8:00s or a woman racing at slower than 9:00s, you may be able to achieve the listed improvements five or six times in a row. On the 10K, that could add up to a 4- to 6-minute improvement. Men running between 7:00s and 8:00s (and women running between 8:00s and 9:00s) can hope for three to four cycles of improvement at the levels shown in the table, while faster runners (men who can run 6:00s to 7:00s without speed training, and women who clock in at 7:00s to 8:00s) can still hope for two or three such successes. The fastest natural speedsters (sub-6:00s for men, sub-7:00s for women) will probably see only one or two rounds of substantial improvement.

TARGET PERFORMANCE IMPROVEMENTS FROM SPEED TRAINING*

RACE DISTANCE	TARGET IMPROVEMENT FROM 4-WEEK TRAINING BLOCK	TARGET IMPROVEMENT FROM 6-WEEK TRAINING BLOCK
5K	0:20	0:30
5-mile	0:35	0:50
10K	0:45	1:00
10-mile	1:10	1:30
half-marathon	1:30	2:00

* Improvements are in overall time, not per-mile pace. Race improvements range from 7–10 seconds per mile.

These aren't hard and fast rules, however. It's not uncommon for high school runners (even the speedy ones) to see their 5K times improve by 90 seconds (30 seconds per mile) in their first seasons of serious cross-country racing. And slower racers can see truly stunning advances. I've known high school runners to advance their 5K cross-country times from the 27-to-28-minute range to 21 or 22 minutes in a mere 3 months. That's nearly a 2-minute-per-mile improvement!

Whatever your natural abilities, eventually you'll hit the point of diminishing returns. By then, though, most people feel just as satisfied knocking 10 seconds off of a personal record as they once did from reducing it by a full minute. After all, any PR performance is a new best, even if the improvement is only by a second. World records have been set by smaller margins than that.

THE VARIETIES OF SPEED WORKOUTS

Different speed workouts are designed to achieve different goals. Some build running efficiency, some boost your ability to handle lactic acid, some help increase your VO_2max. In addition, fast stints on the track can be valuable confidence-builders.

Speed training is also a good opportunity to improve your running form. When you're tiring, your form tends to suffer, but if you can learn to control it in practice, you'll find it easier to do so in races. Longer intervals are more useful for this than shorter ones, because the shortest repeats are over so quickly that you don't spend much time in that tiring, form-failing state.

Top-level competitors design speed workouts around details of their race performances. If they've been dragging in the middle miles, they'll concentrate on one kind of workout; if their weakness is the finish, they'll concentrate on another. They also design workouts around the racing calendar, doing certain types of training early in the season, and others when important races draw nigh.

That's far more complex than anything you should consider unless you've been racing (and running intervals) for several years and can do a 10K at well under a 5:30 pace. (If that's you, consult *Daniels' Running Formula*, by Jack Daniels, which has a highly detailed program geared for faster runners.) What most people need is simply to do a variety of different types of workouts. To facilitate this, I've divided speed workouts into four categories: long intervals, medium intervals, short intervals, and tempo workouts, each with different characteristics and physiological goals.

- *Long intervals.* These are your VO_2max workouts. Repeat miles are the classic, but any distance of 1,000 meters or longer is acceptable. Long intervals are tough because you do them at well faster than race pace. When I did such workouts, I had to psyche myself up almost to the degree I did for a race. You're best off to avoid doing them during the week before a race.
- *Medium intervals.* If you're not in the mood for long intervals, medium intervals offer a good compromise. At distances of 600 to 800 meters, they're

easier than long intervals, even though you'll do more of them and do them a bit faster. Like long intervals, they're designed mostly to boost VO_2max, but they'll also help improve your running efficiency.

- *Short intervals.* These are distances of up to 400 meters, run at the fastest pace you'll ever do in training. They're too short to do much for VO_2max; instead, they're designed primarily to boost your running efficiency—which is why a base of short intervals can help you through not only the race, but also your longer intervals.
- *Tempo runs.* At the opposite end of the distance scale, tempo runs are your longest speed workouts, designed to boost your lactic acid threshold by taking you to the edge of lactic acid overload and holding you there for several minutes. Some runners refer to them as "lactic acid runs." They're not as tough as medium or long intervals because you'll run at slower than race pace—a speed that will feel fast but not unbearably so. Many runners find these to be quite enjoyable.

Your training schedule allows a maximum of two speed workouts per week. With a few constraints that we'll discuss in a moment, you're free to pick workouts from any of the four categories you want. But you shouldn't always do the same workout. Otherwise, you'll be focusing too strongly on one physiological variable, such as VO_2max, at the expense of the others. Also, different types of workouts build on each other.

You could think of it as something like constructing a flight of stairs. When I was targeting on racing 10Ks at a 4:25 pace, for example, I needed to run repeat miles at 4:20s. But to do that, I had to be able to run 1,200 meters (three-quar-

GOALS PROMOTED BY FOUR TYPES OF SPEED WORKOUTS

WORKOUT CATEGORY	DESCRIPTION	GOALS
long intervals	1,000–1,600 meters (1 mile)	higher VO_2max improved running form
medium intervals	600–800 meters	higher VO_2max increased running efficiency improved running form
short intervals	up to 400 meters	increased running efficiency
tempo runs	20 minutes, to one-half of race distance	higher lactic acid threshold improved running form

ters of a mile) in about 3:08 to 3:10. That required a background of 800s in 2:02 to 2:04, which in turn required me to be comfortable with 59- to 60-second quarters. Those quarters drew on a base of 28- to 29-second 200s. Without the 200s, I couldn't have done the quarters, halves, 1,200s, or miles—and 4:25s on the 10K would have been impossible. The short intervals provided a base that supported the long ones.

> **Repeated cycles of racing and speed workouts might allow you to ratchet your speed up by as much as a minute a mile over the course of a year.**

But you won't be building this staircase in strict bottom-to-top order. Instead, you hop back and forth from one level to another, pounding in a nail here and a nail there until the entire edifice is complete. Even when you're running good, hard long intervals, you can't forget the short ones, or the foundation will decay out from under you.

On the other hand, many runners—including some world-class athletes—make the opposite mistake, skimping on the longer intervals. The reason's simple enough: shorter intervals aren't as grueling, and there's a sense of accomplishment from the fact that you can do them at paces dramatically above race pace. You feel like you're flying, and that buoys you up. I knew plenty of runners, though, who could beat me at short intervals but not in races. That was because they got caught up in doing fast repeats at the bottom end of the distance scale and neglected the top end. And it's the top end that's the best indicator of when you're in shape for a race. You know you're ready when you can do long intervals at your target pace, in a modicum of comfort.

In designing a speed program, the basic rule is simple: just as you eat a variety of foods for good nutrition, do a variety of speed workouts for optimum training. Don't draw from the same category for any two successive workouts. Thus, if one speed workout is a tempo run, the next needs to be something else—intervals of one length or another. Within each category, add further variety by not always doing the same workout. Thus, when you're doing long intervals, one session might be 1,000s, another might be miles, and another might be 1,200s. The only other constraint is that you shouldn't do long intervals and medium intervals in successive workouts. Because both are targeted mostly on improving your VO_2max, they're too similar to give you enough variety.

PICKING YOUR BENCHMARK PACE

Speed workouts need to be done at the proper pace, calculated on the basis of your present racing speed. We'll get to the details of the calculation in a moment, but first it's necessary to assess, as objectively as possible, just how fast you currently are. This is important because underestimating your abilities will produce workouts that are too slow; overoptimism will make them too grueling. Unfortunately, for beginners that's a fairly narrow window—less than 20 seconds per mile. The difference between a workout that leaves you feeling "good" tired and one you'd be more apt to describe as "murderous" can be even smaller, sometimes less than 10 seconds per mile.

If you've raced your target distance recently, that performance will be your benchmark. Or, with adjustments to be described in the next paragraph, any recent race can serve as a benchmark, regardless of distance. Otherwise, you need to enter a 5K or run a time trial before you begin speed workouts. Do the time trial on a track or on any other carefully measured, smooth-surfaced course where you won't be impeded by traffic, stoplights, or other obstacles. Go for 3 miles—that's close enough to 5K for present purposes—and run as though you're in a race, pushing as hard as you can. This is the speed you'll be training to beat in your next race, so don't sandbag by loafing.

> **Calculate speed-workout paces based on your recent race performances. Don't substitute goals that aren't performance-based or the workouts will be too tough.**

You can derive a 10K benchmark pace from the same 3-mile time trial or a recent 5K. Simply figure that your pace at the longer distance will be about 15 to 20 seconds per mile slower than for the 3-mile trial or a 5K. The faster you are, the less the difference in pace; at the world-class level, it's about 10 seconds per mile. At 9:00s, it's probably about double that amount.

You can also work in the opposite direction, using a 10K time to estimate your present capability at 5K. For greater precision, or for other race distances, consult the chart on page 213, which shows how to use your performance at one distance to predict your potential performance at any other.

If in doubt, err on the side of being a bit conservative. You'll wind up doing easier-than-optimal workouts, but the race that follows will give you a new, more realistic benchmark. Overoptimism, of course, will also be corrected by race-day reality, but it's a lot more fun to exceed expectations than to fall short. Either way, you'll zero in on your best possible performance as you adjust your training based on your latest race.

HOW TO RUN A SPEED WORKOUT

Interval workouts begin with a warm-up of at least a mile and conclude with another mile of cooldown. But the heart of the workout is composed of the repeats and the intervening recovery breaks. For maximum benefit, you need to do both correctly. (Tempo runs are similar except that generally the speed work is confined to a single, longer segment.)

The repeats should feel fast—unpleasantly so by the time you get to the last one—but they shouldn't be all-out efforts. You want to leave the workout tired but feeling that if you had to, you could have done more. Otherwise, you're either doing too many repeats or being overaggressive in your pacing.

Each repeat should be run at as steady a pace as you can manage. There's no reason not to look at your watch frequently to see if you're on target, adjusting your pace as needed. It's easy to go out too fast in the first portion of an interval because the pace feels deceptively easy. Then fatigue sets in, bringing reality with it, and your speed begins to drop. Being as little as 1 or 2 seconds per lap too fast at the start can catch up with you in the final yards. The fatigue is cumulative; each time you start an interval too fast, you not only create problems at the end of it, but in the next repeat as well.

If, on the other hand, you fall behind pace in the early going, don't attempt to catch back up with a fast sprint at the end; that doesn't train your body to do anything useful. Interval running is intended to make you more comfortable running an even, fast pace. If one interval is off pace, make the adjustment on the next one. If the target pace remains out of reach, consider doing fewer repeats than planned. It's better to do a small number of intervals at the correct pace than a larger number, too slowly.

You should also adjust pace on the next repeat if you went too fast all the way through the previous one. Yes, there are occasional breakthroughs, when interval sessions that once seemed taxing are suddenly easy. It's a glorious feeling, but be leery of it in the early stages of a workout; more often than not, it's an illusion. Ease off on your next repeat and see how that feels. If it still feels good, you can always pick up the pace later on; otherwise, you've averted an unpleasant mistake. If your workout calls for several 1,000-meter repeats at, say, 4:38 each, letting yourself blaze through two fast ones in 4:30 each, then running out of steam, doesn't accomplish the goal. Physiologically, you've not spent enough time at the desired speed to achieve the training goal, and psychologically, you've lost confidence. If you actually do have extra energy, it's better to speed up at the end of a workout than at the beginning.

Proper recovery breaks are nearly as important. They should be done at a slow jog, not a walk (although it's fine to stop for water if you need it). Jogging continues to give you training benefits while you're recovering, and there are psychological gains from not feeling as though you've beaten yourself up so badly that you have no choice but to walk. Jogging also makes it easier to standardize your workouts, so you can compare performances the next time you do a similar one. If you jog, the time spent on recovery won't vary much; walking, you can squander several extra minutes by strolling unusually slowly. That would make it difficult to determine if a change in performance is due to changed conditioning or simply comes from inconsistent recovery breaks.

At least as importantly, jogging flushes lactic acid from your muscles more quickly than does walking. That means that even if it feels tougher than walking, jogging will leave you more ready for your next interval. The jog, however, can be very slow.

OPTIMUM RECOVERY BREAKS FOR INTERVALS FROM 200 METERS TO 1 MILE

INTERVAL LENGTH	OPTIMUM RECOVERY BREAKS, METERS
200 meters (½ lap)	200
300 meters (¾ lap)	200
400 meters (1 lap)	400
600 meters (1½ laps)	400
800 meters (2 laps)	600
1,000 meters (2½ laps)	600
1,200 meters (3 laps)	600
1 mile or 1,600 meters (4 laps)	800

When I was running repeats at paces close to 4:00 per mile, my recovery breaks came in at something on the order of a 9:00 or even 10:00 pace. You may find yourself recovering at 12:00s or even slower—whatever it takes, so long as it's a jog, not a walk.

Recovery breaks should be 50 to 100 percent of the length of the interval. The accompanying table shows recommended recoveries for several standard interval distances. Most are multiples of 200 meters, making it easy to find starting and stopping points on tracks marked in half-lap increments. The exception is the 300s, which wind up as 1¼ laps per repeat/recovery cycle. If there are no quarter-lap marks on your track, start each repeat at the same point and jog back and forth enough to bring the recovery distance up to about the 200 meters recommended in the table.

CUSTOMIZING YOUR SPEED WORK

When I coach, I give my runners individualized workouts that identify the precise speeds and distances I expect them to run, based on their recent performances and upcoming racing schedules. This book could have done something similar by presenting a myriad workout regimens for every conceivable need. But you'll do better by learning to design your own workouts than by having me swamp you with complicated training tables that you're likely to forget to bring to the track anyway.

The table of speed workouts on pages 72–73 offers a menu of workouts in each of the four categories. They are keyed to your race plans: pick the section marked 5K if that's what you're training for, or the section for the 10K or the half-marathon, whatever matches your next race. If you're training for a distance not in the table, pick the one closest to it; it will be close enough to what you need.

Use the table as you would a multicourse menu, with the constraint that you must limit yourself to no more than two courses per week. Also, as we discussed earlier, successive workouts must come from different categories. Which categories is pretty much up to you, although again I strongly advise against doing long and medium intervals in back-to-back workouts.

Within each menu option are two or three choices. Do only one of them. The shorthand should be fairly easy to interpret. For example, "3 to 6 × 800 meters" means to complete three to six runs of 800 meters, plus the appropriate recovery. Exactly how many you do is up to you, although you'll probably want to do only three or four if you're new to running medium-length repeats, if your mileage base is low, or if you're having trouble holding the pace by the time you reach the third interval.

Speed training isn't a race. It works best if done at the proper pace.

If you're training for a 5K, the table tells you to do these 800s at 0:10 to 0:15 (10 to 15 seconds) per mile faster than your current 5K race pace (or your pace on the 3-mile time trial described above). Thus, if your race pace is 8:40 per mile, you'll want to do your 800s at an 8:30 pace or 8:25 pace—or 4:15 to 4:12.5 apiece. If instead you choose to do 600s, they'd be at the same 8:30 to 8:25 pace, which translates to about 3:11 to 3:09 apiece. If the arithmetic confuses you, work it out in advance with a pace calculator (see page 18) or use the Pace Chart in the appendix. The best approach is by computing your desired pace per 400-meter lap, then multiplying by the appropriate number of laps. Fractional seconds don't matter; if your target pace for an 800-meter repeat is the 4:12.5 mentioned above, you're doing OK if you hit anything between about 4:10 and 4:15.

The table gives a range of paces for each speed workout. In general (but by no means always), faster runners will have more experience at pushing themselves hard, and are more apt to be comfortable running at the fast end of the range. Slower runners may be more comfortable at the lower end of the range. Don't worry, either pace will speed you up, and as we've noted before, it's more important to run your target pace consistently throughout your workout than to set a goal you can't maintain.

PRINCIPLES OF DISCIPLINED INTERVAL WORK

Interval workouts are more valuable if they are run according to the following 3 principles:

1. Intervals aren't all-out sprints. They're fast, but never that fast.

2. Each interval should be run as close to the target pace as possible. Pride yourself on hitting the mark, not beating it. If that starts feeling easy, it may be time to change the goal.

3. An interval session includes both the fast running and the recovery. If you take too little recovery, you won't be sufficiently rested to hit your target pace on subsequent intervals; if you take too much, you're not working hard enough.

SPEED WORKOUTS BY CATEGORY AND RACE DISTANCE

RACE DISTANCE	WORKOUT CATEGORY			
	SHORT INTERVALS	MEDIUM INTERVALS	LONG INTERVALS	TEMPO RUNS
5K				
workout choices (pick one)	6 to 10 x 200 meters 5 to 8 x 300 meters 4 to 6 x 400 meters	3 to 6 x 800 meters 4 to 8 x 600 meters	2 to 3 x 1 mile 2 to 4 x 1,200 meters 3 to 5 x 1,000 meters	2 miles continuous 2 x 1.5 miles (with 1-mile recovery) 3 miles continuous
workout pace	0:25 to 0:30 per mile faster than current 5K race pace	0:10 to 0:15 per mile faster than current 5K race pace	0:02 to 0:05 per mile faster than current 5K race pace	0:15 to 0:20 per mile slower than current 5K race pace[1]
8K TO 10K				
workout choices (pick one)	8 to 12 x 200 meters 7 to 10 x 300 meters 6 to 8 x 400 meters	5 to 8 x 800 meters 7 to 10 x 600 meters	3 to 5 x 1 mile 4 to 6 x 1,200 meters 5 to 7 x 1,000 meters	3 to 4 miles 2 x 2 miles (with 1-mile recovery)
workout pace	0:30 to 0:35 per mile faster than current 10K race pace	0:15 to 0:20 per mile faster than current 10K race pace	0:05 to 0:10 per mile faster than current 10K race pace	0:15 to 0:20 per mile slower than current 10K race pace
12K TO 10 MILES				
workout choices (pick one)	8 to 12 x 200 meters 7 to 10 x 300 meters 6 to 8 x 400 meters	6 to 9 x 800 meters 8 to 12 x 600 meters	4 to 6 x 1 mile 5 to 7 x 1,200 meters 6 to 8 x 1,000 meters	4 to 5 miles 2 x 2.5 miles (with 1-mile recovery)
workout pace	0:30 to 0:35 per mile faster than current 10K race pace	0:10 to 0:15 per mile faster than current 10K race pace	0:00 to 0:05 per mile faster than current 10K race pace	0:20 to 0:25 per mile slower than current 10K race pace

RACE DISTANCE	WORKOUT CATEGORY			
	SHORT INTERVALS	MEDIUM INTERVALS	LONG INTERVALS	TEMPO RUNS
12K TO 10 MILES (CONT.)				
(workout pace cont'd)		OR 0:20 to 0:25 per mile faster than current race pace at planned distance[2]	OR 0:10 to 0:15 per mile faster than current race pace at planned distance[2]	OR 0:10 to 0:15 per mile slower than current race pace at planned distance[2]
20K TO 30K (INCLUDING HALF-MARATHON)				
workout choices (pick one)	8 to 12 x 200 meters 7 to 10 x 300 meters 6 to 8 x 400 meters	7 to 10 x 800 meters 10 to 14 x 600 meters	5 to 6 x 1 mile 6 to 8 x 1,200 meters 7 to 9 x 1,000 meters	5 to 7 miles 2 x 3 miles (with 1.5-mile recovery)
workout pace	0:30 to 0:35 per mile faster than current 10K pace	0:05 to 0:10 per mile faster than current 10K pace	Between 0:05 and 0:00 slower than current 10K pace	0:25 to 0:30 per mile slower than current 10K race pace
		OR 0:20 to 0:25 per mile faster than current race pace at planned distance[2]	OR 0:10 to 0:15 per mile faster than current race pace at planned race distance[2]	OR 0:10 to 0:15 per mile slower than current race pace at planned distance[2]
MARATHON SEE CHAPTER 15.				

[1] If you choose the 3-mile option, slow down the pace by an additional 0:05 per mile.
[2] For workouts with more than one alternative method for choosing your target pace, pick the one that uses your most recent benchmark, whether that's a 10K or a prior performance at the distance for which you're training.

FLEET FOOTWEAR

Speed work should be done in the shoes you use for racing. For most folks, those are your training shoes, but if you use racing shoes, wear them. Your pace targets are based on race performances done in the lightweight racing shoes, so trying to speed train in heavier footwear will make your targets too hard to achieve. Also, wearing your racing shoes will help to condition exactly the muscles that you'll use in competition. This might seem to be a small difference—after all, training shoes aren't exactly army boots—but lifting even a few ounces of extra weight per step uses a slightly different set of muscles.

Be alert to incipient injuries, however. The soft surface of the track won't require the amount of cushion found in your training shoes, but extensive use of low-heeled racing shoes can lead to Achilles tendinitis (see pages 132–36) in some runners. Also, if you normally train with orthotics, they'll be doubly important in lightly built racing shoes.

TRAINING FOR THE DISTANCES

Physiologically, your speed work is designed to pursue the same three goals—improvements in VO_2max, running efficiency, and lactic acid metabolism—regardless of the distance you're planning to race. That means that although there are big differences in endurance-training regimens for 5K and the half-marathon, there are only minor differences in their speed programs.

The principal difference is in the number of repeats you'll do and the length of your tempo runs. For short races you'll do relatively few intervals (and relatively short tempo runs) at a fast pace; for long races you'll do more mileage, toning down the pace slightly so you can get through the longer workout. But you won't slow it down by much—just by enough to allow you to do the extra repeats. Thus, even though most people race approximately 10 to 15 seconds per mile more slowly at 15K than at 10K, they'll only relax the pace of their speed training by about 5 seconds per mile when preparing for the longer distance. There's a small physiological benefit from being able to squeeze in an extra repeat or two when preparing for a long race, but mostly, the purpose is simply to let the workout more closely mimic what you'll encounter in the race.

Here's the basic training philosophy for race distances ranging from 5K to 30K (18.6 miles). These descriptions parallel the more-detailed information in the accompanying table of speed workouts. (Speed work for the marathon is covered in chapter 15.)

- **5K.** This is the shortest race covered by this book. As such, it's the fastest. Not surprisingly, your speed workouts for it are relatively short but intense.
- **8K to 10K.** This popular distance category includes 5-mile races as well as the two metric distances. The principal difference between speed work for these distances and the 5K is that you'll base them on your 10K pace rather than your 5K pace. That's enough of a slowdown to make a big difference in the ease of each repeat. Compensate by increasing their number.

- **12K (7.45 miles) to 10 miles (about 16.1K).** These intermediate distances aren't super-popular except in regions where high-profile 12K, 15K, or 10-mile races have created cadres of enthusiasts. But if you can find one, such races are good stepping-stones from the 10K to the half-marathon. Short intervals should be done at the same pace you used for the 10K; longer intervals and tempo runs can be slowed down by about 5 seconds per mile to give you the energy to go a bit farther. Come race day, expect to be about 10 to 20 seconds per mile slower than you'd be in a 10K.
- **20K to 30K.** This looks like a wide range (12.4 miles to 18.6 miles) but training is similar across the entire spectrum. The most popular distance in this category is the half-marathon (13.1 miles or about 21.1K). There are some 25K and 30K races, but their biggest draw tends to be as distance trainers for marathoners seeking company on long training runs. If you race a 25K or 30K seriously, in its own right, you'll be in a small, select group. In speed training for any of these distances, slow down the pace of your long and medium-length intervals by an additional 5 seconds per mile from what you'd do for a 15K, thereby freeing energy for an extra one or two repeats. Also, slow down your tempo runs slightly and lengthen them, as well. If it's your first attempt at the distance, race speed is a little hard to predict, but the chart on page 213 will get you started.

OTHER WORKOUTS

The workouts in the accompanying Speed Workouts chart aren't the only possible forms of speed training. As your training progresses, you'll encounter runners doing quite different workouts, on and off the track.

Pyramid Workouts

On the track, many runners do intervals in which not all of the repeats are the same length. Such workouts have a number of names, *ladders* and *pyramids* being the most common. Rather than repeating the same distance over and over, a ladder might start with a 200-meter run, followed by a 300, a 400, a 600, an 800, and maybe even a 1,200 or a mile. After the longest interval, runners may then come back "down the ladder" by repeating the same progression in reverse.

Popular as they are, these workouts pose serious problems for all but expert racers. First of all, they don't focus on improving either your VO$_2$max or your running efficiency. Rather, they attempt to do both at once—a good way to short-change both. In particular, they tend to be too light on short intervals. Secondly, pyramid-style workouts require you to keep changing pace as you shift from short to medium-length to long intervals. That makes it easy to be continuously off pace. Good pyramid workouts are possible, but they're complex to design, and many of the recreational runners who do them are probably wasting energy on training that doesn't accomplish all that it could.

If you feel the need to mix interval lengths, keep them in the same category. This can actually be a good way to advance your training. If you want to graduate from 3 to 4 repeat miles, for example, you can add a 1,000-meter interval as an intermediate step toward the fourth mile. Alternatively, if you're having a rough day, you might substitute a couple of shorter intervals for longer ones. Coaching, I often do this, shifting a workout to something at which a runner can maintain the pace, rather than forcing him to complete a drill that isn't going to work, that day. One of the most vital things my college coach taught me was that it is very important for workouts to feel like successes; if the original goal is out of reach, step back to something you can achieve. This is easiest, of course, if it's someone else who pulls the plug on the initial plan. Then you can always complain, "But coach, I could have made it!" It's harder to argue with yourself . . . but there's no reason not to try.

Treadmills

There's not much physiological difference between doing interval workouts on the track and doing them on a treadmill. The main difference is that on a treadmill any given speed is slightly easier than on a track because you're not fighting your own self-generated headwind. When I was training for the Comrades Marathon, I did a lot of work on a treadmill, once completing a 35-mile run that way, entertaining myself by listening to the radio.

I like treadmills because they provide a soft surface on which injuries are less likely. But preparing for Comrades, I was concerned about how to make my treadmill workouts comparable to what I'd get on the roads. I was so obsessed about this that one day I did a trio of mile repeats on a treadmill, using a heart-rate monitor to keep track of how hard I was working. Then, still wearing the monitor, I went onto a track and ran the same workout, being careful to hit the same heart rate. I found that I was 17 seconds per mile slower on the track. Additional tests convinced me that a treadmill needs to be set at a 1.5 percent upgrade to duplicate flat, outdoor conditions.

The biggest drawbacks to doing speed work on a treadmill are that most machines won't go faster than 6-minute miles—although this is not a serious limitation for most people—and the need to be alert not to crash spectacularly by stepping off the belt. You may also have a tendency to overheat unless you set up a fan nearby. The biggest advantage to using a treadmill is that you know exactly what pace you're running, and are forced to run it precisely.

Target-Heart-Rate Workouts

Some speed-training philosophies are based on achieving target heart rates, typically measured with a heart-rate monitor (see pages 43–45). Although heart-rate monitors are useful for LSD (long, slow distance) training, I find them too uncertain for speed work. Not only are there individual differences in the effect of effort on heart rate, but it takes too long for your heart rate to reach a stable, meaningful level for the monitor to be of much use for short and even medium-length intervals. Heart-rate-based speed programs therefore tend to concentrate too strongly on long intervals and tempo runs, shortchanging shorter intervals designed to boost running efficiency. The tried-and-true practice of running against the clock is better.

TRACK ETIQUETTE

I grew up on and around tracks. Rick never visited one until he was in his mid-20s. It took him a few interval sessions to become comfortable in this new environment.

The first time you run on a track, you'll probably feel out of place. Just tell yourself you belong there as much as the 5:00-milers do, and squash any temporary feelings of inadequacy. Few racers are going to object to your presence, whatever your pace.

Where you *will* upset other runners is if you don't know how to share the track. A 400-meter track measures precisely 400 meters only on the inside lane, so that's the lane everyone wants to use. The basic rule of track etiquette is that faster runners have priority. Unless you're the only one on the track, move a few lanes to the outside for recovery breaks, using the inner lane only when you need it.

If the track is crowded with fast runners, you may need to run your repeats on an outer lane. If so, figure that each lane that you move out adds about 1.5 to 2 seconds to your time per lap. Running in the third lane, you'd be about 6 to 8 seconds slow for an 800-meter interval. Accept the fact that your 800s are actually 815 or 820 meters, and try to find a less crowded time or place to run.

Other basic rules of track etiquette:

- Always run counterclockwise. This rule may have evolved because it's a little easier for right-handed people to circle the curves that way, but mostly, it's simply a convention, its origin lost in history.
- Don't suddenly stop or change lanes before making sure you're not cutting someone off.
- If runners coming up from behind yell "Track!" they're asking for the right-of-way. Move to the outside if there's time to do so without risk of collision.
- Don't use the track at a time when it's been reserved by a team or club unless you're a member or it's a group that welcomes visitors.

Heart-rate monitors do have two uses in speed training, however. First, they can help you run long intervals and tempo runs on the roads, as described in the upcoming section on road workouts. And on the track, they can tip you off if your heart rate is unusually high. That's a strong signal that you might be starting a workout unduly tired and that you may need to change the day's training goal, even if so far you've been on pace.

Road Workouts

You don't have to confine your workouts to the track. Simply use your watch to do road workouts that mimic what you'd run on a measured course. If your goal is to do repeat 1,000s, for example, you can run at what feels like the right pace, holding it for the time it would normally take for a 1,000-meter repeat. Recover for the right length of time, then move into the next repeat. These workouts are just like running on a track except for the fact that you're doing time-based intervals rather than distance-based ones. You may be impeded by hills or headwinds, but those don't matter because your goal is to duplicate the effort you'd expend on the track, not the precise speed or distance. In theory, you could even do these runs on a trail, although most people are uncomfortable running that fast on uneven surfaces.

Such workouts can be remarkably effective. When I got married, my wife and I went to the Bahamas for 3 weeks, right before the start of the indoor track season. I kept up my mileage but did my speed workouts on the roads. When we returned, I jumped immediately into racing, with no chance to do even one tune-up on the track. My first race turned out to be one of the best of my life—perhaps the best I ever ran on the track. Even though I got tripped up in the pack and fell (losing perhaps 6 or 7 seconds), I was able to get back into the race and finish within one second of the 5,000-meter world record. Obviously, I was in world-record shape, and might have snagged that honor had I not fallen.

Such workouts require frequent returns to the track to verify that you're not drifting off pace. Even the most track-phobic runner should do at least one workout in three on the track. But on vacations and business trips, clock-based workouts are a perfect solution to maintaining your speed training when a track would be hard to find.

You may also find that a heart-rate monitor is a useful aid. Wear it on the track to determine your heart rate at your target pace, then duplicate that heart rate on the roads.

Fartlek-Style Workouts

Fartlek is a Swedish word meaning "speed play." In its purest form, a fartlek is an unstructured off-track workout in which you do interval-style surges by charging up a hill or racing to the next corner, water fountain, or telephone pole. Between surges, you generally recover at a faster pace than on the track, producing workouts

---

GROUP TRAINING

Endurance training is easy to do solo, and many people prefer the contemplative mood that comes with running by themselves. Speed training, however, isn't contemplative. That makes it an arena where workout buddies are particularly useful. Be careful, though, to run at your own target pace, not someone else's. Coaching high schoolers, I frequently separate kids into pace-based groups so the slower ones won't be psychologically downtrodden by being at the back—or physically beaten up by pushing themselves too hard, trying to keep up. Fast runners, on the other hand, may be tempted to slack off if nobody else in the group can seriously challenge them. When possible, try to find speed-training partners of approximately your own ability.

Also, be cautious about group workouts that violate the principles of this chapter and push you into such activities as pyramid intervals with their mixed bag of run lengths, or workouts that give you unusually long or short recovery periods. Even if these are well-designed, you won't know how to pace yourself without individualized coaching. View these as social activities, and do them if you like, but realize that they're unlikely to yield optimal speed-training benefits.

that feel like endurance-training runs or tempo runs with interludes of faster speed
that can mimic short, long, or medium-length intervals.

Many world-class runners have thrived on these workouts, partly because they
free you from the monotony of the track. But it takes years of speed-work experience to know how to do a fartlek that truly accomplishes its training purposes.
Otherwise, it's too easy to get off pace or to over- or underrecover between
surges. For that reason, I only recommend fartleks for marathon training (see
pages 224–25), when the value of a sustained fast run outweighs the risk of getting off pace.

Hill Training

Runners have a love-hate relationship with hills. Racing philosopher George Sheehan called them "the great leveler." Others have called them "good for the soul," a
"supreme test" of mental and physical toughness, or simply "nasty." At race speed
you'll instantly notice even a 1 percent grade (50 feet per mile) and trying to run
too quickly up a 5 or 6 percent grade can feel like wading through molasses.

We talk later about how to race on hilly courses (see pages 193–96), but there
are three main reasons for training on hills—important enough that some world-
class runners have used hills almost entirely as substitutes for the track.

1. *If you're going to be racing on hills, you should be training on them*—not all
   the time, but frequently enough that when you encounter one in a race you
   know how to approach it.
2. *Hill running is great for improving your running efficiency.* Not only does
   the effort give you the same kind of strength training that you get from short
   intervals, but uphill running also is a great way to hone your running form.
   It forces you to lean forward into the slope (otherwise you can't get a good
   push-off with each stride), preventing that backward lean that afflicts so
   many beginning racers. Coaches have long known that if they run their teams
   on hills early in the season, later on they have great form on the track—
   form that soon pays dividends in speed.

3. *Running on hills improves your foot plant at the start of each stride.* At the elite level, athletes seek to land with the foot cocked only slightly, rather than far back on the heel like many recreational athletes tend to land. Even if landing too far back on the heel doesn't come from overstriding, it means that your foot has to flex farther forward to get you onto the ball of your foot for the next push off. While it's flexing, you're having to wait before applying power to the stride. Suppose that this slight delay costs only 1/1,000 of a second per step. If you were a sprinter, that would be about 0.03 seconds in a 100-meter dash. That could easily be the difference between running 9.84 for the gold medal and 9.87 for the bronze. Even for distance runners, these thousandths of a second add up. Most recreational racers put in 1,000 to 1,500 paces per mile. Each millisecond of wasted time eliminated from your stride is therefore at least 1 second per mile of extra pace—a total of 6 to 10 seconds in a 10K. Hill running will help you eliminate it—naturally.

Running hills generally means doing repeats, either by surging up a big hill in small segments, or by finding a series of appropriate-sized hills. In a pinch, you can run the same hill, over and over—a nice way to check the consistency of your pace, but potentially boring. Run at the effort level you'd use for short intervals, and keep the distance short—generally no more than about 400 meters. If you live where hills are in limited supply, try a freeway overpass.

PUTTING IT ALL TOGETHER

During the racing season, when you're targeting on specific events, speed training and endurance training need to be properly combined in your weekly training schedule. Endurance work is the bread and butter of your conditioning, but speed workouts more strongly affect your performance in the short run. In the short run, if something has to give, speed work should take precedence, even if you have to reduce your mileage to accommodate it.

When doing speed work, getting enough rest is more important than ever. This means that you should do your LSD endurance training as slowly as necessary to allow you to hit your target paces on speed workouts. Continue to take at least 1 and preferably 2 days of full rest each week—one after the tougher of your speed workouts, the other whenever you most need it.

The accompanying table of workout schedules shows weekly workouts for distances ranging from 20 to 50 miles, incorporating two speed workouts and one long run per week. Those three are your hard days; the others are for varying degrees of rest. The table is merely a guideline, however. The amount of mileage logged during your long run, as well as during your speed workouts, will vary with your training goals; if you're training for a half-marathon, for example, your speed workouts will be longer than if your target race is a 5K.

WORKOUT SCHEDULES FOR RUNNERS LOGGING FROM 20 TO 50 MILES PER WEEK

TOTAL WEEKLY MILEAGE	SUN.	MON. (SPEED WORKOUT 1)[1]	TUES.	WED.	THURS. (SPEED WORKOUT 2)[1]	FRI.	SAT. (LONG RUN)[2]
20	2	4	rest	3	4	rest	7
25	3	5	rest	4	5	rest	8
30	4	6	rest	5	5	rest	10
35	5	7	rest	5	6	rest	12
40	6	8	rest	6	7	rest	13
45	6	9	rest	5	7	3[3]	15
50[4]	6	9	rest	6	8	6	15

[1] Includes warm-up and cooldown.

[2] This run can be up to 40 percent of weekly total. To run a different "long" distance, compensate by altering mileage on the "easy" days of Sunday, Thursday, and Friday.

[3] At 45 miles per week and higher, it's hard to schedule 2 rest days per week.

[4] Workouts of more than 50 miles per week involve time commitment that is beyond the reach of most recreational runners. If you choose to run higher mileage, structure your workouts according to the principles in this table. Be sure to include at least one full day of rest per week. Only top competitors running 70 or more miles per week should consider training every day.

Adding Weight Lifting to the Mix

When you add weight lifting to the routine, as will be described in chapter 7, it complicates the schedule. Upper-body weight workouts can be done whenever you like, but lower-body ones tire your legs enough that you'll feel it the next day. That means that you don't want to do them on the days before speed workouts or long runs—and most people won't want to do them afterward, on the same day. Weight lifting is ideally done twice a week, but there simply aren't enough days in the week to combine it with twice-weekly speed workouts and once-weekly long runs. Something has to give.

One solution is to shift the length of your "week" to accommodate the extra work, plus the recovery days. A 9-day cycle, for example, would be

Day 1. Long run
Day 2. Easy run; lift weights
Day 3. Easy run or rest
Day 4. Speed workout 1
Day 5. Easy run; lift weights
Day 6. Easy run or rest
Day 7. Speed workout 2
Day 8. Easy run; lift weights
Day 9. Easy run or rest

This could be compressed to an 8-day cycle by dropping the weight lifting on either day 2 or day 8. Or, you could expand the cycle to 10 days by adding an extra easy day sometime between the two speed workouts.

Many people won't be able to schedule long runs except on weekends, however. To get in some weight lifting while meeting this constraint, you could do an alternating-week schedule such as that shown in the next table. This schedule shifts back and forth between weeks with one speed workout and two weight-lifting sessions, and weeks with two speed workouts and one weight-lifting session. It's not as good as the 8-, 9-, or 10-day cycles described above, but it does allow weight lifting and speed training to coexist, without forcing you to do long runs on workdays—an acceptable compromise.

ALTERNATING-WEEK SCHEDULE WITH WEIGHT LIFTING, SPEED WORK, AND LONG RUNS*

	SUN.	MON.	TUES.	WED.	THURS.	FRI.	SAT.
Week 1	easy	easy, weights	speed	easy	easy, weights	easy	long run
Week 2	easy	speed	easy, weights	easy	speed	easy	long run

* "Easy" days may be rest days.

ELITE-LEVEL TRAINING

The training schedules for the top level of racing are brutal—but they're based on the same principles undergirding this chapter. Here's what my schedule looked like during the marathon-training periods when I was putting in 120 miles a week:

- Sunday: 18- to 20-mile continuous run, at about a 6:15 pace.
- Monday: 7 miles in the morning, 8 in the afternoon. The pace was relaxed, which for me was about 6:15 to 6:30.
- Tuesday: 5 relaxed miles in the morning, then long intervals in the afternoon, totaling 11 or 12 miles with warm-up and cooldown.
- Wednesday: morning and afternoon workouts totaling 15 to 17 miles at my relaxed, endurance-training pace of 6:15 to 6:30.
- Thursday: tempo run or short intervals in the morning, totaling 10 miles; 5- to 7-mile easy run in the afternoon.
- Friday: same as Wednesday, but usually totaling 17 miles, not 15.
- Saturday: medium-length or long intervals in the morning, totaling 11 or 12 miles; 5 or 6 miles of gently paced distance training in the afternoon. With the intervals at the start of the day and a second run a few hours later, this was my toughest day.

PART 2

OILING THE MACHINE

LOGGING MILEAGE AND doing speed work are only part of the job of preparing to race. To run your best, you also need to care for your body when you're not running. That, of course, is a very broad assignment—nothing less than a mandate to live an all-around healthy lifestyle—and there is, indeed, a direct link between overall health and racing performance.

A broad discussion of healthy living is beyond the scope of this book. But there are a few aspects that relate particularly well to running. Two fall into realms traditionally viewed as part of athletic training: stretching and weight lifting. You can run without doing either, but you will run faster and with fewer injuries if you do both. Chapter 6 will address stretching, and chapter 7 will address weight lifting. Chapter 7 will also talk briefly about cross-training, which is the use of other sports to augment your training.

Chapter 8 will turn to the linked topics of nutrition and weight control. A good diet will help keep your body in racing tune (and provide fuel for long races and endurance-training runs). You'll also run better if your weight is in your body's ideal range: neither too high nor too low. Much of the chapter is devoted to a discussion of how to find where that ideal lies for your own body.

Chapter 9 offers an extended discussion of a topic we'd all like to avoid: injuries. One goal of the training program outlined in part 1 of this book is to minimize the risk of injuries, but unfortunately *minimize* does not mean *eliminate*. Some people run for years with nary a twinge. Others flit from injury to injury. I myself typically lost about 2 weeks per year to injuries—typical of elite athletes. Recreational racers often fare better because they're not attempting to put in extremely high mileage and can more easily accommodate a few days' rest to nip an incipient injury in the bud. This chapter describes nearly two dozen ailments, ranging from blisters to heat stroke, from tendinitis to altitude sickness. Each includes a discussion of possible causes, suggestions for speeding its healing (hopefully without a layoff), and tips on how to prevent a recurrence.

Finally, chapter 10 will segue back to racing with a discussion of running psychology. We all know that the mind is a very powerful part of the body. Confidence can carry you through a tough race; doubt can undercut months of careful training. New research also indicates that the mind is what governs fatigue—and runners have long known that concentration and careful attention to the body's signals are ways to harness the mind's power to maximize your performance by learning to use your body's abilities as efficiently as possible.

But before venturing onto such ethereal planes, let's limber up the body with some judicious stretching.

STRETCHING

As a full-time competitive athlete, stretching was simply part of my job. I always stretched 10 to 15 minutes before each workout and 10 to 15 minutes afterward. With morning and evening runs, that meant nearly an hour of stretching each day, admittedly a major time commitment. But I was running an average of two hours a day, an even more major time commitment.

Most recreational racers tend to procrastinate stretching, often so badly that they do almost none. Stretching, however, is one of the most important parts of your routine. It's critical to injury-free running because limber muscles exert less tension on tendons and ligaments. They're also less prone to muscle pulls, for the simple reason that they're better able to withstand the shock of modest overextension.

Stretching also enhances performance. Tight muscles have restricted ranges of motion, constraining your stride length. Even if that robs you of only a small-sounding amount of power—say 5 percent—that's roughly equivalent to the difference between running 9:30s and 10:00s. Even a 1 or 2 percent loss in power would add 30 to 60 seconds to your 10K time.

Rather than attempting, and repeatedly failing, to cram a lengthy stretching regimen into a busy schedule, you'll do better with a modest goal that you can actually achieve. Try stretching for at least 5 minutes before each workout and 5 to 10 minutes afterward. More is better, but this will get you most of the benefit, without an undue time commitment. If you're going to scrimp, time spent stretching immediately after your workouts (and races) will produce more bang for the buck than time spent stretching beforehand. If two otherwise identical runners were to do the same stretching routines, one before running and the other afterward, after 6 months the one who stretched afterward would be considerably more limber.

On days when there just isn't much workout time, you'll still get some benefit from stretching as late as several hours after your workout. This is particularly helpful for lunchtime runners who have limited time to suit up, run, stretch, and get back to work. If you have a desk job, try fitting in some stretches during rest breaks. You're supposed to take breaks anyway to reduce the risks of repetitive stress injuries to arms and shoulders; you might as well put those breaks to the best possible use! Some people even stretch while talking on the phone.

THREE REASONS TO STRETCH

- It's relaxing and feels good.
- Stretching reduces the risk of injury.
- Limber muscles allow you to run faster.

STRETCHING BASICS

Proper stretches are *static* or *isometric*. Static stretching involves stretching slowly until you feel a modest pull (not pain) in the muscle. Hold that position for a few seconds, trying to relax the muscle, then cautiously extend the stretch farther, always being prepared to back off. Static stretching is perfectly adequate, and is the method used by most runners.

Isometric stretching is similar, except that between cautious extensions of the stretch, you gently contract the stretched muscle (without allowing the stretched

Take a few minutes to stretch as part of your normal running routine.
(VERA JAGENDORF)

limb to flex) before relaxing it. In contracting the muscle, you are working against the direction of the stretch, so brace the leg (or arm, etc.) against the floor, a wall, or whatever is most comfortable to keep it steady and unmoving. Then you relax the muscle to gently extend the stretch, as in static stretching. A recent revolution in sports training, isometric stretching is counterintuitive but it allows you to get an even better stretch than you do with static stretching. It is, however, a bit more awkward and is therefore not widely used. Most stretches can be done either statically or isometrically.

One of the surprises to come out of recent research is the discovery that there's no need to hold a stretch for more than 20 seconds, and there's virtually no benefit from repeating it. Runners were once told to do each stretch 2 or 3 times, spending at least 30 seconds for each repetition. Now we know you can get most of the benefit from a single repetition, held for as little as 15 seconds at each stage in the stretch-relax-extend process. This allows you to do a lot of different stretches in a few minutes.

Don't bounce when stretching. A sudden stretch makes the muscle think it's about to be hyperextended, and the muscle protects itself by reflexively contracting. The bouncing toe-touches and other calisthenic stretches many of us were taught as children merely fight that reflexive contraction. They can also pull a muscle. Focus on stretching gently.

TEN-MINUTE STRETCHING

Stretching should entail not only the major muscles you use for running, such as the quadriceps (on the front of the thigh), hamstrings (behind the thigh), and calves, but also the muscles of the hip and groin. Some version of the following stretches should form the core of your routine.

STRETCHES TO DO BEFORE AND AFTER EACH TRAINING RUN OR RACE

TARGET MUSCLE GROUP	RECOMMENDED STRETCHES
legs	calf stretch hamstring stretch quadriceps stretch
hips and buttocks figure-four	groin stretch buttocks stretches
upper body (arms, shoulders, and torso)	optional stretches, as desired

Calf stretches. Left: Rear leg straight. Right: Rear leg bent. Do both.

Leg Stretches

Running uses mostly muscles below your waist, and not surprisingly, these should be the primary focus of your stretching regimen. In the legs, three stretches are critical: those for the calves, hamstrings, and quadriceps.

Calf stretch. This looks like it's stretching the Achilles tendon (which links the calf and the heel), but actually it's stretching the calf muscles. Supporting yourself with a wall, railing, desk, or tree, lean forward, feeling the stretch in the calf of the rear leg. Don't cheat by rising up on your toes! Also keep the foot pointing straight ahead, rather than angled out to the side, or you won't get the full benefit of the stretch. Do this stretch first with the stretched leg straight; then bend it a bit at the knee, feeling how that shifts the point of the stretch downward along your calf. If you're on a good, high-traction surface, you can save time by stretching both calves at once, but be careful not to slip and overstretch.

> **Stretching is a crucial element of your training.**
> **Put it off, and you'll eventually regret it.**

Hamstring stretch. There are several ways to stretch your hamstrings. The simplest is the standard toe touch you learned in grade school. If you can't reach your toes, just bend over and reach as far down as you comfortably can, keeping your knees straight. Really flexible people with long backs can put their palms on the floor, but these are usually dancers who've practiced for years. If you have back problems, you may want to avoid the bent-over position of toe touches or at least let your knees bend a bit as you stand back up.

An alternative is to sit on a flat surface with one leg extended, the other comfortably out of the way. Don't sit on your heel; that's hard on the knee. Without locking the knee, lean toward the leg being stretched, feeling the stretch in the hamstring. It's possible to stretch both legs at once, as shown here, but many people will do better by focusing on one leg at a time. Protect your upper body from strain by keeping your back straight, rather than rolling your spine and shoulders forward in an effort to maximize your reach. Remember, you're stretching the hamstring, not your back and shoulders, so reaching forward isn't the goal in and of itself.

Hamstring stretch.

If there's nowhere to sit, you can do a very similar stretch standing up, with your leg propped on a bench or railing, but doing this, you have to be more careful not to apply too much stretching force or get trapped into an overextended position.

Quadriceps stretch. Many runners stretch their quads by sitting on their heels and leaning backward. A variant of this stretch is to stand on one foot, pulling the other toe upward toward your buttocks. These are indeed the most effective stretches for the quadriceps, but they should be viewed as no-nos because they also stress the front of the knee. You may be able to get away with them (I can), but

Quadriceps stretch. This can be done standing or seated, whichever is more comfortable. For minimum stress on the knee, the stretch should come from rocking the hip forward, not from pulling the foot upward toward the buttocks.

you don't need that much flexibility unless you're a serious competitor or a ballet dancer.

A safer stretch is to stand on one foot, holding the other in your hand, anywhere between the toe and the ankle. If your balance is unsteady, use your free hand to brace yourself against a wall or railing. Now, without pulling your foot up toward your buttocks, let your hip rock forward as the foot moves horizontally backward. If you do this right, you'll feel the stretch not only in the quadriceps but also along the front of the hip, an area that isn't stretched by the conventional quadriceps stretch. Men will feel a more substantial stretch than do women. (In fact, some women will find that they can't get any stretch out of this at all; these people have no alternative but to do the traditional stretch, but only if their knees don't hurt.)

An alternative version of this stretch is done sitting on the ground. Again, remember that the stretch comes from pressing forward with the hips, not from yanking the toe up toward the buttocks.

Hip and Buttock Stretches

Once you've stretched your lower legs, don't overlook your hips and buttocks. Here, there are five main stretches.

Groin stretch. In this stretch, done sitting on the floor, your knees should be spread wide and the soles of your feet should be together. Put your elbows on your knees and your hands on your shins or ankles—whichever is convenient. Use your elbows to press your knees down and sideways until you feel a good stretch in the groin. It's OK to lean forward and place your chin on

Groin stretch. Try not to hunch forward.

your clasped hands if that helps you get a better and more controlled stretch. There is also a standing version of this stretch, done by standing straddle-legged and leaning toward the side of your groin that you want to stretch. Women and very flexible men, however, may not feel much stretch from this version.

Figure-four stretch. This stretch is a bit complex, but it's good for the hip when you get it right. Sit on the floor, with the right leg extended comfortably in front of you. Draw the left leg closer, so that its knee rises above the floor. Now, lift the left foot and put it flat on the floor on the far side of the straight leg's knee, maintaining your balance with a hand splayed out behind you. Finally, reach past the right side of your right knee so that the back of the arm, somewhere near the elbow, is pressed against the knee's outside. It's an odd-feeling but not uncomfortable position.

*Figure-four
stretch.*

So far, you've contorted but not stretched. To stretch, rotate your torso clockwise and look backward over your right shoulder, while using the left elbow to press counterclockwise against the knee. You should feel the stretch on the outside of your right hip. As with any one-leg-at-a-time stretch, reverse sides and stretch the other leg equally.

Buttocks stretches. The next three stretches are for the buttocks, and are most conveniently done in the order shown here. Unwind from the figure-four and lie on your back, legs extended comfortably in front of you.

For the first buttocks stretch, bend one leg about 90 degrees at the knee and rotate it at the hip so the shin is raised off the floor, roughly crossways to your body. This will bring the knee and ankle close enough to you that you should be able to reach them easily. Grasp one in each hand and pull with equal force to draw the entire lower leg toward your head. *Do not* twist the knee; rather, use both hands to move the lower leg as a unit.

For the second buttocks stretch, release your grip on the ankle and, keeping the leg raised off the ground, knee bent, rotate it so the shin now lines up with your body. Clasp your hands around the knee, anywhere convenient between the knee-cap and the top of the shin. Then pull

Buttocks and upper hamstring stretch number one. In all three stretches, do not twist the knee or strain back and shoulders by reaching higher than is comfortable. Most of you will be able to rotate the shin farther sideways than I can, but it's important to avoid twisting.

the knee toward your nose, stretching a slightly different part of the buttocks.

For the third buttocks stretch, extend the foot higher above the ground, but don't completely straighten the leg, or you'll wind up stretching the

Buttocks and upper hamstring stretch number two.

hamstring rather than the buttocks. (Even so, part of this stretch will be felt in the upper hamstring.) If you can comfortably reach that far, clasp your hands behind

Buttocks and upper hamstring stretch number three.

STRETCHING DOS AND DON'TS

- Do make stretching a regular part of your training routine and your prerace warm-up.
- Don't overcommit. A 5-minute routine that actually fits your workout schedule is better than a grandiose plan that never happens.
- Do stretches with a sequence of extension, relaxation, and additional extension, repeated until you can obtain no additional extension. Isometric contraction can be added after each extension to give you an even better stretch.
- Don't do bouncing stretches or stretch to the point of pain.
- Do include gentle stretching as part of an injury-rehabilitation program (see chapter 9), but be very careful not to aggravate the injury by overstretching the injured tissues. Consult a doctor or sports trainer for injury-specific advice.

the ankle and pull, again more or less toward your nose. Remember, though, that this isn't a shoulder or back stretch, so reach no higher than is comfortable, even if that's only to mid-thigh. Repeat the entire sequence, of course, with the other leg.

Extend stretches to the point where you feel a good stretch—not pain.

Arm and shoulder stretch number one. All three easy stretches are great for office work, as well as loosening up for the run.

Upper-Body Stretches

You're not likely to get a running injury by failing to stretch out the upper body, but tight arms and shoulders won't help your performance. The following three stretches will limber up your arms and shoulders in about a minute.

For the first stretch, clasp your hands behind your back. Keeping your arms straight at the elbows, extend them backward, feeling the stretch mostly in the front of your shoulders.

For the second stretch, unclasp your hands and wrap one arm—we'll start with the right arm—around the front of your body, under your chin to reach over the top of the other shoulder as though you were trying to scratch a hard-to-reach itch. Park the hand flat on your shoulder blade, or as close to

Arm and shoulder stretch number two.

that as you can comfortably reach. Alternatively, you can simply let the hand dangle in midair, somewhere behind or to the side of your shoulder. Either way, the right elbow should be sticking out in front of your chin. Place your left hand on the back of the right elbow or on the lower part of the upper arm, and gently pull as though attempting to wrap the right arm tighter around your body.

The third stretch begins by reaching one arm—again we'll start with the right arm—over the top of your head, more or less getting your hand within scratching distance of your left shoulder. Grasp your right wrist with your free hand and rock your head, neck, and torso to the left to stretch

Arm and shoulder stretch number three.

your side and a new group of shoulder muscles (as well as some of the muscles of your side). Switch arms and repeat the second and third stretches. Congratulations, you're finished.

STRETCHING WITH YOGA

Do you have a problem area that's always tight? Or would you like to learn more about stretching parts of the upper body, such as the torso, not described in this book? Take a yoga lesson and ask the instructor for specific tips. Yoga-derived stretches are also useful for people who work a lot with computers or other repetitive tasks and are trying to avoid (or rehabilitate) occupational injuries.

WEIGHT TRAINING AND CROSS-TRAINING

COACHES ONCE BELIEVED that all that you needed to do to strengthen your body for running was to run. But it's been shown that runners who lift weights are stronger and better runners—as well as in better overall condition—than those who don't. This is because weight lifting allows you to isolate specific muscles and stress them heavily in brief but intense workouts.

Equally important, weight lifting can be used to strengthen muscles like the abdominals and shoulders that don't get much exercise during running but that help maintain proper running posture. Keeping these muscles strong will help prevent backaches, stiff necks, and tired shoulders. Weight lifting can also reduce your susceptibility to injury and can even cure specific injuries, such as shin splints or runner's knee, which are often associated with specific muscle weaknesses.

Chapter 9 discusses how weight lifting can be focused on these and other specific injuries. Here we address weight training, which involves a regular weekly program designed more for prevention and overall strength and speed than for the elimination of specific problems.

This chapter also talks, to a lesser degree, about cross-training (the use of sports other than running) as part of your overall conditioning, and about plyometrics, a system of bounding exercises used by many world-class athletes to build strength and quickness. But the most important of these topics is weight training.

By weight-room standards, your workouts will be fairly easy, because bodybuilding isn't the goal. As a runner, in fact, excessive bulking up is counterproductive because you would have to carry all that muscle around with you in races. As little as an hour of weight training a week, though, will help tone your entire body. It will also add strength to your legs to help you run faster and more comfortably.

Even "fairly easy" weight lifting is intense enough that your legs will still feel it the next day. There are times when elite athletes cannot lift weights—not because they don't believe in it, but because their speed workouts are so intense and frequent that they can't handle the additional stress of weights. You too will have some problems cramming weight lifting, long runs, and a full complement of speed work into a 7-day cycle. As was discussed in chapter 5, you'll need at least an 8-day "week," or an alternating-week rotation (see pages 81–82). Nevertheless, you'll benefit from lifting weights, even if it forces you to cut back to only 1½ speed sessions per week. During parts of the year when you're not doing speed work, weight lifting is easier to schedule and even more useful.

The benefit of weight lifting comes from the combination of the amount of weight you lift and the number of times (*repetitions* or *reps* in the jargon of the weight room) that you lift it. Each group of reps, with an intervening rest break, is called a *set*. There's nothing magic about the order in which you do the exercises

FIVE REASONS TO LIFT WEIGHTS

- Running can tone your legs, but on its own won't do much for the rest of your body.
- Weights can strengthen muscles that play a limited role in running, but which you need for balance and posture.
- Lifting adds power to your primary running muscles, making you faster.
- Weight lifting reduces injury risk, and plays a role in the rehabilitation of some injuries.
- Weight workouts offset the loss of muscle mass that comes with aging.

or the precise amount of time you take to recover between sets. You do, however, need at least a 60-second rest break between sets, and you will probably feel you're getting a better workout if you let no more than 5 minutes elapse between them. But you don't have to stand around doing nothing during these recoveries; you should have plenty of energy to move directly from one muscle group to another. For exercises that work one leg at a time, you may find that you can rattle off two or three sets in fairly rapid-fire succession simply by alternating legs.

Power lifters puff and strain to heave close to the maximum possible weight skyward with each repetition. They'll rarely accomplish more than five of these lifts per set. Your purposes are better served by doing more reps with smaller weights. Choose the weights so you can do 12 to 15 reps per set. This will result in a lot less grunting and a lot less of the muscular protests that power lifters call "a good burn."

Old-school weight-lifting wisdom recommended doing three sets each time you work out, with three workouts a week for each muscle group. But you can do less and still get most of the benefit. In fact, three times a week is slightly too often; the best research indicates that you'll get better results if you work each set of muscles every third day. Twice a week is adequate, and you can drop your lower-body workouts back to about once every 5 days if you're also doing speed training.

Nor is it vital to do the traditional three sets. Studies have shown that you get at least 90 percent of the benefit from doing only two. Dropping to one set, however, probably cuts the benefit by nearly half.

Power lifters always raise and lower weights slowly, concentrating on the muscle as they flex it, then gradually release it. You can do this if you want, but it's not mandatory for your purposes. Just don't pump the weights so quickly that you risk pulling a muscle or tendon. And make sure you lower the weight slowly enough that you're working the muscle not merely as you lift the weight, but also while the weight is on its way back down. The two types of motion are different, and you need to strengthen both of them.

With the light weights you should be using, each set of 15 will take well under a minute. You might get slightly more benefit if you slow the rhythm down a bit, but if time is a factor, you can rattle the lifts off fairly quickly.

When beginning, make sure to err on the light side when choosing which weights to lift. It's amazingly easy to work yourself so hard in a few minutes that you have a memorable set of sore muscles for days afterward. You'll be a lot happier if you're conservative, adding a little more weight with each workout until you've learned what you can comfortably lift. Within a month you should be getting noticeably stronger. If you want, keep a log of the weights lifted and the numbers of reps and sets, but all you really need to record are the dates on which you've worked out and whether those workouts involved the upper body, the lower body, or both.

As with other types of training, weight training strengthens muscles by tearing them down slightly so that the body rebuilds them stronger than before. Because it's more intense than running, however, you need a longer recovery period, which is why you shouldn't lift more often than every third day. If you want to visit the gym more frequently, alternate between upper- and lower-body workouts. It's more efficient, though, to work out less frequently and do everything all at once. If you lift and run on the same day, run first.

There are two basic types of weights: free weights (barbells and dumbbells) and machines. Athletes in sports like basketball, football, and baseball prefer free weights because they force you to develop greater balance. They also build strength connections among related muscle groups. But these connections are needed only in sports that draw on explosive bursts of coordinated power. You can get your job done with either type of weights, but working solely with free weights takes a good deal longer. The program presented in this chapter, therefore, mostly uses machines.

Strength training is easiest if you have access to a well-equipped health club or gym. (Weight lifting was an important enough part of my training that I have my own weight machines at home.) On your own, you might be able to do a partial workout via calisthenics such as pushups, pullups, lunges, squats, and abdominal curls, but it's difficult to find calisthenic-style exercises that isolate certain important muscles, such as the hamstrings. Ankle weights and rubber tubing might also help, but both have limitations and are not covered in this book. Sadly, if you don't have access to a gym, you're going to have trouble doing a well-focused weight-lifting program. Get a book on bodybuilding and seek out whatever exercises you have the equipment to do that can substitute for those recommended below.

concentric contraction

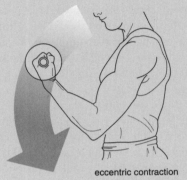

eccentric contraction

Muscles use "concentric" contractions when they flex to lift a weight (top). Easing the weight back to ground (bottom) uses "eccentric" contractions. You gain the most strength by working both parts of the cycle.

CONCENTRIC VS. ECCENTRIC CONTRACTIONS

Muscles are capable of two types of work, termed *concentric* and *eccentric* contractions by exercise physiologists. When you flex your biceps to lift a heavy object, that's a concentric effort—the type of motion you ordinarily think of in terms of weight lifting. When you use that same muscle to lower the weight without allowing it to crash back to earth, that's an eccentric contraction. It's the same muscle, but it's doing a different type of work—the difference between walking up or down a flight of stairs.

To get the most from your weight lifting, practice strengthening the muscle on both parts of its cycle. For the concentric contraction, lift the weight briskly (but not with a muscle-pulling snap). To strengthen the eccentric phase, lower the weight gradually, in a controlled manner. That will add a second or so to the time consumed by each rep, but it will pay dividends in increased strength.

DON'T FORGET TO BREATHE

Holding your breath—the beginning weight lifter's natural tendency—causes a buildup in pressure in the chest as the rib cage is squeezed by your exertions. This can cut off blood flow to the heart—an obviously bad idea. With the light weights you'll be using, this is a low risk, but it's still good to practice safe lifting methods: exhale as you lift; inhale when lowering the weight back to rest.

LOWER-BODY EXERCISES (CORE PROGRAM)

At a minimum, there are four weight-lifting exercises for your lower body. These are designed to exercise the quadriceps, the hamstrings, the calves, and the hip flexors.

BASIC WEIGHT-LIFTING ROUTINE

EXERCISE	MUSCLES WORKED
LOWER-BODY EXERCISES (CORE PROGRAM)	
quadriceps extensions	front of thigh (quadriceps)
hamstring curls	back of thigh (hamstrings)
calf raises	calves
hip flexions	hip flexors
hip extensions	gluteus muscles of the buttocks
OPTIONAL LOWER-BODY EXERCISES	
lunges	quadriceps (mostly)
squats or leg presses	quadriceps (mostly)
dead lifts*	upper hamstrings
UPPER-BODY EXERCISES (CORE PROGRAM)	
crunches	abdominals
back raises*	back muscles
OPTIONAL UPPER-BODY EXERCISES	
biceps curls	biceps (front of upper arm)
triceps extensions	triceps (back of upper arm)
lat pull-downs	back and shoulders
lat rowing pulls	back and shoulders
butterfly curls	pectorals (chest)
double-leg reverse crunches*	lower abdominals

* People with back problems should consult an expert before doing this exercise.

Quadriceps Extensions. The quads are the big muscles on the fronts of your thighs. The best way to strengthen them is on specially designed machines, where you sit with a padded bar across the top of your ankles. Using one leg, raise the bar until your leg is nearly straight, but don't lock the knee—that puts heavy stress on the tendons around the kneecap, risking injury. The only way to be sure you're exercising both legs equally is to work them in separate sets. At the bottom of the cycle, however, your quads are in their weakest position, and you may need an assist from the resting leg. Do so to first lift the weight off its blocks, then avoid the need in subsequent reps by not lowering the weight all the way back down until you've finished the set. In fact, try to bend your knee no more than 45 degrees between lifts; repeatedly lifting from a lower position can be hard on your knees.

Quadriceps extensions.

Hamstring curls. The machine for hamstring curls has you lie on your stomach, with a padded bar behind your ankles. Again, you may need to use both legs to raise the bar for the first few inches without overstraining, but after that you should exercise each hamstring separately, lowering the bar no farther than you can easily raise it back up with one leg.

Hamstring curl. Some people point the toe for a slightly different lift.

Calf raises. Calf raises can be done at a health club, on a sidewalk curb, or at home. All you need is a step, with something nearby to hold onto for balance. Stand with your heels hanging out over empty air; then alternately drop your heels as far as they will comfortably go and rise up on your toes to the top of your comfortable range of motion. Because you're lifting only your own body weight, this exercise will be relatively easy. Compensate by building up to sets of 30, doing 10 reps with your toes pointed straight ahead, 10 with toes outward, and 10 with toes angled inward. That sounds like a lot of reps, but they don't take long.

Hip flexions and hip extensions. If there's a single muscle whose strength is most strongly correlated to running speed, it's the hip flexor. This midsized muscle lies at the top of the leg, in front of your hip. High-step with your knee,

Calf raises.

The multihip machine allows you to work either the hip flexors or the gluteus muscles. This woman is working her glutes. To work the hip flexor, put the leg below the bar and lift forward, rather than back. To work the other leg, turn around and face in the opposite direction.
(LIFE FITNESS)

and you'll see it, above the quadriceps, helping you bend the thigh forward from the hip. It's important for running because this is what lifts your knee and drives your leg forward with each stride; strong hip flexors mean a more rapid stride.

The best hip-flexor exercise uses a *multihip machine*. This device has a bar that you lift by raising your knee, one leg at a time. To work the other leg, you have to turn around and face the opposite direction, adjusting the machine to reverse the direction of the resistance. That sounds complex, but once someone has shown you how to do it, it's easy. While you're getting assistance, ask the attendant to show you how to adjust the height of the bar so it's comfortable.

The same machine—with yet another adjustment—creates resistance when you push down rather than up. Swinging the leg down and out behind you allows you to work out the gluteus muscles of the buttocks, a useful supplemental exercise.

> **For optimal weight-lifting benefits, work each muscle group every third day, and do three sets of each exercise.**

Optional Lower-Body Exercises

There are lots of other lower-body exercises, but three of the best are lunges, squats (or leg presses), and dead lifts.

The lunge.

Lunges. This exercise starts from a standing position, with your feet about shoulder-width apart. From this position, step forward, dipping your front knee toward the floor like a fencer on the attack, keeping your torso straight. Unlike the fencer, however, do this with your arms immobile, hands on hips or simply hanging at your sides. It's the forward step that gives the exercise its name, but most of the work comes from pushing backward as you return to your original standing position. The amount of exercise depends on how far forward you step and how deeply you bend your knee. When the exercise starts becoming too easy, increase the effort by holding dumbbells in your hands or a weight bar across your shoulders.

Squats or leg presses. The squat is done standing while holding a weight bar or dumbbells. It's a good exercise, but many people prefer working the same muscles on a leg press machine, which gives you somewhat finer control. Either way, you're doing the equivalent of standing up and squatting down, while lifting more than your body weight (the leg press machine does this by having you press against a plate, attached to a stack of weights). To avoid knee strain, however, this exercise does not involve a full squat: never bend your knees more than 90 degrees. Some experts advise against bending them by more than 45 degrees.

Squats (above) *and leg presses* (right). *You only need to do one or the other.*

Dead lifts.

Dead lifts. The dead lift shouldn't be attempted by people with back problems, unless they've first consulted a doctor, trainer, or physical therapist. And whatever you may have seen in televised power-lifting competitions, this isn't a good exercise for nonexperts to engage in as a macho endeavor to test their limits. The lift itself is simple. Set a weight bar on the floor; then bend over to grasp it, making sure your knees, as in the drawing, are bent enough that your torso never has to lean forward more than 45 degrees. Lift the bar by standing back upright, raising the weight with your legs more than with your back. The primary purpose isn't to strengthen your back muscles; it's to work the top part of your hamstrings. After each repetition, lower the weight back to (or near) the floor with the same bent-legged posture you used to lift it.

SAFETY TIPS

If in doubt about how to do any of these exercises, ask for a demonstration from a trainer at your gym or health club: the best way to learn is by watching someone else. Also, health clubs typically post detailed instructions near each machine.

Never lift weights without warming up for a few minutes, perhaps by walking briskly on a treadmill or spinning gently on an exercise bicycle. I've never pulled a muscle in a weight room, but it's possible with cold muscles, and it's a really silly way to temporarily disable yourself. Five or 10 minutes of warm-up should be sufficient—just enough that you begin to sweat.

If an exercise causes pain other than the normal "burn" of a well-worked muscle, stop immediately and consult an expert. You may be doing something wrong, or you may have a physical condition that makes it unwise to do that particular exercise. For the same reasons, start any new exercise at a weight that feels relatively easy, until you're sure your body can handle it.

UPPER-BODY EXERCISES (CORE PROGRAM)

For racing, exercising the upper body is mostly a matter of working the major muscle groups enough to give you good overall muscle tone. If you're after more upper-body strength than that, a weight-lifting book or a health club trainer can recommend additional exercises.

There are only two upper-body exercises that should be considered mandatory for runners: crunches and back raises.

Crunches. These are the successor to the sit-ups you probably learned in grade school. The difference is that you focus the exercise more strongly on your abdominal muscles by not actually sitting all the way up. Lie on your back, knees bent, feet on the floor, arms folded on your chest. Initially, the exercise is almost static, as you tighten your abdominal muscles and flatten your spine against the floor. As you gain strength, curl your head and shoulders upward to increase the resistance. You can do crunches in sets of 15, just like any other strength exercise, or you can build up to a single large set of perhaps 50.

Crunches.

Back raises. These can be done on special machines or by simply lying on a padded mat. As with dead lifts, if you're prone to back problems, don't do back raises without first consulting a back specialist. This exercise is like a reverse crunch. Lying on your stomach, with your hands clasped behind the small of your back, use your back muscles to curl your head and shoulders an inch or two above the mat. If that's too much, raise only one leg and the diagonally opposite arm (as in the drawing), reversing sides with each rep. Go easy, and don't strain.

Back raises.

Optional Upper-Body Exercises

The rest of your upper-body workout can involve any combination of lat pulls, biceps curls, pushups, triceps extensions, or any of a number of other exercises. As a runner, you need not be as worried about minor upper-body imbalances as you should be about exercising your legs equally, so there's no reason to devote separate sets to each arm. Nevertheless, try to exercise them equally. Following are a few suggested exercises.

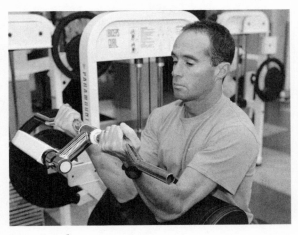

Biceps curls. The curls can be done on a specialty machine or with free weights. Either way, simply lift the desired weight by flexing your arms.

Biceps curls.

Triceps extensions. These extensions work the muscle on the side of the upper arm opposite the biceps. The biceps flexes the arm; the triceps straightens it. Hard races can sometimes tire this muscle, so it's a good one to work on. In running, your arm swing makes more use of the triceps than the biceps. The easiest way to isolate the triceps for weight lifting is with a triceps extension machine, which allows you to work your triceps without straining your shoulders.

Triceps extensions can be done on a weight machine (as shown here) or with a weight bar.

Lat pull-downs. These are best done with a machine that uses a chain or a strap to suspend a bar over your head. Grasping the bar by its handgrips, pull it downward in front of your head until it reaches the bottom of your neck. It's OK to lean back slightly. Some people do this exercise by pulling the bar down behind their necks, but experts warn that this can be hard on the rotator cuff muscles of your shoulders. *Lat*, by the way, is short for latissimus dorsi, which are the major pulling muscles of the back and shoulders.

Lat rowing pulls. Another pulling exercise is the lat rowing pull. The difference is that this one is done horizontally rather than vertically. Pull with your arms and shoulders, not your back. Doing lat rowing pulls, by the way, isn't the same thing as working out on a rowing machine; rowing machines use both the arms and legs at a much lower level of intensity and are a form of cross-training, not weight lifting.

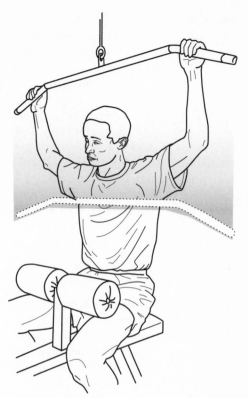

Lat pull-downs.

Lat rowing pulls.

Butterfly curls. The aptly named butterfly curl is designed to strengthen the pectoral muscles of the chest. The machine looks complex, but once you've figured out how to get your arms into it, the only way you can move is by swinging your elbows toward each other in front of you—like an enormous butterfly flapping its wings. A foot pedal helps you get started from the initial wings-open position, where your pecs are too weak to lift much weight. Between reps, don't return all the way to the start-up position; for the safety of your rotator cuffs, your elbows should never be behind the plane of your shoulders when you're exerting pressure.

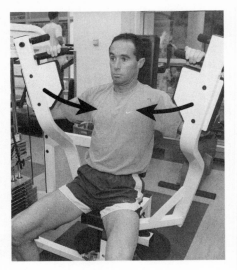

Butterfly curls.

Double-leg reverse crunches. This exercise is for the lower abdominal muscles, not the legs. Start by lying on your back, with your legs raised high. Now slowly lower them, feeling the burn in your abs. Raise them again and repeat. Don't go so low that your back arches. Consciously tighten your stomach muscles before you begin, to flatten your spine against the floor. If you have a bad back, consult with a physical therapist or professional trainer before attempting this exercise.

Double-leg reverse crunches. If you need to reduce the strain on your back, try bending your knees slightly.

PLYOMETRICS

Plyometrics is a system of jumping and bounding drills created in Eastern Europe to add explosive power to your stride. It's a form of strength training, but is done with a fluid, dynamic motion that is more akin to the demands of actual racing than is weight lifting.

> **Strong muscles are good. Strong, inflexible muscles aren't so good. Don't forget to temper your weight lifting with stretching.**

In the 1950s, athletically gifted children in the Soviet Union were placed on these drills from a young age, with phenomenal results. But plyometrics was virtually unknown in the West until one of those children, Valeri Borzov, grew up to win the Olympic 100 meters, usually a North American specialty, in 1972. U.S. coaches quickly realized what they were missing, and plyometrics entered American sprinting and jumping—with the result that the U.S. soon reclaimed its traditional prominence. More recently, elite distance runners have taken up the discipline, making it an integral part of their training.

A typical plyometric drill might have you hop as quickly as you can onto and off a 12-inch wooden box, in sets of 10 repeats. Some sets might use a double-legged

MUSCLES, MUSCLES, AND MORE MUSCLES

The body has many muscles. To say that racing uses them all may be an exaggeration (you're not likely to need much hand strength, for example), but it does use enough of them that a hard race may leave you sore in unexpected places. I've been coaching a talented 15-year-old, for example, who was startled to discover that his arms were sore from pumping them harder and longer in races than he was accustomed to from training. The solution was to increase his upper-body weight lifting.

The same can apply to lots of other muscles. Rick says that in his first couple of years of racing, he had sore adductors (groin muscles) after his first spring race—a problem he'd then address with a few weeks' work with rubber tubing. Other runners may find that their own weaknesses lie in any of several other muscles associated with balance or foot or leg motion.

It's important to address these weaknesses as soon as you identify them. Otherwise, you can strain the muscle by racing too hard on it, substantially slowing its recovery.

In-depth discussion of all possible weight-lifting workouts is beyond the scope of this book, but health club trainers can help you identify exercises that isolate the muscles you need to strengthen. Cross-training, particularly in sports that test your balance, will also help keep these smaller muscles in tone. Rick's adductor problems disappeared after he took up cross-country skiing during the winter off-season.

hop, others might exercise one leg at a time. A complete workout might use a total of 30 or 35 sets, with 10 or 12 different drills.

Equipment needs are minimal but specialized: sturdy, no-tip boxes of various heights, and a smooth, high-traction surface on which to work. But plyometrics is an advanced training method, used by only a few people. If you're interested, many health clubs have the equipment, with trainers to teach you some drills. For an entire book on the subject, consult *High-Powered Plyometrics*, by James Radcliffe and Robert Farentinos.

VACATION AS CROSS-TRAINING

Sometimes you can benefit from a vacation that gives you a brief break from running, while still giving you a lot of exercise from other activities. Here's Rick:

An active vacation can keep you in surprisingly good shape, even if you never run a step. That's especially true for trips involving such sports as backpacking, bicycling, or cross-country skiing, which rack up enormous amounts of cross-training.

The first time I interrupted my training with such a trip, it was a weeklong backpacking trip in the high mountains of northern Utah. In theory, I could have gone trail running each evening; in practice, hiking was as much work as I wanted. My running was a bit sluggish for a few days afterward, but within 10 days, I was doing better speed workouts than before I left, and shortly after that, I rewrote all of my PRs (personal records) from 5K to 10 miles. Clearly, the trip hadn't set me back, and the shift in activities had actually given my running muscles a valuable rest.

I've repeated this experience since then, most recently following a 2-week hiking, backpacking, and mountain-biking trip on which I only managed to run on the first day and the last two. Two weeks later, I ran the fastest half-marathon of my masters career, winning my age group.

CROSS-TRAINING

The term *cross-training* is coaching jargon for investing part of your work in a sport other than your principal one. Reasons to cross-train vary. Some people want to exercise different sets of muscles; others seek activities that closely mimic their main sports for occasions when their first love is impossible. Cross-country skiers, for example, need cross-training to keep in shape during the snow-free months.

Elite runners don't do much cross-training, unless you broaden the definition to include weight lifting and stretching—which are better viewed as parts of your core training. If your goal is to become the best possible runner, the most efficient way to train is by running as much as your body will tolerate.

Sometimes, though, you'll want to engage in cross-training either for fun, variety, or as a way to keep in shape during a layoff. Bicycling is probably the most popular way to do this, partly because it doesn't require a trip to a swimming pool or health club. Other options include

- swimming
- stair climbing
- stationary cycling
- using a rowing machine
- hiking
- cross-country skiing

Just remember that none of these uses exactly the same muscles as running. You need to be careful, therefore, not to hurt yourself by taking them up too quickly. And realize, too, that none of them will keep you in perfect running shape.

NUTRITION AND WEIGHT CONTROL

NUTRITION BASICS

French gastronomist Anthelme Brillat-Savarin had it right a long time ago with his now-famous pronouncement: "Tell me what you eat and I will tell you who you are." The only thing missed by that proverb (usually condensed to "you are what you eat") is the degree to which people divide into warring dietary camps.

Mostly, dietary advice for athletes is the same as for anyone else:

- Eat a variety of foods (in Japan, health authorities encourage "30 flavors" each day).
- Eat at least five half-cup servings of fruits and vegetables daily, and make sure that at least some are fruits. Nine servings per day is better. Examine a 4-ounce measuring cup to get the idea of what a half-cup looks like. It's not all that large; a big apple or banana, for example, might be two servings. French fries and potato chips, incidentally, don't count.
- Don't substitute vitamin pills for fruits and vegetables. Scientists haven't figured out what it is in fruits and vegetables that does the good, but it appears to be more than the individual chemicals sometimes extracted from them and sold as supplements. If you choose to take supplements, eat fruits and vegetables as well. Also, read as much as you can about supplement pros and cons before you take them. Some have risks, some shouldn't be mixed with common medications, and some are excreted by the body so quickly it's often quipped that their only effect is to give you expensive urine.
- Keep fat to no more than 30 percent of total caloric intake, and minimize the saturated fat (mostly of animal origin). Just because you're a runner

doesn't mean you're immune to atherosclerosis. You don't need to add up fat grams fanatically to make substantial progress in this arena. You can achieve a lot with common sense: save fried foods, fatty meats (except for oily fish, which has a healthy form of fat), whole milk, and high-fat bakery goods for special occasions. Eat mostly low-fat meats, low-fat or skim milk, low-fat cheeses, and so forth.

- Don't forget calcium. Many adult Americans, particularly women, don't get enough of it. Look for it in milk (preferably skim), cheese, orange juice, spinach, broccoli, and related foods, and take pills if your doctor recommends them. Don't go beyond the recommended doses of the pills, though; that can give you kidney stones.

> **Eat a basic healthy diet: a variety of foods, lots of fruits and vegetables, not too much fat (especially saturated fat)—and read the nutrition labels so you know what you're actually eating.**

- Eat a high-fiber diet. Most people obtain much less than half of the fiber that nutritionists recommend. When possible, eat whole-grain breads rather than highly refined grains, and eat beans, high-fiber breakfast cereals, and a lot of those all-around-good-for-you fruits and vegetables.
- Make a habit of reading nutrition labels on packaged foods. That can teach you a lot about what foods contain what nutrients. In particular, it's a good way to seek out sources of fiber and to avoid hidden fat.
- Remember that unless you suffer from a food allergy or intolerance, there's no such thing as a "good food" or a "bad food." Instead, there are good and bad *diets*. Rather than feeling guilty about wanting an occasional treat, keep the serving size small, make sure it's really a treat and not a staple, and retain balance by adjusting other parts of your diet.

Two nutrients not included in the above list are salt and sugar. That's because they are controversial, and it's hard to give specific advice. The official U.S. dietary guidelines still recommend limiting your salt intake, but many scientists are increasingly convinced that calcium deficiency is a more significant cause of high blood pressure than is excess salt consumption. Sedentary lifestyles are also an enormous factor, one that you've eliminated by becoming a runner. Nevertheless, monitor your blood pressure at least twice a year and consult your doctor if it's high or creeping upward.

As for sugar, vast amounts have been written—and disputed—over the effect of sugar and other carbohydrates on the risk of developing diabetes. With diabetes on the rise in Western cultures, this topic deserves discussion, but some of the advice flatly contradicts conventional sports nutrition wisdom by steering you away from carbohydrates, the athlete's primary fuel. On the other hand, there's no reason not to be selective about which carbohydrates you eat. Whatever their impact might be on diabetes, refined sugar and highly processed flour don't carry the fiber and micronutrients found in fruits and whole grains.

Special considerations, however, apply to the meals you eat the night before and morning of a race, particularly for long races. These are discussed in part 3 of this book, about the race itself.

FUELING THE SERIOUS ATHLETE

If a study were to announce that a mixture of artichokes, pineapple, and anchovies could shave a minute off your 10K time, there would undoubtedly be a boom in exotic pizza combinations. The truth appears to be considerably more prosaic. Diet is indeed important, and dietary errors can destroy your performance as thoroughly as an injury, but there are no magic bullets that will make you instantly faster. At least two dietary factors, however, are critical: carbohydrates and protein. Fats are also important, but mostly because there are limits to how far health-conscious people should cut back on them.

Carbohydrates

Carbohydrates are your primary running fuel. In chapter 2, we talked about glycogen, the form in which your muscles and liver store carbohydrates. Your body draws on its glycogen stores every time you run, but those supplies can only be replenished if you eat carbohydrates. Otherwise they stay depleted, and performance suffers as your body shifts to lower-grade fuels.

If you don't believe in the importance of carbohydrates, you could become persuaded quickly enough by trying the depletion phase of the carbohydrate depletion-loading diet described in chapter 15 on marathon training. This diet is a weeklong effort to tweak the body's glycogen supply by first depleting it, then allowing it to rebound so quickly that it overshoots its norm—potentially useful in long races. In the depletion phase, you eat virtually no carbohydrates, with the result that in a few days you can barely walk comfortably around the block, let alone go for long runs. Anyone who's ever tried this knows that carbohydrates are important.

Carbohydrates are your primary fuel. They need to be replaced after each run, or eventually you'll become depleted and sluggish.

The carbohydrate depletion diet is extreme, but it's possible to become accidentally depleted enough to feel an effect. Sometimes, particularly when I was away from my normal home routine, I would find myself feeling unexpectedly sluggish. I'd mentally catalog my past few days' meals and realize that they were low in carbohydrates. A big spaghetti dinner would fix that, and the next day I'd be running my normal 17 miles, feeling just fine. You just can't run happily if you don't eat enough carbohydrates.

Another problem from not eating enough carbohydrates is that it forces the body to look elsewhere for energy. That's why high-mileage runners sometimes look emaciated. Not only do they have no body fat, but their muscles have been cannibalized for fuel. If you eat enough carbohydrates, there's no reason for this to happen. You can run 100 miles a week without losing muscle.

How much carbohydrates should you eat? The answer depends on how much you're running. Traditional nutritional advice is to obtain 55 percent of your calories from carbohydrates, the rest from a mixture of fat (no more than 30 percent) and protein (at least 15 percent). But that's for inactive people. Elite athletes generally jack the carbohydrates up to 70 percent, dropping the fat and protein to 20 percent and 10 percent, respectively.

Looking at these in terms of percentages is misleading, though, because it makes it look as though the elite athletes have lowered their fat and protein consumption. Actually, consumption of all three nutrients is elevated, but the total diet has increased from the 2,000 calories a day that is typical for sedentary individuals to perhaps 3,500 calories per day. If we convert the percentages to calories, we get the results shown in the accompanying table. It shows that despite the radically different percentages, there is a very simple difference between the elite athlete's diet and the average person's: the elite athlete is obtaining almost all of the extra calories from carbohydrates.

You won't be running as much mileage as an elite runner, but you can apply the same dietary principle. Running burns off approximately 100 calories per mile, and you should eat most of those calories as carbohydrates. That's about the equivalent of a big bagel and a banana after a 4- to 5-mile run. You could get the same number of calories from a donut, but the donut's higher fat content means that it won't be as effective at replenishing the spent glycogen.

DIET COMPARISON

NUTRIENT	STANDARD U.S. RECOMMENDATIONS FOR DIETARY INTAKE, CALORIES (GRAMS)*	ELITE ATHLETE'S CONSUMPTION, CALORIES (GRAMS)*
carbohydrates	1,100 (275)	2,450 (610)
fat	600 (65)	700 (80)
protein	300 (75)	350 (95)
Total	2,000	3,500

* Gram figures are calculated as follows: carbohydrates and protein have 4 calories per gram, fat has 9 calories per gram. Values are rounded off to the nearest 5 grams.

COMPLEX VS. SIMPLE CARBOHYDRATES

In the world of carbohydrates, "complexity" is good. *Simple carbohydrates* are refined sugars. They can play a role in your carbohydrate intake, but the main player should be *complex carbohydrates*, which are molecules made by linking sugar molecules into chains. Flour, starches, and fruit sugars are complex carbohydrates; candy bars are not. Nutritionally, the difference is that simple carbohydrates are more easily digested and will give you a sudden flash of energy that's soon gone. Complex carbohydrates are parceled out more gradually—the difference between a slow, steady burn and an explosion. If you're totally wiped out from a hard workout, you may want the rapid burst of energy from a sugary snack, but most of the time, trickle-charging via complex carbohydrates works better.

Eating these carbohydrates predominantly from whole-grain breads or other high-fiber sources—or as parts of meals that also contain protein or modest amounts of fat—will also improve the sustained-energy effect because the fiber, protein, and fat slow your digestion, thereby releasing the energy more gradually.

Protein

Exercise strengthens muscles by tearing them down, then allowing them to rebuild, stronger than before. Protein provides the biochemical building blocks for the rebuilding. The body can scavenge some of these building blocks from damaged proteins, but part of the original protein is irretrievably lost. In addition, a small but not negligible amount of it is burned up for fuel, particularly in hard workouts. All of this needs to be replaced.

Scientific research increasingly shows that the 50 grams per day of protein set as a minimum on U.S. food labels (itself lower than the 15 percent figure discussed earlier in this chapter) may be on the low side. The best research focuses on football players and other high-performance athletes, but it is beginning to look as though college-level track athletes need about three-quarters of a gram of protein per pound of body weight—well more than most of them get. Football players need a full gram.

The average person probably needs about half a gram of protein per pound of body weight. But if you're running more than 30 miles a week, you might want to step that up to two-thirds of a gram. If you weigh 150 pounds, that's double the food-label recommendation, and 33 percent higher than you'll get from a 15-percent-protein, 2,000-calorie diet.

There are two ways to get the extra protein. One is from standard dietary sources, such as meat and dairy products. Just make sure you use mostly heart-friendly, low-fat, low-cholesterol sources. Unless you're lactose intolerant, skim milk is perfect. A couple of glasses a day has 16 grams of protein, only 160 calories, and a big shot of calcium. Alternatively, you can get extra protein from high-protein nutritional products packaged either as food bars or beverage powders that taste a lot like milk shakes (try mixing one in skim milk for a snack that can pack 20 grams of protein into a single dose).

An extra 50 grams of protein has about 200 calories. Preferably, you should make room for that in your diet by cutting back on fat, but if it winds up coming out of your carbohydrate allotment, 200 calories isn't enough to interfere noticeably with glycogen recovery.

Eat more protein than the minimum recommended on food labels. If you weigh 150 pounds, 100 grams per day is a good target.

Fat

It's easy to view fat as nothing but a dietary evil, but in moderation it's as vital for health as protein and carbohydrates. Cellular metabolism, nerve function, and the absorption of certain fat-soluble vitamins (most notably vitamins A, D, and E) depend on fats. People who force themselves onto absurdly low-fat diets can fall prey to a variety of highly unpleasant ailments. Don't cut your fat consumption below 20 percent or do anything else that involves an unusual manipulation of fat intake (such as restricting yourself to only one type of fat) without first consulting a doctor. Besides, one of the joys of running is that you're burning off enough energy that you can occasionally indulge in a hot-fudge sundae, bag of chips, chocolate bar, or other treat.

On the other hand, don't eat enormous amounts of fat just because you can do so without gaining weight. We've already mentioned the risk of atherosclerosis. On the more mundane side is the fact that fat crowds protein and carbohydrates out of your diet. It can also make running uncomfortable by taking longer to digest than other foods.

Food Allergies and Intolerances

Food allergies are potentially life-threatening reactions to specific foods, such as peanuts or walnuts. Their primary relevance to racing is that if you have an allergy, you need to bring your own food to the finish line or make sure that the race organizers have provided something you can safely eat.

Food intolerances are less dangerous, but they can interfere with training by giving you diarrhea or other digestive problems. Some runners have reported that the stress of running, particularly speed work, can bring to the fore a minor intolerance that had never before affected them enough to be noticeable. If you suspect that you have a food intolerance, you're going to have to play around with your diet to weed out the cause (see page 154).

THE RIGHT WEIGHT FOR YOU

"What should I weigh?" If there's a single question that's most apt to give speakers heartburn at running clinics, that's the one. There's actually a simple answer: your ideal weight is that which is best for your health and your performance. If you weigh too much, you'll be slow, easily injured, and subject to health problems. If you weigh too little, you'll be slow, easily injured, and subject to other health problems.

Ideally, I'd just leave it at that. But in racing or in training, runners tend to check each other out. And what everyone notices is that while runners as a group tend to be lean, fast runners tend to be leaner yet. That leads to the inevitable question: If runner X, who always beats me in the races, is 5 pounds lighter than I am, could I beat him if I were to reduce by 10 pounds?

The answer is maybe yes, maybe no. *Extra* weight does indeed slow you down. But comparing yourself to other runners won't tell you your ideal weight. A better way to assess where you stand is with height-weight formulas, but even these are far from perfect. A very simple, older formula that describes a lot of speedier runners is the "double-the-inches" formula. This said that your ideal weight was twice your height in inches. At 6 feet, 2 inches, I should weigh 148 pounds according to the formula, which is very close to what I did weigh for racing (144 pounds).

The double-the-inches formula, however, is derived from the heights and weights of elite male racers, who almost always are extremely fine-boned. It worked for Rick, who at 5 feet, 6 inches, weighed 132 pounds when he set his lifetime PRs, but he too is very fine-boned. To assess your bone structure, circle your wrist with the thumb and fingers of the other hand. If they meet with room to spare, you're fine-boned. If they barely touch, you're medium-boned. If you can't make them touch, you're large-boned. Even if you're substantially overweight this test should work, because most people don't carry much fat in their wrists.

Medium-boned people shouldn't strive for the double-the-inches target weight. If they make it, they're going to be far too thin. Target instead on something about 10 percent higher. Heavy-boned people should set their target weights higher yet, probably 20 percent above the level appropriate for fine-boned people.

That's for men. For women, the double-the-inches formula gives weights that are a bit on the high side. Bob Glover, a respected New York sports and fitness consultant and running author, recommends that women begin from a base of 120 pounds, adding or subtracting 3 pounds for each inch above or below a height of 5 feet, 6 inches. By this formula, a 5-foot-4 woman "should" weigh 114 pounds; a 5-foot-9 woman comes in at 129 pounds.

Although Glover doesn't state it in this fashion, his formula appears to be targeted on medium-boned women. Heavy-boned women should expect to be 10 percent higher; fine-boned women can go 10 percent lower. Women, however, have to be a lot more careful about not cutting too much weight than do men; as we'll discuss in a moment, they need more than twice as much body fat for basic health.

Body Mass Index: The New Height-Weight Measure

Although both of the above height-weight formulas are popular in the running literature, sports physiologists and nutritionists rarely use either of them. Instead, medical research tends to evaluate body weight in terms of *body mass index* (BMI).

BMI is simply your weight in kilograms divided by the square of your height in meters. As a mathematical formula, that would be stated as

$$BMI = \frac{\text{weight in kilograms}}{(\text{height in meters})^2}$$

I'm 1.88 meters tall and raced at 65.5 kilograms. That gave me a BMI of 18.5—well on the lean side.

To start from pounds and inches, divide your weight in pounds by 2.2 and divide your height in inches by 39.4. Or, you can do the whole thing in English units and multiply by 705 to make the unit changes automatically. The formula would be

$$BMI = \frac{\text{weight in pounds}}{(\text{height in inches})^2} \times 705$$

"Normal" BMI is about 20 to 25, which is a fairly broad range. If you're fine-boned, you'll probably look and feel best at the lower end of the range; if you're large-boned, you'll want to be at the upper end. Average-boned people will be closer to the middle.

Even BMI, however, isn't a perfect measure of leanness. A fine-boned body-builder is going to be heavier than a heavy-boned person who has never wanted to bulk up. If your BMI is in the 20 to 25 range, you're considered normal, regardless of bone structure. A BMI below 18 is definitely considered "underweight."

A BMI of 25 or above, on the other hand, is the medical definition of being overweight (although a few muscle-bound hunks may have BMIs over 25 without carrying significant excess fat). A BMI of 30 or above is the clinical definition of obesity. The table on page 120 shows normal, overweight, and clinically obese weight levels for a wide range of heights, giving you the opportunity to compare these to your own weight. There also is a column for BMI 18, but please note the accompanying caveat: this is *not* a target; it's a weight at which most nutritionists would consider you excessively thin. Depending on your bone structure and other factors, you could be underweight even if you weighed 10 or 20 pounds more than this.

A major advantage of BMI over other height-weight measures is that it recognizes important differences in tall and short people that are overlooked by simpler formulas. Thus, although Rick and I both looked the same under the double-the-inches weight formula, his BMI was a low-normal 21.4, while mine was barely over the underweight category, reflecting the fact that I was much more the "string bean."

BODY COMPOSITION: MEASURING THE FAT

The ultimate in height-weight testing is to measure your body composition. That's because what really matters in assessing fitness is your percentage body fat. If you're carrying a lot of muscle, you can be fit, compact, and heavy. You may not be

BODY WEIGHTS AND BODY MASS INDEX (BMI), BY HEIGHT

BMI (Body Mass Index)

Height*	18—CAUTION LEVEL FOR EXCESSIVE THINNESS	20—LOW END OF NORMAL RANGE	25—BORDERLINE OVERWEIGHT	30—BORDERLINE OBESE
4'11"	91 lb.	101 lb.	126 lb.	151 lb.
5'0"	94	104	130	156
5'1"	97	108	135	162
5'2"	100	111	139	167
5'3"	103	115	144	172
5'4"	107	119	148	178
5'5"	110	122	153	183
5'6"	113	126	158	189
5'7"	117	130	162	195
5'8"	120	134	167	201
5'9"	124	138	172	207
5'10"	128	142	177	213
5'11"	131	146	182	219
6'0"	135	150	188	225
6'1"	139	154	193	231
6'2"	143	158	198	238
6'3"	147	163	204	244
6'4"	150	167	209	251
6'5"	154	172	215	257
6'6"	158	176	220	264

* To determine your BMI more precisely, and for people outside this height range, use the formula on page 119.

hyperfast, but there's not much you can do about it unless you want to give up the activity that built all those muscles.

Conversely, it's possible to be lightweight and flabby. Height-weight calculations won't reveal this because your weight is right where it should be, but a body composition test will catch it. Here, your solution isn't to lose weight, but to get busy training (and perhaps weight lifting) to convert some of the fat into muscle that can speed you up.

There are three standard ways of measuring body composition: underwater weighing, the skin-fold test, and skin conductivity. Any can be done in minutes by a qualified technician for about the cost of a race registration fee. Sometimes, skin-fold and skin conductivity tests are done for free or very inexpensively at pre-race expositions.

Underwater weighing is the most accurate. It's done exactly as the name implies, by having you sit on a scale in a large tub of water. This takes advantage of the fact that fat floats, while bone and muscle sink. By comparing your submerged weight to what you weigh outside the tub, the technician can determine how much fat you're carrying. The primary limiting factor is your ability to expel all of the air from your lungs—something that the technician will teach you how to do. The only method of measuring body composition more accurately than this would involve expensive imaging techniques such as MRI or CAT scans of your entire body. Most researchers believe that underwater weighing is accurate to within about 2 or 3 percentage points.

The skin-fold test is simpler and produces results that are probably accurate to within 3 or 4 percentage points. It's related to the "pinch an inch" test occasionally advocated for seeing if you're overweight. According to that old rule of thumb, if you can pinch an inch-thick roll of skin and fat at your waist, you can benefit by going on a diet. Skin-fold tests use calipers to measure exactly how big a roll you can pinch, and instead of relying solely on the waist, they also test other parts of the body, typically the shoulders and the thighs. That way, the test accounts for the fact that different people accumulate fat on different parts of the anatomy. This test can be fooled by loose, stretched-out skin if you've recently lost a lot of weight. In those cases, it may give measures that are a bit too low.

COMPARISON OF METHODS OF DETERMINING BODY FAT

METHOD	ADVANTAGES	DISADVANTAGES	ACCURACY
underwater weighing	most accurate measure available	skilled technician and special facilities required costs about $30	±2–3 percentage points
skin-fold	simple and quick inexpensive needs no special facilities (can be done in health club or gym)	accuracy depends on skill of technician reduced accuracy for people who've lost large amounts of weight	± 3–4 percentage points
skin conductivity (electrostatic)	takes only a minute inexpensive highly skilled technician not required needs no special facilities	results vary with factors affecting body electrolytes	± 4–5 percentage points

CLYDESDALES AND BONNYDALES

Large-framed runners are at a competitive disadvantage. That doesn't mean you can't race, but it has encouraged some races to create special heavyweight divisions. Typically these are called Clydesdale divisions, in honor of the big, strong draft horses. Sometimes the women's division sports a more feminine name such as Bonnydale, but Clydesdale can apply to either gender. If the term sounds like an insult, think about what a draft horse looks like. They're not fat; they're just tall and powerful, not especially built for speed. Why should you feel inferior because you can't beat those fine-boned thoroughbreds at their own game? Clydesdale competition is the best thing that ever happened to large-boned runners. Races that make a specialty of this often have multiple weight divisions. The Portland (Oregon) Marathon even has divisions set by how much you can bench press!

There's no standard, but the Clydesdale category often begins at about 145 pounds for women, and 185 pounds for men. View that as naked, first-thing-in-the-morning weight, not what you weigh fully dressed after a big meal and a huge drink of water. You may have to prove your claim by standing on a scale in running clothes at registration.

Skin conductivity tests are even quicker than skin-fold measurements, which can be done in a couple of minutes. The conductivity tests work by applying electrodes to your body, typically the arms or legs. Fat and muscle conduct electricity differently, so the amount of current your body conducts can be used to determine how much you have of each tissue. Such measurements are complicated, however, by a variety of factors, including your level of hydration and how long it's been since your last run. Academic laboratories estimate that this measure is accurate to within 4 or 5 percentage points, but you may not get such good results at prerace exhibitions. When we were writing this book, Rick tried this test and was told he had negative 5 percent body fat—an obvious impossibility. A friend of his was then given a reading 50 percent higher than what she'd obtained from a recent skin-fold measurement.

Skin conductivity is the one test, however, that's easy to do at home. Tanita makes a moderately priced bathroom scale with electrodes beneath the soles of your feet, so you measure your weight and your body fat, simultaneously. Even if skin conductivity isn't the most accurate measure of body composition, these scales may allow you to monitor month-to-month changes.

The smaller your percentage of body fat, the more muscular you are for your size. But that isn't necessarily better. Modest amounts of fat are vital for health. Men need at least 2 to 4 percent fat; women need 10 to 12 percent for proper hormone functioning, among other things (see table on page 123). Maintaining that minimum isn't an enormous concern for men; it's pretty hard for most people to get their body fat down into the single digits, let alone below 5 percent. Women can more easily dip into their vital reserves, thinking it will help them eke out an extra iota of speed. If you're already racer-thin, check your body composition occasionally to make sure you're not pushing too closely against that margin of safety. Don't wait until you start missing menstrual periods to discover that you're too thin.

GENERAL BODY-FAT PERCENTAGE CATEGORIES

	WOMEN	**MEN**
essential fat	10 to 12	2 to 4
athletes	14 to 20	6 to 13
fitness*	21 to 24	14 to 17
acceptable*	25 to 31	18 to 25
obese	32+	25+

* Many runners fall into these categories. The "athletes" category applies mostly to elite and celebrity athletes.

Source: American Council on Exercise. Reprinted with permission.

Elite male and female runners tend to have about 6 and 14 percent body fat, respectively (mine was between 4 and 5 percent). Healthy nonrunning men and women tend to be about 18 and 25 percent, respectively. Don't target on the elite levels, though; hitting and maintaining them requires an extraordinary amount of training. As a recreational racer you probably want to be somewhere between the population-wide average and the elites. (On the other hand, I've managed to retain my competitive body composition even though I've gained 16 pounds since I retired from racing. I now weigh in at 160, with a still-lean 4.5 percent body fat—something I've achieved mostly by a lot of weight lifting.)

For heavy people, percent body fat is a better indicator of obesity than is the body mass index (BMI). The table also gives cutoffs for clinical obesity for both sexes.

You can alter your body composition by diet and exercise. Exercising while eating enough to keep your weight stable is the way to convert fat to muscle without losing or gaining weight. Your normal training will already have started you down this path, but you can make additional progress by lifting weights or adding some cross-training.

Losing weight, you presumably want to shed as much fat and as little muscle as possible. Weight-loss diets alone rarely accomplish this. Your training will help you retain muscle, but you also need to make sure you get enough protein.

Losing Weight

Detailed discussion of weight loss methods is beyond the scope of this book, but here are a few tips.

- Slow and steady is best. Losing more than about a pound per week increases the fraction that comes from muscle.
- Counting calories can be useful. Running burns about 100 calories per mile, regardless of pace and fairly independently of body weight. A pound of fat

has 3,600 calories. That means that a 36-mile-per week running program, coupled with the diet you'd eat if you weren't running, should shed a pound per week of fat. If you're losing weight faster than your diet and exercise program would predict, you're probably losing muscle, which contains only 1,600 calories per pound.

- The average 150-pound person burns about 2,000 calories per day, not counting what they use for exercise, but the precise amount varies. Equipment now being marketed to health clubs may allow you to measure your own *base metabolic rate* with a precision previously available only in research laboratories.

- Keeping track of the number of calories eaten in a day requires a good memory and perhaps a diet scale to measure portion sizes. Most people eat about 30 to 50 percent more than they realize.

- The best way to cut calories is by reducing fat consumption. Fat has 225 calories per dry ounce; protein and carbohydrate have 100. Nutrition labels can help you dodge hidden fat.

- When you diet, the body thinks it's starving and may try to defend its current weight by reducing its base metabolic rate. It also institutes food cravings, even if you're not physically hungry. Most people can still lose weight with perseverance and careful avoidance of sneak eating, but there are documented cases of people whose weight steadfastly refuses to decline. Luckily, running appears to help offset this starvation response, making it easier to lose weight—but not for everyone.

- Beware of fad diets that upset the basic nutrition principles at the start of this chapter. In my opinion, that includes popular high-protein, low-carbohydrate diets. People do lose weight on them, but it's hard to imagine how they can give you the energy to run well. They can also have frighteningly high amounts of fat and cholesterol.

For additional information from trustworthy sources, consult your doctor or visit the Web sites of such organizations as the American Dietetic Association (www.eatright.org) or the American Heart Association (www.americanheart.org).

RICK'S STORY

I never worried much about my weight. Training 110 miles per week, I was going through close to 4,000 calories a day—about double the average person's diet. Like most elite runners, I ate all day long just trying to keep up. Even after a large dinner, I'd often wake up hungry at 2 A.M., needing a couple of bowls of cereal as a snack. Rick's experience is different, and may be inspirational for those who would never view themselves as naturally thin.

I've always had to watch my weight, even on superactive vacations such as bicycle tours, which can burn off 6,000 to 8,000 calories per day. This has made me a strong believer in the *metabolic set-point theory,* which says that our bodies have innate amounts that they "want" to weigh, controlled by a feedback mechanism scientists have dubbed the *adipostat*—a combination of the terms *adipose* ("fat") and *thermostat.*

Thin people often presume that heavy people got that way because they consistently overindulge. But studies have shown that many heavy people eat less than their thin counterparts. Their problem isn't a character flaw; it's metabolic treason from an improperly set adipostat. I suspect that I myself am a naturally obese person who has kept thin (most of the time) by heavy exercise and obsessive weight watching. Worse, my adipostat setting, like that of many middle-aged people, seems to be gradually creeping upward. For more than a decade, I took a hiatus from running. Even though I remained extremely active, I watched my weight gradually mount. Ultimately, I was horrified to find that I was 59 pounds above my one-time racing weight, with a BMI of 30.8—not just overweight, but clinically obese.

Again, the culprit didn't appear to be an easily controllable lifestyle factor. I'd gained all that weight not in a series of spectacular splurges but as a slow creep that had averaged about 40 extra calories per day—equivalent to about 10 minutes less of walking, one bite of a bagel, or half of a small apple. That's a trivial imbalance for someone who was backpacking hundreds of miles a year and biking 100 miles a week, but if it had continued, I was only a decade away from being 100 pounds overweight.

That 30.8 BMI was an enormous motivator. Over the course of nearly a year I took off 55 pounds (I deliberately retained the other 4 pounds). I've kept them off for three years, weighing exactly what I did at the end of the diet. My method is a combination of exercise and rigorous calorie-counting. When I need to lose weight, I seek a daily 1,000-calorie difference between my calorie input and the number of calories I burn—a target that usually allows me to lose weight even if my counting isn't quite accurate. When I need extra exercise, I don't add running mileage; instead I add low-impact cross-training such as hiking, biking, and rowing.

My new racing friends find this story hard to believe; to them I look like the type of person who's always been thin and always will be. But my experience makes me sympathetic with anyone struggling with weight creep. I can also bring two pieces of good news: it really is possible to lose weight and keep it off; and the intense exercise of running appears to help. But I can also attest that my adipostat isn't fully reset. Keeping my weight down remains a constant battle, one that I wage by weighing myself every morning and writing the result in my training diary. I've drawn a metaphorical line in the sand, 2 pounds above my preferred weight. Any morning when I weigh in at even a half-pound too high, I'm back on the diet, no excuses. I've had to lose the same 2 pounds at least a dozen times in three years—but that's a lot better than waiting until I had to lose 24 pounds all at once.

ACHES AND PAINS

SOME PEOPLE RACE injury-free for decades. Others seem to spend half their time on injured reserve. Partly, this is luck of the genetic draw: If you're blessed with a biomechanically perfect body, you'll not only be inherently speedy, but you can train a lot harder without triggering an injury. But the correlation isn't as strong as you might think. Many back-of-the-pack runners have fewer injuries than the elites, probably because they're more cautious about their limitations.

There is an extremely fine line between peak performance and injury. Racing involves pushing for the peak without overshooting. Ironically, the time to be most cautious is when you're feeling strong, seemingly on the verge of smashing all of your PRs. Feeling invincible, you do too many races, too many hard workouts, too little recovery—and *bang*, you're injured. The peak fades away, its potential never fully realized.

This book's training program is deliberately conservative, designed to minimize your chances of injury. But nobody can promise a lifetime of pain-free running. All sports carry some injury risk; part of running mostly injury free is learning to recognize symptoms when they crop up so you can nip incipient problems in the bud.

Calling these ailments *injuries*, incidentally, can be misleading. For many people, references to sports injuries draw forth images of wounded football heroes or "agony of defeat" photos of crashing skiers. Fortunately, running injuries are rarely so dramatic. Unless you sprain an ankle, break a bone, or suffer a severe muscle pull, you're unlikely to encounter significant discomfort that stays with you when you're not running (although a few minor ailments such as blisters are notable exceptions). That's good news for those of us who don't like pain, but it makes it easy to brush off an injury as minor, when it isn't. By trying to run through a seemingly minor problem when you shouldn't, you gradually entrench it, making the recovery slower and more difficult.

This chapter will help you identify common problems, treat them, and prevent them from recurring. But first, let's discuss some basic sports medicine principles.

SEVEN RULES OF INJURY PREVENTION

One of this book's primary philosophies is that it's better to stay healthy by progressing slowly than it is to risk injury setbacks from overly aggressive training. Tips for doing so are scattered throughout the text, but here are seven of the most important.

1. Warm up properly.

2. Never skimp on rest and recovery.

3. Don't run hard workouts back-to-back.

4. Stretch religiously.

5. Phase in all changes in training.

6. Use weights to combat known weaknesses.

7. Heed the signs of overtraining.

BASICS OF FIELD REPAIRS

Top athletes don't survive without learning something about sports medicine. I've learned not only from my own injuries but also by swapping war stories with friends and teammates. Just by reading this chapter, you'll know more than many of your friends do about the most common injuries, but you can continue learning by talking to longtime runners.

Even if you never suffer a running injury, you can benefit from a basic understanding of sports medicine. The same principles apply if you pull a muscle or sprain an ankle in a household accident.

Although doctors are important for treating some types of running injuries, general practitioners generally aren't your best sources of information. They may be able to help cure the ailment, but far too often they don't know what caused it. When pressed, they're too likely to shrug and say: "Well, if it only hurts when you run fast, don't run fast." Like many experienced runners, I've concluded that I can often give better sports medicine advice than the average medical doctor. Of course, the best of all possible worlds is to find a physician who's also a dedicated runner. Fortunately, such people are becoming more and more common.

Even if your family doctor is a runner, you won't be scurrying to the clinic with every injury. Often, the best treatments are ones you can do perfectly well yourself, without waiting for the doctor's say-so. The following sections describe three basic concepts to help speed your recovery from most running ailments.

Remember RICE

RICE—an acronym for Rest, Ice, Compression, and Elevation—is the standard prescription for injured runners. These are particularly important during the first 48 hours after an injury, while the body is more or less deciding how badly it's hurt. Whether your problem is a sprained ankle or an overuse injury, attentive care at this stage can substantially speed your recovery.

Rest can be anything from a complete layoff to simply slowing down a bit while the injury heals. If a misstep has left your ankle looking like a purple football, you obviously need a complete layoff. With a slower-onset injury that you've caught early on, it's often OK just to try running at a reduced level and seeing how well that works. But be realistic; if backing off partway isn't doing the job, bite the bullet and take a true rest now, before you have to take a longer one later on. To keep fit while laid off, switch to some other sport, such as cycling, swimming, or working out on a rowing machine. As long as these activities don't hurt, you're unlikely to be causing harm. In fact, most sports medicine experts believe that keeping active promotes healing by pumping more blood through the injured tissue, which speeds recovery and reduces swelling. But you really have to let pain be your guide—and you have to be willing to take a total rest if that's what your body is asking for.

Icing an injury can be done either with a bag of crushed ice or by rubbing ice cubes directly against the skin. The ice bag works best with injuries that require longer application, because it's not so unpleasantly cold to the touch. Ice cubes are faster with more superficial injuries, and you can usually tolerate them for a few minutes. Don't frostbite yourself with super-chilled ice cubes taken directly from the freezer, however. Even a thin plastic bag will provide some insulation to reduce this risk.

ICE VS. HEAT

One of the most common questions in sports medicine is, "What about heat, rather than ice?" After all, it's a lot more pleasant to get into a hot tub than to slather your skin with ice.

The bottom line, sadly, is that ice is better, at least during the initial stages of healing. Heat can make an injury worse by increasing the swelling. Not long ago, getting in a whirlpool was a postgame ritual for banged-up football players. Now, ice baths are preferred (brrr!). Some coaches advise the same for runners seeking to speed recovery after hard races, but you have to be pretty dedicated to try it.

Hot tubs can be part of your treatment, though, once an injury is well on the road to recovery. Some people insist that heat is never as good as ice; others advise trying both approaches and seeing which works best for any given injury. If you're really dedicated, try alternating heat and ice, with the ice coming second, after you've climbed out of the hot tub. The heat opens the blood vessels and flushes nutrients to the site of the injury—then the cold shuts the blood vessels back down again and prevents inflammation. But heat should be completely avoided until the injury is on the road to recovery—several days or longer after its onset.

Older sports medicine books may tell you to ice the tissue for 20 minutes at a time. Actually, all you have to do is get it good and cold. This will take longer with a deep muscle pull than with a sore Achilles tendon. But once the tissue is well chilled, you've achieved most of the benefit you're going to get; you'll spend your time more efficiently if you ice the injury again later, rather than continuing to do so now.

Compression and elevation are often done simultaneously. Whenever you get the chance, wrap the injured extremity in an elastic bandage and prop it on a footstool.

TRICKS OF THE (ICE) TRADE

It's easy to procrastinate icing an injury. "I'll do it in a few minutes" becomes a few hours, and then a few days. Obviously, the more convenient it is to apply the ice, the more likely you are to do it. Here are two common methods for simplifying the process:

- Put water into paper cups and freeze them. Pull back the paper to expose the ice, and wrap all but the business end in a small towel to keep your fingers warm and to sop up drips. One paper cup can last for several icings, but remember, there's no insulation between this subfreezing ice and your skin. Don't frostbite yourself!
- For deeper injuries for which an ice bag is better than an ice cube, try using a bag of frozen peas or other vegetables. Not only is it leak-proof, but it's also reusable (at least until repeated freezing and thawing glues the peas into awkward lumps). Or use it once, then cook up the veggies for dinner!

Anti-Inflammatories

Along with RICE, anti-inflammatory drugs are one of your best friends. These medications kill pain by combating the inflammation process that causes it. This means you're not just doping yourself up so you can go out and worsen your injury without knowing you're doing so. You can be fairly confident that you're OK doing anything that doesn't hurt.

Over-the-counter anti-inflammatories include aspirin, ibuprofen, and naproxen sodium. If you use aspirin, you'll probably need to take more than two at a time; many people use three. Just don't take so many that your ears ring, the first sign of aspirin overdose. With the other anti-inflammatories—which most runners today use instead of aspirin—you'll get no such overdose warning, so don't exceed the label doses without first talking to a doctor. Your chief concerns should be for your stomach and kidneys. Try not to take them on an empty stomach (taking them with milk is ideal), and keep well hydrated so the drug is nicely diluted when your kidneys excrete it in your urine. Don't use these drugs without first consulting your doctor if you have ulcers or kidney problems, and read the label carefully before using any of these medications on children.

Chemically, anti-inflammatory drugs must serve two functions. One part of the molecule fights inflammation; another tracks down inflamed tissues so the inflammation fighter can be concentrated where it's needed. Which medication works for what injury isn't very predictable. If ibuprofen isn't doing the trick, try naproxen sodium or aspirin.

Aspirin, ibuprofen, and naproxen sodium are the big three of sports medicine anti-inflammatories, but new ones are being developed all the time. Any non-steroidal anti-inflammatory drug (NSAID) designed for arthritis is also of potential benefit in sports medicine. Acetaminophen (Tylenol) is in a different class of medications. It has some anti-inflammatory effect, but it's also a direct painkiller. That means that if acetaminophen dulls the pain, you can't be sure you aren't continuing to damage the injured tissue.

Stretching and Weight Lifting

Injured tissue has generally been overstretched, either from prolonged overuse or a sudden pull. Your natural tendency, therefore, will be to avoid stretching it for fear of making the injury worse.

This instinct is correct, but only partly so. Reinjury is a definite risk, but total immobility can actually increase this risk. Not only will the increased blood flow from cautious motion speed the healing process, but you'll need gentle stretching to keep the injured tissue from becoming less flexible—and more injury-prone—as it heals.

Muscle, tendon, and ligament injuries form scar tissue, just as your skin does after a cut or scrape. This tissue will begin forming in about a week, binding the injured area back together like natural sutures. It grows randomly, however, in starburst patterns that can become inflexible knots. *Gentle* stretching encourages the scar tissue to line up in the right direction while it's still malleable. It doesn't take much stretching to achieve this: just enough to move the injured limb through its pain-free range of motion. Do it once a day, starting about a week after the injury, being careful not to stretch to anywhere near the sharp pain that signals additional injury.

Weight lifting can also be beneficial for some injuries, but it requires even greater care. A pulled hamstring, for example, is going to be weak for months, even after you've returned to running. Weight lifting will speed its rehabilitation, but initially you need to keep the weights very light to avoid a new pull. And you shouldn't even start lifting weights until such an injury is fairly well healed. Other injuries, such as runner's knee, respond more quickly to weight lifting because here you're not attempting to strengthen the injured tissue itself. Rather, you're strengthening the surrounding muscles to eliminate the stresses that gave you the problem in the first place.

STAGES OF INJURY

Except for ankle sprains, stress fractures, and such traumas as running into a lamppost (don't laugh: it happens), running injuries seldom appear full-blown. Rather, they creep up on you in an orderly progression of stages, ranging from a barely perceptible onset to a time when the injury has made an unmistakable alteration in your lifestyle. Happily, this needn't be a one-way street. With proper treatment, injuries can move either direction on the scale of severity. Minimize your downtime by knowing the stages, objectively charting your progress (or lack thereof), and taking action appropriate for the injury's current stage and its history.

There is no uniform scale for measuring an injury's severity. Podiatrist Joe Ellis, in his 1994 book *Running Injury-Free*, rated injuries on a 10-point scale; Tim Noakes, in *Lore of Running*, uses four grades. The simple chart here splits the difference and distinguishes seven stages. The double-headed arrows indicate that injuries can progress in both directions.

Stage 1 injuries rarely require layoffs. But they are calling on you to find the cause and eliminate it before they move on to Stage 2 and beyond. Stage 2 and 3 injuries require more rest. At a minimum, you'll have to cut back, at least for a few days, on the activities that produce the most pain; they're simply making the injury worse. At Stage 4, and especially Stage 5, this has become pronounced. A complete layoff may not be required, but you need to eliminate hard workouts and keep the easy ones gentle enough that "pain" recedes back to Stage 3 "discomfort." The moment you reach Stage 6, where you're limping, even slightly, a layoff has become mandatory. Otherwise, you'll move rapidly to Stage 7, where nature will force you to take the layoff you've been putting off.

Stage 6. Normal running mechanics are affected. You're limping or otherwise altering your stride as your body tries to reduce stress on the site of the injury.

Stage 7. It hurts too much to run, even slowly. You may be limping when you walk.

Stage 5. Discomfort during the run becomes pain, especially during hard workouts or races. Racing performance and speed work are impaired.

Stage 1. It doesn't hurt to run, but you notice minor discomfort a few hours later. (In the very earliest part of this stage, the discomfort might not show up until the next day.)

Stage 4. Discomfort now does not fully abate between workouts. You know you're injured even as you lace up your shoes, but as in stage 3, it doesn't affect performance.

Stage 2. Discomfort is similar to stage 1, but it has progressed to something you're more apt to call pain. It lasts longer and comes on more quickly after you stop running.

Stage 3. You feel the injury while you run, but can easily ignore the discomfort. Stride mechanics and running speed are unaffected. Pain continues after your run, as in stage 2.

COMMON HURTS

A treatise on running injuries is beyond the scope of this book, but the following sections provide basic information on the most common injuries, with tips for their treatment and prevention.

If you want to read more, there are several books dealing exclusively with running injuries. George Sheehan's classic *Medical Advice for Runners* contains many useful tips, and Tim Noakes's 804-page *Lore of Running* is about as thorough as anything written for the layman can possibly be (Noakes, an ultramarathoner, devotes more than a quarter of this tome to medical issues). Additional information, including the latest research, can be found in the medical advice sections of *Runner's World* and other running magazines.

SEEKING HELP

See a doctor immediately in any of the following situations:

- you suspect a stress fracture
- the injury begins with a sudden pop or snapping sensation
- a joint, particularly the knee, "locks" or "gives out"

A stress fracture is always a major injury, and pops, clicks, and "giving out" sensations indicate that you may have ruptured a tendon or torn some cartilage.

You should also see a doctor for any injury that's getting progressively worse despite a layoff, hasn't improved significantly after 2 weeks of rest, or causes you to limp when you walk, even after a 4- or 5-day layoff. It's possible you've misdiagnosed the problem.

"Seeing a doctor" needn't mean going to an M.D. Physical therapists, sports trainers, and alternative health-care providers may be less expensive and more knowledgeable. Make sure you start, however, by consulting someone with enough background in conventional medicine to spot a major medical problem (such as cancer, diabetes, or blocked arteries) masquerading as a sports injury.

Achilles Tendinitis

Any injury whose name ends with *itis* is an inflammation. In this case, the inflamed tissue is the Achilles tendon, which connects the calf muscles to the heel. There are two basic ways to injure it: overuse and overstretching. With overuse, the Achilles tendon doesn't quite have time to recover between workouts and gradually becomes sore; you can often find the sore spot by squeezing the tendon gently between thumb and forefinger. Other early symptoms are pain in the tendon when you first get out of bed in the morning, pain at the start of your run, or pain when you walk, particularly in low-heeled shoes. Severe cases will produce a grating sensation when you flex the foot, but you should have done something about the problem long before it gets to that point.

Overstretching typically occurs from changing some variable in your workout too rapidly. Even world-class athletes can get Achilles tendinitis if they suddenly

CAUSES AND TREATMENTS OF MAJOR RUNNING INJURIES

Injury	Location	Most Likely Causes	First Line of Attack[1]	Prevention of Recurrence[2]
Achilles tendinitis	between calf and heel	tight calves	RICE and anti-inflammatories stretching heel lifts	calf stretching calf strengthening new shoes orthotics
plantar fasciitis	bottom of arch or heel	poor arch support	RICE and anti-inflammatories foot roller or massage	new shoes orthotics
muscle pulls	any	tight, weak, or cold muscles	RICE (layoff needed) and anti-inflammatories	stretching adequate warm-up strengthening known muscle weaknesses
sprains	any joint, especially ankle	misstep	RICE (layoff needed) and anti-inflammatories consider seeing M.D. may need professional rehab	strengthen muscles surrounding affected joint surgical repair (severe sprain only)
iliotibial band (ITB) syndrome	outside of knee or, rarely, of hip	minor trigger leads to cycle of increasing inflammation	RICE (especially ice) and anti-inflammatories	ITB stretches (including figure-four stretch) minimize running on slanted surfaces new shoes orthotics

[1] Short-run treatments to abate the problem while the cause is determined.
[2] Listed in order of implementation difficulty or expense. Not all will be needed.

(continued next page)

INJURY	LOCATION	MOST LIKELY CAUSES	FIRST LINE OF ATTACK[1]	PREVENTION OF RECURRENCE[2]
stress fractures	any bone, *especially* in foot, shins, or hips	repeated pounding anorexia or near-anorexia in women	layoff see doctor may need cast	well-cushioned shoes soft running surfaces build up or alter training gradually women should avoid excessive thinness
shin splints	front of shins	impact stress radiating up from feet	RICE and anti-inflammatories switch running to soft surfaces	avoid sudden changes in workout intensity or running surface water-bucket lift
runner's knee	kneecap or vicinity	abnormal stresses in knee, radiating from other parts of the leg	RICE and anti-inflammatories patellar strap	strengthen quadriceps avoid downhill running use patellar strap in training stretch all muscles above and below the knee isolate and strengthen specific sections of quadriceps motion-control shoes orthotics

[1] Short-run treatments to abate the problem while the cause is determined.
[2] Listed in order of implementation difficulty or expense. Not all will be needed.

start doing interval workouts in low-heeled track shoes. Suddenly taking up hill running can do the same thing.

Treatment. As with any inflammation, begin with anti-inflammatories and RICE (Rest, Ice, Compression, and Elevation). Also, try putting a firm, quarter-inch pad into the heel of your shoes. Called *heel lifts*, these pads should be available at a modest price from any orthopedic appliance store. For a temporary substitute, fold up a piece of moleskin or any similar material and put it under your shoe's sole insert—anything to jack up the heel a bit.

Use an equal amount of lift in both shoes, even if only one heel hurts, to avoid creating an imbalance. If possible, avoid the foamy heel cushions commonly sold in drugstores. They compress under pressure, giving you less lift than you think you're getting and subjecting the back of your heel to blister-inducing rubbing. As the tendinitis abates, reduce the amount of heel lift to an eighth of an inch, then to nothing. Although entrenched Achilles tendinitis can take months to resolve, most cases should be substantially improved in a couple of weeks.

If you've not seen any improvement by then, consult a doctor. It's possible that you have a much more serious *Achilles tendon tear* or *partial rupture* requiring surgical repair. Even if your problem is simple Achilles tendinitis, a doctor may be able to refer you to a physical therapist or sports medicine clinic that can speed recovery with ultrasound or massage. Some chiropractors can provide the same services. A sports-medicine professional may also teach you kinesiotaping (which uses a stretchy, skin-fitting tape) or recommend a neoprene wrap, such as that made by Pro-Tec (which appears to absorb at least a little of the stress that might otherwise be transmitted into your Achilles tendon).

Don't ignore Achilles tendinitis, even when it's minor. Not only will the pain gradually get worse until eventually you can't even walk, but prolonged inflammation can weaken the tendon, making it more apt to rupture if you keep abusing it,

ADVANCED THERAPIES

If an injury is slow to heal, it may benefit from any of a number of therapies available from sports-medicine clinics. These include

- ultrasound
- electrical stimulation
- massage
- assisted stretching
- injury-specific strengthening exercises
- athletic taping

Elite athletes, seeking to minimize lost training, draw heavily on all of these (I even bought my own ultrasound machine). Recreational racers may find them too costly. Because most injuries will heal perfectly well (albeit a bit more slowly) on their own, your health insurance may not foot the bill.

month after month. The ultimate in Achilles abuse is a *total rupture* of the tendon. This is a catastrophic injury, which makes it impossible to flex the foot. Luckily, it's not very common.

The Achilles tendon isn't the only tendon that can become inflamed by running. You can also aggravate the big tendons behind the knee, which link the hamstrings to the lower leg. And there are many others throughout the body, any of which can become inflamed. Treatment is similar to that for Achilles tendinitis: RICE, anti-inflammatories, gentle stretching to reduce stress on the tendon, and a search for the reasons the tendon became inflamed.

BURSITIS

An *itis* not discussed at length in this chapter is bursitis, which comes from inflammation of the tiny fluid-filled *bursae* that cushion the numerous places where tendons run over the top of bones (the knee alone has 14 bursae). Some types of activities can give you bursitis in the shoulders; runners are probably the most vulnerable in the knees and the hip.

Bursitis can be hard to distinguish from tendinitis, but luckily, the initial treatments are similar: RICE, anti-inflammatories, and religious stretching (so long as the stretching itself doesn't add to the pain). If you're lucky, that will get rid of it quickly. Prevention is also similar to tendinitis, including stretching, muscle strengthening, avoidance of slanted running surfaces, and replacing worn-out shoes.

Entrenched bursitis can be excruciatingly slow to heal, and may require a cortisone injection. Suspect bursitis if you have a tendinitis-like pain that gets worse with gentle activity rather than abating as the muscle limbers up. That, however, is by no means a sure way to distinguish it from tendinitis. If you get bursitis, take it seriously. If you ignore it, the bursa's membrane will eventually thicken, creating a chronic problem.

Prevention. Increase workout mileage very gradually. Make sure your shoe has good heel support and that the heel is built up at least three-quarters of an inch above the ground. Good impact cushioning in the heel may also help, although that has yet to be proven. Also, lace your shoes as tightly as is comfortable; if your foot slops around inside them, it can stress the Achilles tendon. In addition, you should use the calf stretch (see page 88) before and after all workouts. Calf raises (see page 101) may also help, both by increasing the calf's ability to absorb shock and by directly strengthening the Achilles tendon. If you change your workouts to add more speed work, hills, or even a different running surface, phase in the change gradually, over the course of a couple of weeks, and don't simultaneously increase your mileage.

Plantar Fasciitis

The plantar fascia is the ligament that connects the heel bone to the toes. It has been compared to a bowstring, because it applies the tension to your foot that creates the arch. You can find it easily with your fingers, just a little to the outside of the foot's centerline.

Like any other connective tissue, the plantar fascia can become overstretched and inflamed. It has a poor blood supply, so once it becomes inflamed, it's slow to heal, typically producing sharp, tingling pains at the point of injury, most notably at the start of your run. The tingling may be in the middle of your arch or beneath your heel, where the plantar fascia wraps around to meet the base of the Achilles tendon. Prolonged plantar fasciitis near the base of the heel may cause the growth of bony *heel spurs*. Years ago, doctors would remove these surgically, but they often grew back. Nowadays, heel spurs are generally treated by treating the plantar fasciitis. Once that is cured, the spurs usually are no problem.

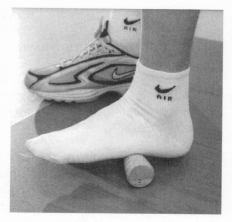

A foot roller allows you to massage the plantar fascia. Press firmly, even if doing so hurts.

Remember RICE:
R-est
I-ce
C-ompression
E-levation

Treatment. Use RICE and anti-inflammatories, and consider massage. Massage can most easily be done with a plastic or wooden foot roller (available from an orthopedic supply store for about $15 to $20). Standing on your good leg, step on this device with your shoe off, centering it under the arch of your afflicted foot. Pressing down firmly, rock the roller back and forth on the floor, beneath your arch. Don't worry if this hurts. In fact, it works best when producing as much pain as you can tolerate. Try to find a spot that feels knotted, at the point of injury. When you find it, the roller will produce a crunching sensation that you may almost be able to hear. The knot represents scar tissue forming at the site of the injury; massaging it softens the scar tissue so that it doesn't contract the ligament even further. If you don't have a foot roller, massage the lump with your thumb and forefinger. In most cases, the problem should be pretty well healed in a week or two, even without a layoff. But if it's really entrenched, you may need a cortisone injection.

Prevention. Plantar fasciitis is caused by poor arch support. Imagine what would happen if you inverted a plastic bowl on the floor and then stomped down on it, hard. That's what happens to your arch if there's not enough support. (Downhill skiers have a similar problem when, seeking extra control, they fasten their boots so tightly that they squash the arch flat for hours on end. Many develop plantar fasciitis.) Change to more supportive shoes or invest in custom orthotics. Plantar fasciitis sufferers who buy orthotics rarely have a recurrence.

Muscle Pulls

Muscle pulls are actually muscle tears. If there's only a small amount of damaged tissue, you tend to call the injury a "strain" rather than a pull and count your blessings. Any sharp, stabbing muscle pain is likely to be a pull. Severe ones can drop you in your tracks. You can also pull a tendon or the area where the muscle and tendon join. In general, the closer the pull is to the tendon, the slower it will be to heal, due to reduced blood supply.

Treatment. Immediately apply ice; then rest. Even a minor pull requires a few days' layoff. Picture your muscle as a rope: the pull has nicked a few fibers; if you continue to use it right away, there may be additional fraying. You'll also benefit from anti-inflammatories and the remainder of the RICE treatment.

Recovery to the point where you can resume running will take anything from a few days to a few weeks. Most cases will take about 5 to 7 days, but you'll have to be careful on your first outings.

There are also slower-onset ailments that Tim Noakes, author of *Lore of Running*, likes to call chronic muscle tears. Such pseudo-tears form tiny, painful knots that have a tendency to recur at the same locations. The tear (if there truly is one) is generally very tiny; most of the pain comes from spasms in nearby muscle fibers. It's mostly a problem of elite athletes engaged in intensive, high-volume training. Chronic tears respond well to *cross-frictional massage* by a sports-medicine expert (this technique can also be applied to other running ailments, such as Achilles tendinitis). But beware, the massage itself can be excruciatingly painful.

Prevention. Elite runners are particularly wary of muscle pulls, largely because they're so preventable. Stretch regularly. Also, most pulls are caused by running too fast before you're adequately warmed up. Run slowly for at least the first mile of all training runs, longer if it's cold. On a chilly day, it might take 10 minutes to warm up to the point you'd reach in 2 or 3 minutes on a hot day. You should also allow extra warm-up time for early morning runs because your body temperature dipped while you were asleep. I've always avoided hard morning runs until I've been out of bed for at least an hour and a half.

Sprains

With some injuries, familiarity breeds contempt. For example, because few of us escape childhood without twisted ankles, we don't take these injuries very seriously, painful as they are. But sprains can be more damaging and slower to heal than broken bones.

When you are running, your most vulnerable point is the ankle. Any twist you can't "walk off" in a few minutes is potentially serious. Luckily, serious sprains are relatively rare among runners who stick to flat surfaces. But if your fancy includes trail or cross-country racing, you may have to cope with these painful interruptions.

Treatment. Use RICE and anti-inflammatories. If the sprain is serious—which may be a bit hard to diagnose on your own—consider seeing a sports-medicine specialist to have it evaluated and to be put on a rehabilitation program. Beware that for at least 6 weeks after a major sprain—and maybe much longer—you're a sitting duck for a second, worse one. Many a collegiate cross-country runner or soccer player has damaged an ankle for life by trying to get back out on it too soon. Don't be misled by basketball and football players who suffer major sprains and are back in the game within minutes. These people have had their ankles taped by experts who know how to make sure they won't sprain them again. Don't be tempted, incidentally, to tape up your own ankle and try to run on it. If you don't know what you're doing, that can cause a great deal of damage.

Prevention. Some medical experts say that a badly sprained ankle never fully recovers. Minor twists recover well enough that you'll never know the difference, but major ones severely stretch the ligaments—and stretched ligaments remain stretched unless they're surgically repaired. You can compensate for even a severe sprain, however, by strengthening your ankle muscles. Try flexing and rolling your feet any time you're sitting where you don't have to wear shoes. Another exercise is to stand first on the outside edges of your feet, then on the inside edges. If you want to really strengthen your ankles, take up ice-skating. The high-top boots will guard against sprains, but the need for balance will test—and build—muscles you never knew you had.

As a collegiate cross-country runner, I had my share of twisted ankles and have learned to give this injury a great deal of respect. Many is the time I've turned an ankle slightly, stumbled a bit, then powered on through the run—only to discover the next morning that the ankle was surprisingly swollen and discolored. Now, if I take a misstep, I slow down or stop and walk for a few minutes to see if the pain will pass. If there's even the slightest twinge after 4 or 5 minutes, I abandon the run and walk home. Pressing on, I've learned, worsens the injury substantially.

Iliotibial Band Syndrome

The iliotibial band (ITB) is a ligament that runs along the outside of your thigh, wrapping across the point of your hip at one end and around the outside of your knee at the other. Its purpose is to keep your leg from bowing outward. Normally, it does this job unnoticed, but occasionally it becomes too tight, possibly because you've irritated it with unnatural stresses, such as from running constantly on a slanted surface or with worn-out shoes.

The tightness may lie anywhere along the length of the band, but the point of stress is almost always where the band crosses the outside of the knee. The band is supposed to pass smoothly through a notch on the knee's side, but if it's overly taut, it pops out of place with each stride, sometimes with a palpable clicking sensation. That rubs the backside of the band, inflaming it. The inflammation worsens the fit of the band in its notch, setting off a vicious cycle of increasing pain.

Treatment. Initial treatment is simply to take down the inflammation. Ice and anti-inflammatories are the best weapons, but stretching the band as described next may be all that's needed to alleviate tension enough to reverse the inflammatory spiral. DMSO, a rubbing liniment (see pages 147–48), is particularly useful for this injury, sometimes working a miracle cure in a matter of hours.

Prevention. Stretching alleviates the tightness that can cause iliotibial band problems. The figure-four stretch (see pages 90–91) stretches the upper part of the band, where it passes across the hip, but it's difficult to find a suitable stretch for the band's lower portions. Your body just wasn't made to bend that way. Still, there are two stretches that work somewhat (see photos opposite). One is to lie on your side on a low, solidly built table or bench, long enough for your whole body. Your sore leg should be on top. Now, let the sore leg droop off the side of the bench behind you, stretching its upper side. You'll probably stretch multiple small muscles, but you should also get some stretch along part of the iliotibial band.

A similarly cumbersome stretch is to stand upright, with the sore leg crossed behind the other, feet parallel and touching. (It's OK if the toes aren't equally far forward.) Now, using a hand for balance, bend sideways at the waist, away from the hip of the crossed-behind leg. You should feel some stretch in the hip, near the upper part of the iliotibial band.

You can also reduce iliotibial band problems by avoiding sudden changes in your workout that might stress the ligament. Such changes include running on slanted surfaces—such as crowned roads or beaches—or stepped-up interval training, particularly on short, indoor tracks. Also, make sure your shoes are in good condition, and consider investing in orthotics if you tend to overpronate.

Stress Fractures

Stress fractures are hairline cracks brought on by workouts that cause more pounding than your bones are conditioned to handle. They start as deep, dull aches, usually in the foot or shin, but possibly anywhere up to the hip. The pain comes on quickly but not instantaneously, taking about a week to progress from its first twinges to being debilitating enough that it may even hurt to walk.

Treatment. Stress fractures need to be diagnosed by X-ray, which entails a doctor's visit. Since the break is only a hairline crack, you probably won't need a cast unless you abuse the bone by continuing to run. And stress fractures will almost always heal completely, a major advantage over other kinds of fractures. You'll have to take a layoff, but you should be able to do any other exercise that doesn't hurt during or afterward, such as walking, biking, or swimming. Even with bone injuries, such exercises can speed recovery by helping to increase blood flow.

Prevention. Practice moderation in advancing your training. It also helps to use well-cushioned shoes and to run as much as possible on moderately soft surfaces, such as asphalt, treadmills, running paths, or well-designed tracks. If you

Two stretches for the iliotibial band. The figure-four stretch (see pages 90–91) also helps.

have no choice but to run on harder surfaces such as concrete, let your bones adjust by phasing in the change gradually, over the course of several weeks. If you're a woman, be careful not to cut your weight too far. Excessive thinness causes amenorrhea (interruption of the menstrual cycle), and a few months of this can make you prone to stress fractures for the rest of your life. This is a shockingly common problem among hyperthin collegiate runners. There are also concerns that some women may suffer from this problem even without the advance warning of missed

HOW TO TURN AN INJURY INTO A DISASTER

The worst injury I've ever had didn't come from running per se. Rather, it was an ankle sprain from stepping in a hole in my backyard.

The original injury was bad enough—a severely ruptured tendon that should have been surgically repaired. Unfortunately, the rupture was masked by the widespread pain and swelling of a major sprain, and wasn't properly diagnosed and repaired until much later. Even more unfortunately, I was determined not to miss any training. I continued to run 80 to 90 miles per week, even though I was always limping on the injured ankle.

The limp put unnatural stresses on my feet, leading to a pair of stress fractures so severe that both needed the surgical insertion of metal pins. After that healed I returned to running—still limping. This time, the unnatural stresses radiated all the way up my legs, and produced a ruptured hip flexor, requiring yet another surgery. All three of these operations could have been avoided if I'd taken the layoff my body was demanding while my doctors and I concentrated on the underlying ankle problem.

Today, when I see runners trying to train through stride-affecting injuries, I have no sympathy for the common plea: "But coach, it doesn't hurt all that much." "You're limping," I say. "That means you've got to take a break."

menstrual periods, so don't presume you're safe simply because you're not missing periods. Excessive thinness is all too easily a career-killer for women athletes.

Stress fractures can also be caused by problems in your feet that give you an unnaturally jarring stride. If there is no obvious explanation for the fracture—such as suddenly doubling your mileage—get your feet checked out by a sports medicine expert who knows something about orthotics. People who've had one stress fracture are predisposed to others if they don't find and eliminate the cause.

> **Gentle activity and gentle stretching can promote healing. But don't do either if it hurts—that means the injury is still too fresh.**

Shin Splints

Shin splints are sharp pains in the front of the shins, sometimes radiating downward to the top of the foot. You'll feel them most strongly when your foot hits the ground or if you vigorously flex it back and forth to its limits. Medical professionals debate the details of what's going wrong: some view shin splints as ligament or tendon injuries; others see them as minor stress fractures of the shinbone. Most likely, there is a gamut of injuries, with stress fractures being the worst. There is definitely a gamut of pain, ranging from mild discomfort to excruciating pain with each foot strike.

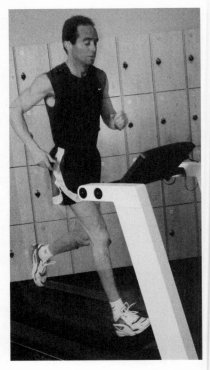

Treatment. Use ice and anti-inflammatories. Also, give your shins a respite while the condition is still mild by taking a couple of days off. Then shift your training to a softer surface for a week or so, icing the shin after each workout. Shin splints generally respond well to this treatment. A compression wrap such as that made by Pro-Tec may also help alleviate stress while the injury heals.

Prevention. Avoid sudden changes in running surface or workout intensity. An exercise called the "water-bucket lift" sometimes helps, too. Hook the comfortably

Running on soft surfaces such as a treadmill is a good way to reduce stress on all parts of the body. (PETER FIELD PECK/GETFITNOW.COM)

padded handle of a bucket over your toes and flex the foot, if you can do so without aggravating the injury. The goal is to strengthen the muscle that attaches to the shin so that it can absorb impact shock, rather than passing the shock on to the muscle's point of attachment to the bone. As you gain strength, add water to the bucket to increase the resistance.

Mild shin splints are a common beginner's problem that will abate as you become better conditioned. With experience, you'll also learn to recognize incipient shin splints before you have any discomfort you could truly call pain, allowing you to cut back a bit to dodge the overwork that produces them.

Runner's Knee

Runner's knee—also known as "jumper's knee," "cyclist's knee," and a host of ailments named for other sports—is an inflammation of the kneecap, although it can also come from tendinitis of the patellar tendon, the big tendon below the kneecap.

Runner's knee used to be called *chrondomalacia*, but this term has gone out of vogue. Technically, chrondomalacia is an uncommon arthritislike roughening of the back of the kneecap—a problem that can occur if you run with a sore knee for so long that you begin to plow grooves into the kneecap. There's no excuse for letting a knee problem persist this long.

Runner's knee typically arises from unnatural motion in your kneecap, which normally slides up and down in a groove in the underlying bones. If for some reason the kneecap tracks diagonally in its groove, runner's knee is the usual outcome.

Treatment. Use RICE and anti-inflammatories. Sometimes a gadget called a *patellar strap* will help (see sidebar page 145); the leading brand is made by Pro-Tec. A pair costs about $40 from any good orthopedic supply house. The strap is simply a padded band of neoprene that wraps below the knee, passing over the top of the patellar tendon, across the indentation you can feel just below the kneecap. It straps on with Velcro; it should be snug but comfortable.

Prevention. Despite the fact that many people think they have "weak" knees, knee pain rarely originates in the knees. Typically the cause lies elsewhere and the knee suffers indirectly, from unnatural jarring or twisting transmitted up or down the legs. One solution is to strengthen the quadriceps (see page 100). A weak quadriceps may not cause runner's knee, but a strong one helps prevent it by keeping the kneecap properly aligned in its groove.

Other potential runner's knee causes and their solutions include

- excess pronation or supination (buy motion control shoes or be fitted for orthotics)
- reaching out with your stride (review chapter 4 on running form)
- running too much on slanted surfaces (avoid steeply crowned roads and find low-traffic or off-road routes where you can safely run down the center)
- running downhill (avoid training routes with long, knee-pounding downgrades, and be particularly careful not to overstride on shorter descents;

reduce pounding in races by learning proper downhill running style; see pages 194–95
- inflexibility in the hamstrings, quadriceps, or calf muscles (review the stretches in chapter 6)
- leg-length discrepancy (not everyone's legs are of equal length: if this describes you, check with your doctor or a sports trainer; the solution is to build up the shorter leg with specially designed shoes or insoles)

Solving these problems will also reduce your risk of iliotibial band problems. If runner's knee nevertheless recurs, you may suffer from *patello-femoral malalignment*, which can be caused by a problem in knee structure (correctable by surgery) but which most commonly comes from overdeveloping the outside portions of the quadriceps compared to the inner portions. This overdevelopment pulls the kneecap diagonally, irritating it with each stride. Patellar straps and taping will help hold the kneecap in place, but you need to talk to a sports trainer about how to correct the underlying muscle imbalance.

Running rarely creates patello-femoral malalignment, but other sports do. Perhaps one in three serious cyclists, for example, suffers from it, particularly the cyclist who likes to climb steep hills. Suspect patello-femoral malalignment if you have persistent knee problems and bicycle more than a few miles a week, even if bicycling itself is pain free. Even if you don't bicycle, suspect patello-femoral malalignment if you have recurrent runner's knee with no other obvious cause.

EXCESS PRONATION AND ITS CONTROL

Excess pronation isn't an injury, but it's a leading cause of injury—perhaps *the* leading cause.

In normal foot motion, the foot lands on the outside of the heel, then rolls inward as the arch compresses under the stress. The foot then rebounds and rolls back outward enough that you push off for the next stride more or less from the center of the forefoot. The inward roll is *pronation*; the recovery is *supination*.

Pronation is part of the body's natural shock-absorbing system. People with high, rigid arches that won't roll inward in the normal manner are among the most injury-prone runners there are, because their bodies jar strongly with each step (these people are referred to as *excess supinators*). *Excess pronation* occurs when the foot rolls too far inward and fails to supinate adequately. It's common, particularly among older runners, whose ligaments have stretched with age and no longer provide their youthful support.

The effects of excess pronation can be felt all the way up the leg. Not only do the knees receive unwanted sideways torques, but you can also get stress at the ankles, shins, Achilles tendons, hips, and even the lower back. Fellow runners or trained shoe clerks can spot the problem by watching you run. Or you can identify it by looking at the soles of well-used shoes (see illustration page 146). The normal wear pattern is heaviest on the outside of the heel, where you strike, and near the center or slightly to the inside of the forefoot, where the normal foot toes off. If you overpronate, you'll probably strike correctly on the outside of the heel, but the wear pattern will then shift too strongly to the inside. In extreme cases, the toe wear will be all the way over at the inside edge of the shoe. (An excess supinator will show the reverse wear pattern, starting correctly on the outside of the heel but then staying on the outside of the foot rather than moving toward the middle.)

Solutions are twofold. You may be able to control the problem with *motion-control shoes* specifically designed for overpronators (many such shoes are on the market). Alternatively, you may need *orthotics*. These are shoe inserts designed to compensate for abnormalities in your feet. They come in a variety of construction materials and styles, and cost upward of $150. Luckily, they're durable, although changes in your feet may require that they be replaced about every three years.

You can obtain orthotics by prescription from your doctor, but a prescription isn't necessary unless it's required by your health insurance company—and many insurers won't pay for orthotics, anyway. If you decide to buy orthotics on your own, skip the doctor and go straight to the specialists who make them. Ask for referrals from other runners, a running store, a podiatrist, or even a chiropractor interested in sports medicine. Or check the yellow pages for makers of "orthopedic appliances."

PATELLAR STRAPS

I've never used patellar straps, but Rick has for other sports that stress the knee as running does. Here's what he has to say:

Patellar straps don't immunize you from sore knees, but they can extend your pain-free mileage range and give your knees a break while inflammation subsides. For one-time use, you can fashion a makeshift strap with first-aid tape. Simply wrap the tape tightly around your leg below the kneecap, just as you would a patellar strap. You can double the effect by wrapping another piece of tape around the leg, about 2 inches above the kneecap. Do this with your leg extended straight, snugging the tape tightly enough that you'd be uncomfortable squatting on your haunches, but not so tightly it digs into the back of your leg when you run. Shave the leg beforehand or use a nonstick layer of gauze beneath the tape, or you'll be sorry when you rip the tape off later.

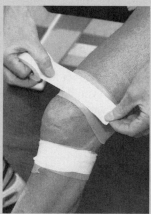

Makeshift patellar strap made from athletic tape.

Tape and straps work by clamping down on the tendons above and below the kneecap, shutting off the forces that tend to pull it sideways. When it works, it's like a magic switch, instantly shutting off the pain. Don't view this as a long-term cure, though. What you've done is to buy time so you can track down the underlying causes.

Don't get orthotics merely because you overpronate. Some overpronators run perfectly well without orthotics, and it may be best to leave well enough alone. The classic sign that you may need orthotics is if your body repeatedly breaks down when you hit a particular level of training, regardless of how slowly you progress. That typically means something's wrong with your stride, and the feet are the most likely culprit. You may also need orthotics if any one of the following are true:

- you're an excess supinator
- you have Morton's foot (a common but "abnormal" foot shape in which the second toe is longer than the big toe; the undersized big toe reduces the ability of the foot to supinate properly)
- you've ever broken an ankle (the bones may not have set correctly)
- you have a history of ankle sprains (the orthotic will help stabilize your foot and reduce its tendency to twist)
- you have degenerative arthritis in your knees (orthotics can alter the stress points so you can be active, without pain)

COMING BACK AFTER AN INJURY LAYOFF

Nobody likes a layoff. You start to lose fitness within a few days in a detraining process that becomes particularly noticeable after the first week. Coming back from a layoff of a month or more feels frustratingly like starting over from scratch.

Nevertheless, some injuries require rest, and if you ignore this reality, you're just lengthening the layoff they'll ultimately impose on you. You'll need at least a short layoff for any injury that gets progressively worse despite treatment, or that hobbles you sufficiently to alter your stride, raising the specter of a second, "compensation" injury from the unnatural stride mechanics.

Returning to running after a short layoff (up to about a week) is fairly easy. You may feel sluggish for a day or two, but you won't have had time to detrain significantly, and you'll bounce back quickly. Even elite competitors can be back into racing form within a couple of weeks, and you'll probably feel that you've made a 90 percent comeback in half that time.

The wear pattern on your shoes reveals much about your foot motion.

normal wear   excess pronation   excess supination

Coming back from a longer layoff takes, well, longer. An old rule of thumb is that it takes 2 days for each day you were laid off, although in the latter part of that interval what you'll notice is more a lack of speed than a reduction in stamina.

Minimize the time needed for your comeback by finding a cross-training sport that you can do during the layoff. As little as 20 minutes of the other sport, three times a week, will greatly slow your fitness decline. The key is to pick a sport that doesn't aggravate the injury. If you're laid off with runner's knee, for example, stair climbing is probably a bad choice. But swimming or "pool running" (done with a flotation vest in a swimming pool) might be exactly the ticket. Bicycling is also a popular way to maintain fitness during a layoff, although it's not quite as easy on the body as swimming. Let pain be your guide; if one activity hurts, try another.

One other tip: tempting as it is to try to come back full force once the injury appears to be healed, you need to start up slowly. I never ran more than a mile on my first 2 or 3 outings after a layoff, just to make sure I was indeed ready to go. After that, you can build up your running time fairly quickly, as long as you don't worry about the fact that you'll be running relatively slowly. If you've been cross-training during the layoff, you'll probably be able to get back to your normal volume within about 2 weeks of a 2-week layoff—and you should have your speed back 2 weeks after that. Without cross-training, it may take the entire 4 weeks simply to build your volume back to normal. There's nothing magic about these numbers, however, and you have to let your body be your guide. If you try to power back too quickly, not only will you feel awful, but you'll set the stage for another cycle of injury, layoff, and recovery frustrations.

DMSO

DMSO is dimethyl sulfoxide, a solvent made as a by-product of the wood-products industry. It's been used for 30 years as a rubbing liniment for superficial inflammations. I myself have used it since 1980, even appearing on national television with the medical researcher who is the substance's leading proponent. Other runners generally find that it's either completely miraculous or doesn't work at all; there doesn't seem to be much middle ground. It works best for inflammation that's close to the surface—half an inch deep at most. If you have a deep muscle pull, DMSO will probably disperse in the blood before it penetrates far enough to help.

What makes DMSO unusual is that it rapidly penetrates the skin—so rapidly that if you touch the sweaty body of another runner who's been using it, you'll experience the chemical's distinct taste (sometimes compared to garlic or to clams or oysters) in your mouth only a few seconds later.

DMSO is widely regarded as safe, but it has never been approved by the U.S. Food and Drug Administration, partly because the taste makes it impossible to do the double-blind placebo-controlled studies required to prove that it works. Because of the taste, test subjects who are receiving the real stuff know it immediately, a problem that makes it impossible for scientists to sort out the substance's direct effect from the placebo effect.

Many athletes—including me—are sure of its efficacy, however. It's approved for veterinary purposes, but you don't have to go to a veterinary supplier to track it down. Many pharmacies carry it, labeled somewhat humorously as "not for human use." Chiropractors and alternative-medicine stores may also sell MSM (methylsulfonylmethane), a related chemical. Usually, MSM is taken orally in the form of capsules or dissolvable crystals, but it is also available as a lotion; DMSO is always used topically.

DMSO appears to work by increasing blood circulation to inflamed tissues. That flushes away inflammation by-products and reduces swelling—often almost immediately. Its one drawback is that it is such a good solvent that it will also carry through the skin any other substance lurking in the vicinity.

For safety, therefore, wash your hands and the site of the injury before using DMSO, and be careful what you touch afterward. I once made the mistake of putting on dark socks shortly after using DMSO on an Achilles tendon. Later I discovered that I'd chemically tattooed myself with dye that the DMSO had dissolved out of the socks. It took weeks for the dark spots to disappear. Now, when I see athletes incautiously slapping the stuff on in locker rooms, I point out to them they're sucking anything they've touched through their skin and into their bodies. If you choose to use DMSO, be careful what else you touch.

LESSER AILMENTS

The injuries discussed so far in this chapter are the ones for which runners most commonly seek advice. But there are a few others worthy of at least brief mention.

CAUSES AND TREATMENTS OF MINOR (BUT OFTEN PAINFUL) RUNNING INJURIES

Injury	Location	Most Likely Causes	First Line of Attack[1]	Prevention of Recurrence[2]
side stitch	below rib cage may radiate to shoulder	spasm of diaphragm	slow down or walk bend over, touch toes, and breathe deeply	avoid running with full stomach adequate warm-up belly breathing
heel bruise	bottom of heel	misstep	RICE and anti-inflammatories	change running surface

[1] Short-run treatments to abate the problem while the cause is determined.
[2] Listed in order of implementation difficulty or expense. Not all will be needed.
[3] Caution: if this doesn't respond quickly to treatment, it may be a stress fracture, a much more serious injury.

Injury	Location	Most Likely Causes	First Line of Attack[1]	Prevention of Recurrence[2]
(heel bruise cont'd)		cumulative effect of pounding aging of heel's fat pad		buy new shoes use heel cup
shoelace bruise[3]	pain on top of foot, beneath shoelaces	pressure from shoelaces	add padding beneath shoelaces	re-lace shoes to reduce pressure
bruised or black toenails	any toe, but usually on big toe	lack of toe room in shoes downhill running	ice and anti-inflammatories wear roomy shoes or sandals while pain subsides have hole drilled in nail by an M.D. to alleviate pressure	better-fitting shoes improved downhill running technique
blisters and chafing	toes, groin, armpits, nipples	rubbing, especially when sweaty	moleskin	petroleum jelly moleskin test all clothing, socks, shoes under controlled conditions men should tape nipples before long runs; women should be sure sports tops fit comfortably
back pain	any portion of spine	numerous	consult doctor	strengthen abdominal muscles stretch hamstrings lose excess weight consider orthotics

[1] Short-run treatments to abate the problem while the cause is determined.
[2] Listed in order of implementation difficulty or expense. Not all will be needed.
[3] Caution: if this doesn't respond quickly to treatment, it may be a stress fracture, a much more serious injury.

(continued next page)

Injury	Location	Most Likely Causes	First Line of Attack[1]	Prevention of Recurrence[2]
muscle cramps	any, usually calves or hamstrings	dehydration and hard exercise pushing muscles "to their limit"	keep well hydrated	train for expected conditions
digestive upsets ("runner's trots")	diarrhea during or after race or hard workout	poorly understood; some cases may be food intolerances that only appear under stress of racing	none; resolves itself within a few hours	experiment with prerace diet
bloody urine	appears on first urination after hard workout, especially in hot weather	bruised bladder	heals on its own within hours if it persists, consult M.D. immediately; could indicate more serious ailment	keep well-hydrated don't urinate immediately before running, to retain a protective "cushion" of urine

[1] Short-run treatments to abate the problem while the cause is determined.
[2] Listed in order of implementation difficulty or expense. Not all will be needed.
[3] Caution: if this doesn't respond quickly to treatment, it may be a stress fracture, a much more serious injury.

Side Stitch

A side stitch is a stabbing pain deep in your side, below the rib cage. Often it's accompanied by a satellite pain in the shoulder, due to some odd nerve linkage. Adults who never had side stitches in childhood are often frightened, thinking it's a heart attack. Actually, a side stitch is a spasm in your diaphragm. It comes from making the diaphragm work too hard—either by pushing yourself to your limit or by doing something else that overtaxes it.

One good way to overtax the diaphragm is by running too soon after a meal. Some people are more prone to this problem than are others, so you may have to learn from experience what your body can and cannot tolerate. Personally, I avoid running within 4 hours of any sizable meal (although you can snack or eat a light breakfast much later than this, as we'll discuss in the section of this book dealing with racing).

Another leading cause of side stitches is breathing too hard, too soon. Like any other muscle, the diaphragm needs to warm up for maximum efficiency. So take it easy at the start of your training runs, and warm up for races.

If you get a stitch in training, the ideal solution is to slow down immediately. Walk if you need to. Usually, the stitch will pass in a few minutes regardless of what you do, but the harder you push, the longer it's likely to take. Also, check your breathing pattern. Side stitches can be brought on by erratic, haphazard breathing—the type of whooping breaths that indicate you've pushed yourself close to the point of exhaustion. In addition to slowing down, you may be able to eliminate the stitch by consciously controlling your breathing to bring it back into a nice, rhythmical pattern. Another aspect of proper breathing is to belly breathe, rather than chest breathe (see page 54). Rick has known several beginning racers who've had stitch problems associated with chest breathing.

In a race, you may have no choice but to gut it out. The worst stitch I've ever had lasted 5 miles in my first New York City Marathon. When I was done, it hurt for 3 weeks afterward, indicating that I must have actually torn the diaphragm rather than suffering the usual minor spasm. It's a price I was willing to pay to win; but if you get a stitch during a race, you'll have to make your own decision about whether the pain is worth it!

Heel Bruise

Some runners also call this a *stone bruise*, although it can be caused by factors other than encounters with pebbles. Unless you stepped on something and got an instant stab of pain, the origin of this injury is sometimes hard to fathom, but it doesn't take much of a bruise to be excruciatingly painful. Some unfortunate people become increasingly prone to these as they age and lose part of the normal shock-absorbing fat pads beneath their heels.

Minimize bruises by wearing good shoes and not running on extremely hard surfaces such as concrete. Most bruises will heal enough to allow you to run within a few days, although you might have to take a week or more off from speed workouts or downgrades. The issue here is simply allowing the bruise to heal, without constantly aggravating it. If a bruise persists, specialized *heel cups* sold at orthopedic supply houses will minimize pain, help you heal, and perhaps prevent recurrences. Since these invariably have some degree of heel lift, you'll want to add some lift (or a second heel cup) to the uninjured foot, to keep your stride balanced. Beware of blisters from ill-fitting cups.

Shoelace Bruise

Pain that occurs directly beneath your shoelaces can be caused by the pressure of tight laces on bones or nerves. (A deep ache can also signal a stress fracture of the underlying bones.) If the problem is simple bruising, the solution is to eliminate the

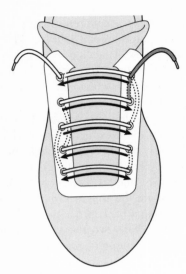

Pain on the top of the foot can often be alleviated by lacing your shoe in a way that distributes the pressure more evenly.

pressure. The usual cause is the standard crossover method of lacing shoes. Re-lace as shown in the drawing, if necessary, leaving a gap at the most tender location. If that doesn't bring immediate relief, insert a piece of foam padding beneath the laces to distribute the pressure. You can't run efficiently without tightly laced shoes, but with persistence and creativity you can ensure that the pressure of the laces isn't painful. If the problem persists, consult a doctor to make sure it's not a stress fracture.

Bruised Toenails

Too-short shoes or fast downhill running (as in a hilly race) can produce painful bruises beneath your toenails, most likely on your big toes. Like any bruise, this will abate in a few days, but if it's painful enough, you may want to have a doctor drill a tiny hole in the toenail to alleviate the pressure. Eventually a badly bruised toenail turns black from the dried blood beneath it. A few months later, it falls off, revealing a new, healthy nail underneath. Leave the old toenail alone until it's ready to fall off; that will protect the tender skin beneath it while the new nail grows in. Meanwhile, buy shoes with more toe room so it won't happen again. Improving your downhill running technique as discussed in chapter 13 may also make you less susceptible to this injury.

Blisters and Chafing

Chafing and blisters both come from unwanted rubbing. Hot, humid weather makes them more likely. Both can hurt a lot during the race, and even more walking to your car afterward, when the body's natural painkillers have begun to wear off. The solutions all lie in the realm of prevention. Never wear clothing in a race, particularly shoes or socks, that you've not tested in training. Swab chafing-prone regions with petroleum jelly or some other lubricating salve before you start.

Fabric rubbing on your nipples can abrade them enough to bleed, particularly in long races or long training runs. Women should make sure that their sports tops are comfortable; men should put first-aid tape across their nipples before they start. (This is critical for marathons.) On long runs, men should never wear any shirt with a heavy, abrasive transfer at nipple height, and men and women should beware of underarm chafing from tank tops and sleeveless racing singlets.

You may also chafe on the insides of your thighs, especially if you're not superthin (and some running shorts will do this to the thinnest of us). If petroleum jelly won't do the job, consider wearing tight spandex or Lycra shorts that come partway down your thighs, like cycling shorts. Loose-fitting shorts may keep you slightly cooler, but it doesn't take much chafing to undo their advantages.

Some runners attempt to stave off blisters in the same way they do chafing, by swabbing large amounts of petroleum jelly between their toes and onto their feet. Others can't stand all that goo slopping around their feet. Better than lubricants is moleskin, a slightly cushioned tape obtainable in any drugstore. Cut off a piece large enough to cover the blister-prone region and stick it in place (avoiding wrinkles). Be careful not to dislodge it when you put on your socks. Walk or jog to glue the moleskin firmly in place, and don't also use petroleum jelly, which will interfere with the moleskin's glue.

Moleskin sticks best when applied to dry feet, so put it on before you start warming up. Even if you only blister during races, practice using moleskin on training runs; improperly applied, it can create new rub spots. You particularly don't want it coming loose in a race and forming a big lump beneath your arch or your toes. Other antiblister products are also available; my favorite is a gelatinous substance called 2nd Skin, which works wonders for taking the pressure off blisters that formed despite your best efforts to forestall them.

Even if you don't normally blister, be wary of blisters on courses with extended, steep downgrades.

Back Pain

Lower-back pain can put a severe crimp in your style, in running as in virtually any other activity. And while there's no indication that running is any more dangerous to your back than many other activities (lack of overall fitness, in fact, is a risk factor for back pain), some people do get sore backs when they run.

Diagnosing and treating back problems is beyond the scope of this book. If you suspect a ruptured disk or torn muscle, you need the help of a back specialist. But for low-grade aches and pains, there is some standard advice that might help:

1. Don't do any of the stretches or weight lifts in chapters 6 and 7 that are identified as contraindicated for people with back problems.
2. Stretch your hamstrings religiously. Tightness there can radiate upward into the back, aggravating back pain.
3. Do crunches (see page 104). Mild to moderate back pain is often associated with weak abdominal muscles, and runners often forget to strengthen their abs.
4. If you're overweight, reduce pounding by losing weight.
5. Have your stride examined for abnormalities that might be transmitting stress all the way up to your spine. Amazingly, orthotics can be the cure for back pain.

Muscle Cramps

Excruciating, charley-horse-type muscle cramps are rare among runners. More common are minor spasms, sometimes called *heat cramps*, which come on when muscles are simultaneously dehydrated and worked hard for extended periods of time. Since these are largely a problem in longer races, they are discussed in chapter 15, on marathon running.

Digestive Upsets

Digestive problems during a race are usually due to eating too soon before the event or eating or drinking the wrong thing before or during the race. Some runners, however, experience digestive upsets a few hours after the race. Sports medicine author Tim Noakes, who suffers from this problem, dubs it the "runner's trots," and posits that it might be due to some dietary factor, such as lactose intolerance, which is normally too mild to notice but is exacerbated under the stress of racing. Try abstaining from dairy products for 2 or 3 days before the race, Noakes suggests; if that doesn't work, try abstaining from other foods that can provoke intolerances, such as gluten (in wheat).

RUNNING WITH A COLD

Many older running books (and doctors) habitually told runners never to run with an acute infection (including the common cold). When it came to colds, however, this was advice that no serious racer ever followed. If I'd taken a 10-day layoff every time I had a cold, I'd have then needed to spend the next 3 weeks getting back into shape for racing—an unthinkable interruption in my training.

From my more recent medical reading, I've decided that the smart thing to do is to split the difference, cutting back your training by about 50 percent when you first feel a cold coming on. Medical research has shown that runners can continue to run at moderate levels without causing their colds to linger any longer than if they'd just stayed home and vegged out. And my own experience is that moderate running counteracts some of the lethargy that comes with a cold. The splitting-the-difference approach also keeps you at an acceptable level of training; even with a week or 10 days of half-length workouts you won't see a noticeable setback.

If you have a fever, though, you really need to take a few days off, lest you turn your flu into something worse, such as pneumonia.

Bloody Urine

Blood in your urine is scary. In ordinary life it can signal any of several medical emergencies. But runners sometimes get it simply because they've bruised their bladders from the continual pounding of a hard race or long workout. This only happens if your bladder starts the race empty and stays that way, so the solution is simple: be well-hydrated before the race and leave a little cushion of urine in your bladder by not urinating immediately before the start. If you do spot blood in your urine after a marathon or a hard workout, it's a tough call whether to see a doctor. On the one hand, you risk ignoring the first signs of a bladder infection or kidney stone; on the other, you may simply set into motion a series of medical tests for a trivial problem that will heal itself in a couple of days.

OTHER MALADIES

A number of other running-related medical problems, although less common, hold potentially serious consequences for the runner.

Morton's Neuroma

A painful foot problem, though not common, is Morton's neuroma, which can produce a marble-sized swelling of a nerve that runs near the base of the big toe. Even if there's no swelling, suspect a neuroma if you have burning, shooting, or tingling pains in this part of the foot, all of which are characteristic of nerve injuries. This isn't an injury that's likely to respond to self-treatment, although it may be

CAUSES AND TREATMENTS OF OTHER RUNNING-RELATED INJURIES

INJURY	LOCATION	MOST LIKELY CAUSES	FIRST LINE OF ATTACK[1]	PREVENTION OF RECURRENCE[2]
Morton's neuroma	near base of big toe, beneath foot	inflamed or pinched nerve	rest orthotics cortisone injection surgery	not well understood
heat stroke	can be life-threatening not always accompanied by cessation of sweating may give early warning via sense of being chilled on a hot day	rapid rise of body temperature	immediately stop running get help drink	train for expected weather conditions drink before and during race or training run don't go all-out in hot weather
altitude sickness	headache, nausea, loss of appetite, difficulty in sleeping, other symptoms	going up too high, too quickly	descend	give the body time to acclimate

[1] Short-run treatments to abate the problem while the cause is determined.
[2] Listed in order of implementation difficulty or expense. Not all will be needed.

alleviated with orthotics designed to alleviate pressure on the nerve. A cortisone injection may resolve it; otherwise, surgery is the only answer. Luckily, the surgery is almost always successful, and the injury is unlikely to recur.

Heat Stroke

Most running injuries are no more than frustrating interruptions to your training schedule. Heat and dehydration, however, can kill. We'll talk more about keeping hydrated in part 3, on racing. For purposes of this chapter, just remember that heat and dehydration problems are insidious, sometimes creeping up even on people who think they're well acclimated. In training, take frequent water breaks and drink more than a few sips. Contrary to popular belief, you can't train your body to be more water efficient by reducing your water intake, so don't even attempt it. Look at your fingertips occasionally, particularly on hot days. It's not a sure sign, but if they're starting to wrinkle up like you've been washing dishes, you're probably dehydrating.

A not-to-be-overlooked sign of dangerous dehydration (and incipient heat stroke) is a sudden feeling of being chilled (often starting on your arms or the back of your neck) on a day you know is hot. Stop running immediately and seek shade and water (but don't go hide out of sight where nobody will see you if you collapse). If you're in a race, tell other runners to send back help from the next aid station. On training runs, always take it easy on hot days and run with friends. Dehydration and heat stroke cause disorientation, and that's easier to spot in each other than in yourself.

Feeling lightheaded on a hot day is also not good but generally not as dangerous. But it does mean that your body's cooling system is so overloaded that you're not getting enough blood to your brain and are about to faint. Lie down (preferably in the shade), knees elevated (or head downhill).

Altitude Sickness

Running at high elevations can produce headache, nausea, dehydration, or any of a number of other symptoms collectively known as altitude sickness. In extreme cases, these can be accompanied by potentially deadly fluid buildups in the lungs or brain, but that's not likely to happen unless you attempt a running vacation in Tibet.

Although there are prescription medications that can help you out, the simplest solution is acclimatization. A rule of thumb used by mountaineers is not to ascend by more than 4,000 or 5,000 feet per day. Another is that you can speed acclimatization with gentle exercise—which means walking or easy hiking, not running. Even at altitudes as low as 7,000 feet, it takes several weeks to fully adapt, and you never reach a point where altitude feels 100 percent as comfortable as sea level. High-altitude training can be used to boost your VO_2max for sea-level racing (it's one reason why many world-class runners come from mountainous countries), but when the race is at altitude—even altitudes as low as 3,000 feet—everyone's performance suffers. If you race at altitude, don't expect to match your personal record, and be careful not to push yourself too hard in an effort to compensate.

THE RUNNER'S MIND

ALL THE TRAINING in the world won't help you if on race day you undercut it with a poor mental attitude. Mental preparation is a complex and amorphous subject. Before this chapter is over, I'm going to tell you to relax, work hard, accept failure, visualize success, concentrate, and not to think too much—all at the same time. It sounds self-contradictory, but at its heart lies the important psychological distinction between "trying" and "doing."

"Trying" is hard work that can rob you of energy better spent in the simple act of racing. Feeling pressured to succeed reduces your chances of doing so. In racing, we call that "trying too hard." Other sports call it "choking under pressure."

"Doing" is a state in which focused action replaces fear and frazzle. Elite racers and many other athletes call it "being in the zone." It entails finding a mental state where you're racing without thinking about those success-or-failure pressures. This does not mean that you've spaced out. Rather, you're concentrating so thoroughly on the task at hand that you may be semi-oblivious to other matters. If you're in the zone, racing feels natural and unforced.

The distinction is comparable to the difference between trying to play an instrument and making music; the goal of this chapter is to help you to discover how to immerse yourself in the racing equivalent to making music. The outcome will then be whatever it will be, but if you've done your training and followed the racing tips in part 3 of this book, that outcome will probably be good. Regardless, the closer you come to being in the zone, the better you'll do.

PAYING THE PRICE

Before you can work on achieving a proper race-day mindset, you must resolve a preliminary matter: deciding how much you really want to achieve your best possible performance.

Racing, to put it bluntly, involves pain. Running philosopher George Sheehan loved to describe this in dramatically masochistic terms. In the race, he said, you took whatever part of your body hurt in the early miles and made it hurt worse later on. I won't be that extreme, but I will advise you that you can't fun-run your way to your full potential. If you never feel discomfort during training and racing, you're jogging, not racing. The first part of your mental preparation is to determine how much discomfort you're willing to tolerate. Experience will then teach you how hard you can go at each point in a race without exceeding this threshold.

If you decide to go all out, the discomfort will be substantial enough that midway through the race, you may ask why you're doing this to yourself. Have an answer ready, because along with the question comes a temptation: *gee, if I slow down only a few seconds per mile, much of the discomfort will go away.* Having your goals well in mind will help you stare down that temptation. You'll know whether, later on, you'll deeply regret backing off, or whether you really won't care one way or the other.

> **How close you can come to your ultimate racing potential depends on how much discomfort you're willing to put up with in racing and in training.**

On the other hand, discomfort is also part of your more intense workouts, so the race shouldn't carry you into whole new realms of pain. If the midparts of the race hurt significantly more than anything you're used to, you're probably pushing harder than your training will support, and you really do need to back off. Wisdom also dictates backing off from pain that feels like incipient injury. The pain that you need to brace yourself for is the normal discomfort of running through mounting fatigue.

The serious racer's attitude toward fatigue-related pain is: *I was tired, but I kept going as well as I could.* The opposing attitude is: *I got tired, so I slowed down.* You won't achieve a good performance without being willing to extend yourself into areas of discomfort—both in races and in speed workouts—but this isn't an all-or-nothing decision. If you don't want to put up with the pain required to do your absolute best, you can obtain an intermediate level of results from an intermediate level of effort. Typically, it's the last few seconds per mile of extra speed that account for the lion's share of the pain—but they also account for the difference between a good race and a great one.

BUILDING CONFIDENCE

Once you've decided how hard you're willing to race, your next step is to boost your confidence that you can indeed achieve your goal. There are three basic steps: setting realistic goals; believing in your training; and visualization.

The setting of performance goals was covered in chapter 5. Basically, you shouldn't target on more than a 7- to 10-second-per-mile improvement from one race to the next—less if you've not been speed training. Larger breakthroughs are possible, but if you deliberately try for one, you run a large risk of not achieving anything. A fundamental tenet of this book is that you'll reach your potential more comfortably and with fewer setbacks if you do so by a series of incremental goals. You'll also get repeated positive feedback along the way.

Believing in your training is also important. The program outlined in chapter 5 is geared for specific racing targets. If you do the training and hit the target paces for your speed workouts, you are adequately prepared for the goals listed in that chapter. That doesn't mean you're guaranteed to achieve your goal in your next race; there are simply too many factors that can get in your way. (If nothing else, the weather might preempt your PR by being brutally hot, or so cold you have to bundle up like a snowman.) But doing the training proves that you're in shape to make the goal. If that doesn't come in this race, it will probably come in the next one.

Visualization

Visualization is a fancy word for daydreaming. The difference is that rather than letting your mind wander, you often take conscious control and entertain only thoughts that will help your running.

It's a technique that holds an honored role in skill sports. Basketball players imagine the feel of perfectly shot free throws, and downhill skiers mentally swoosh through perfect, linked turns. This mental rehearsal helps ingrain the correct sequence of motions so that when the time comes to do it for real, you're more likely to ski or shoot hoops correctly.

Running is less of a skill sport, with fewer opportunities for this type of visualization. Mental rehearsal can probably help, though, if you're trying to correct deficiencies in your running form. Memorize what it feels like to run correctly, then replay that memory over and over again, concentrating on the rhythm and flow of good form. If nothing else, this should make it easier to distinguish good form from bad in your actual workouts.

Visualization works. Take control of your daydreams and turn them to positive images of running a great race.

The most important use of visualization in running, though, is to boost your confidence. Psychological research has conclusively demonstrated that people who see themselves succeeding are more likely to do so than those who visualize themselves as failing. At the elite level, the effect is dramatic. Polls of elite runners have found that those who repeatedly do well have been envisioning themselves as breaking the tape, setting a record, or otherwise achieving a goal. Those who are mired in a string of poor performances have been visualizing failure. It's the difference between having daydreams and day-nightmares.

To some extent, this positive and negative visualization is the result of these athletes' recent performances. People who are doing well will naturally have positive thoughts; those who are in a slump may be depressed. But when runners are asked to change their visualization habits, the research has proven that positive images will indeed help you to do better. Visualization involves a strong element of self-fulfilling prophecy.

There are, of course, limits to this. You can't use visualization to bootstrap your way into achieving things that aren't supported by your training. But imagining yourself succeeding helps you fulfill that training's promise. Not doing so makes it difficult to exceed your negative expectations.

Visualizing success comes automatically to some people but not to others. When I was young, I naturally daydreamed about winning medals and setting records. Later, as the dreams came true, it was easy to continue doing the same. Rick doesn't visualize winning per se, but sitting in an armchair he finds it easy to slip into the zone of his best-run races. He's daydreaming about the *feel* of running well.

Other people have to learn to visualize, or at least to visualize success rather than failure. There's no magic formula—only a process of taking deliberate control over your thoughts. Turn aside from the negative ones and envision yourself as running a perfect race, in which everything goes according to plan. It takes practice, but even a natural pessimist can learn to set aside the negative thoughts, at least in this one, narrow arena.

DEAR DIARY

Prior to a race, I would always look over my training diary, reminding myself that I'd done all of my planned workouts and that I'd generally performed well. Knowing that I'd done the work always left me confident that the race would go well.

Sometimes, of course, your workouts haven't been going all that well and your training diary will be a source of added anxiety. If you're merely in a short-term slump, scan your diary for other occasions when you've suddenly pulled out of similar slumps. If it's a long-term slump, though, your diary may be telling you to readjust your goal for the upcoming race.

Fighting Doubts

However confident you may be a week before the race, doubts mount as the start draws near. By race day, the list can be quite impressive: the starting time is too early, you didn't sleep well, you ate too much the night before, there's an odd pain in your knee—or any of a myriad other possibilities. Particularly worrisome are tiny aches and pains that you'd never have noticed if you weren't thinking about the race. Such doubts are so common that Bill Dellinger, my college coach, once told me that one of his main prerace duties was to reassure his runners that this, that, or the other soreness wouldn't stop them from running well.

Here are three suggestions for keeping doubts from undermining your confidence:

- Ask yourself if the problem is one that you'd worry about (or even notice) before a training run. If it isn't, it probably won't affect your race, either.
- Remember that very few races are ever perfect. The vast majority of imperfections are so minor they'll have no impact.
- Draw on your racing and training experience to judge whether a concern is important. When I won the Boston Marathon, I had a sore hamstring from a minor pull about 9 days before the race. I didn't let that bother me, though, because worse problems than this hadn't stopped me from doing well in other races.

Obviously, if you've sustained a real injury, you may have to drop out of the race. But try to be as objective as possible about such matters, realizing that on race day, everyone's a hypochondriac.

LETTING GO

Being confident doesn't mean pretending that failure is impossible. Every race is a calculated risk, and you won't always achieve your goals. But failure is unpleasant, and the threat of it contributes to prerace jitters.

There are several ways to fight this nervousness, but the first and most important step is to convince yourself that you don't *have* to run a great race. It's similar

MIND GAME

There's no single, best way to let go of self-defeating pressures to succeed. Coaching kids, I remind them that there will always be good races and bad ones. Rick's approach is to play mind games with himself:

I'm one of those runners who likes to have his excuses lined up well in advance of the race. Even if I know I'm in personal-record shape, I'll seldom tell anyone, or even admit it overtly to myself. In my early years, a family member would commonly accompany me to races. "When should I look for you at the finish?" she'd ask.

My answer was so much by rote that it could have been part of my prerace ritual. "I feel like death warmed over," I'd say. "I don't know what's wrong but I just don't have it today."

She'd heard this so many times that she always laughed, then predicted a finish very close to my own secret goal.

"No, no," I'd protest. "This time I mean it!" Then the gun would sound and I'd instantly fall into a more aggressive race plan. Often enough, it would end with a PR.

Even as I was making my excuses, I knew they were bogus—designed solely to free me from undue pressure. A quarter-century later, I'm still playing this game, and it still works, erasing just enough pressure to make it easier for me to do what I'm actually confident that I *can* do.

to the distinction between "trying" and "doing" discussed earlier in this chapter. Feeling that you "have" to do something wastes mental energy.

Don't worry that letting go in this manner will ruin your confidence or strip you of the desire to run well. Your goal is to reach the starting line confident but not feeling that something horrible will happen if you have a bad race. Ironically, once you've let go of the *need* to succeed and convinced yourself that it's only a race, you'll actually run better.

> **Psychologists say that running a great race feels better when you're under no pressure to succeed. Instead of immediately feeling that you now have to repeat your success, you can simply say, That's nice, and not worry about the future.**

Fear of Success

Some runners never reach their full potential because they're afraid of success. It's a quite common problem. If you suffer from it, you'll tend to run every race very conservatively. If you do any speed training at all, it will probably be fairly secretive, so that nobody else knows what you're capable of doing. Or you'll hold back, just as you do in races.

The underlying fear isn't really of success, but of the consequences of success. Running a breakthrough race proves that you're capable of doing more than you've done in the past, and that puts you under pressure to do it again. You dodge this pressure by never letting yourself run a truly good race; it's like being afraid of falling in love for fear of being hurt.

The solution is similar to that for letting go of prerace pressure to succeed. In this case, you're thinking two races down the road rather than one, but psychologically the issues are identical. Try reversing the action-movie cliché and tell yourself that failure *is* an option.

Other suggestions:

- Carry the incremental-improvement approach to its logical extreme. If you can beat a prior performance by only a few seconds, you've advanced without putting yourself under much pressure.
- Remember that all running careers have ups and downs. That means that you're not obliged to follow up a triumph with another success because you can always write the next race off as one of those periodic troughs between the peaks.
- Tell friends, family, and other would-be coaches that their attempted cheerleading is putting you under unneeded pressure. Keep your race results secret from those who can't respect this request.

Think about the old proverb about success and failure: "Show me a person who's never failed, and I'll show you a person who's never accomplished anything." Like a lot of proverbs it's corny—but true.

PANIC AVOIDANCE

Prerace jitters can be hard to avoid, but two major worries aren't:

1. Get to the start with plenty of time to spare.

2. When you get there, locate an outlying toilet that's unlikely to have a long line when you need it. Most other runners won't wander far from the starting line.

RELAXATION

Most runners suffer strongly enough from prerace jitters that they have no need to psyche themselves up like football players bumping helmets before a big game. In fact, psyche-up routines are usually counterproductive because the short-term excitement wears off in the first mile or, worse, inspires you to start out too fast. It can also burn up energy as you wait for the start, champing at the bit.

You run best when you're relaxed. The goal is to hit your target pace while making the effort feel as easy as possible. Runners who've just run great races almost always say it felt so easy they're sure they could have done even better. Prior to the start, therefore, your job is to stay as relaxed as possible. Experienced racers often seem almost withdrawn, off in their own worlds as they marshal their energies for when they'll be needed.

If you're too keyed up, try doing a few simple calming exercises. Some runners listen to soothing music or use "centering exercises" of the type used before meditation or prayer. You can also try repeating a simple mantra—something like *I'm relaxed. I'm confident. My training's gone well.* Psychologists have demonstrated that you can indeed become more relaxed by telling yourself you're relaxed, but it takes practice. Pick a message that fits your personality and your prerace mood, and make sure it's something you really believe. "My training's gone well" isn't a good

COPING WITH FAILURE

If a race is disappointing, shrug it off. Bad races happen, and if you can't learn to accept this, you won't last long as a racer. Soften the blow by telling yourself that it's just one race, and that there are many more to come. Continue to have faith in your training. Great runners stick with the plan, knowing it will eventually pay off.

Sometimes disappointments can teach important lessons. Even if the day was one you'd rather forget, describe it in your training diary so that later on, you may be able to find patterns that will show you how to run better in the future.

choice if actually you've skipped the last six speed workouts. Then your mantra might have to be a bit milder: *I'll do OK.*

A related trick is biofeedback, but for this you need a heart-rate monitor. Rick can drop his heart rate by 5 to 10 beats per minute simply by staring at the monitor and willing himself to relax. Playing with this at home has helped him perfect an array of personalized calming techniques that he can apply whenever he wants.

One good way to relax before a race is to establish a prerace ritual and stick with it, race after race. Drink the same beverages, eat the same breakfast, and do the same warm-up exercises. By controlling your routine, you'll feel more in control of the race itself, and the ritual nature of your preparations is calming.

Elite runners are pretty focused on their prerace preparations, but at the recreational level, you may face some distractions. In the hour before a race, many recreational racers chat with friends or otherwise act like they're at a party rather than a race. Rick says he tries to stay aloof from such activities. Talking to friends at this time pulls him out of his routine, steals time from his planned warm-up, and distracts him from the task at hand. Rick talks with old friends at the finish, not the start.

THE MENTAL RACE: FIGHTING FATIGUE

The moment the race starts, the fears and jitters vanish. Now the job is to run. At first that's easy—too easy, in fact, because you'll tend to start too fast. In future chapters, we'll discuss pacing strategies, but for now we'll talk about another aspect of the mental race: running through the fatigue that will start setting in all too soon.

Everyone has their own way of doing this. One common technique is to divide the race into bite-sized subsections, concentrating on them one at a time. In short races, the halfway point is often a convenient target. Once you reach it, you can shift focus to the three-quarter mark, and so on, with each target goal reached more quickly than the one before. That works particularly well in a 5K, where you might pass the half with only 10 to 15 minutes to go. Pretty soon you're down to 5 minutes, and while you might wish that these minutes would pass more quickly, that's still an easily manageable number.

In a marathon, on the other hand, being halfway through the race could mean having 2 hours to go or longer—a long way if you're having a bad day. And among ultramarathoners in South Africa's 54-mile Comrades Marathon, the joke is that when you get to the midpoint, you only have a marathon left to go. The solution is to break the race up into smaller chunks and take them one at a time. Make the chunks short enough that they're not too daunting but long enough that each one gives you a real sense of progress.

In short races—up to about 10 miles—fatigue mounts steadily as you progress. That means that you shouldn't feel too bad for the first one-third of the race, even if you know you'll be hurting in the final third. The exception is the 5K, which seems like a sprint the whole way. It's difficult to ever really relax into it because it feels as though you're into that final push practically before you've started.

In long races, fatigue and pain don't rise quite so linearly. Instead you'll experience a mix of good stretches and bad ones. Weather the bad ones by realizing that they don't last forever; in a mile or two you'll probably be feeling better. In marathons, there's also a general pattern in which fatigue mounts steadily for about the first 8 miles, then hits a plateau that typically lasts until mile 18 or 20. In those middle miles, many runners report that they feel as though they could run forever. They're not totally free of discomfort, but the discomfort is mild and not getting any worse.

Then the plateau ends and the fatigue again starts climbing. Some people hit *the wall* (see pages 235–36), a point in the race where there is a sudden, dramatic increase in discomfort. The only good thing that can be said about this is that once it happens, the discomfort probably won't get much worse. If you're lucky enough not to hit the wall before mile 20, you will instead start feeling a steady increase in fatigue, starting somewhere around that mileage. This will progress until you either do hit the wall or the race ends, whichever comes first. Either way, the sensation of feeling that you can run forever has ended.

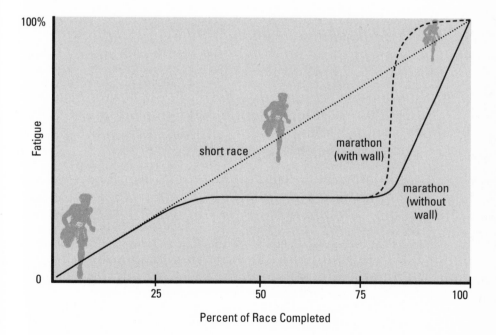

Fatigue mounts steadily in races shorter than about 10 miles. In marathons, it mounts in two stages. The pattern varies, though, depending on whether you hit the "wall."

MYTH OF THE SECOND WIND

Runners often talk about the "second wind" that kicks in to rescue you after a tough patch in a race. Sadly, no such mysterious energy source exists. What's happened is that you've been running too hard and are forced to back off—possibly so much that you overcompensate. The second wind is simply the sense of recovery that comes from correcting a pacing error.

The last 6 miles of a marathon can feel so much tougher than what came before that some runners have quipped that psychologically, mile 20 is only halfway through the race. This is such a daunting thought that I don't believe it's useful. Yes, the last 6 miles are the toughest, but they'll be over a lot more quickly than were the first 20 miles. Divide them into pieces, just as you would a shorter race, and run the pieces one at a time.

LONG-TERM MOTIVATION

After they've been racing for a few years, some runners start to lose motivation for continued training. Many factors can enter into this, ranging from changes in family or career to the simple sense that you're falling into a rut. Here are a few suggestions that have helped some runners:

- Change your training routine. If you're a morning runner, run a few evenings. Find new training routes, run your Tuesday route on Wednesday, or reverse the direction of loop courses.
- Take a break from the track and run less structured speed workouts instead, such as fartleks or hills.
- Find a workout group and make running more of a social event.
- Try some trail running.
- Take a total break for perhaps 2 to 4 weeks. You'll bounce back from it in a couple of months.
- Cut back your training for several months or even a year. Don't worry too much about backsliding, so long as you're still out jogging 4 or 5 days a week. Sure, you'll lose your competitive edge, but that will come back when you return to speed training. Each mile you run is like putting money in the bank. Physiologically, you continue laying groundwork for future racing even if you reduce the rate at which you're making these deposits.

Be aware, though, that mind and body are linked. A sudden shift of attitude, such as a loss of motivation or becoming cranky and irritable, may be an early sign of a physical problem: overtraining. Take a break now, before it gets worse.

Alternatively, some runners start to lose motivation when, either because of age or because they've reached their full potential, they can no longer set PRs.

When that happens, it's time to set new goals. Chapter 16 suggests how older runners can age-adjust their times to account for the passage of years, and chapter 17 offers a variety of new challenges that jaded racers can use to spice up their racing calendars.

RUNNING ADDICTION

As your career develops, it's likely that a few friends or acquaintances will refer to you as a "running addict." Don't worry about these passing comments: they tend to come from nonrunners who are baffled (and perhaps slightly threatened) by your passion. True running addiction occurs if that passion becomes an obsession. Suspect it if you realize that any of the following is occurring:

- Running is jeopardizing other parts of your life—family, career, social life. Conflicting schedules and family compromises are a normal part of life; irrational refusal ever to put anything ahead of your training schedule is not.
- It's difficult to force yourself to take rest days. Your family life may be fine, but here, your obsession is threatening your running itself by courting overtraining and injury.
- You have the sense that you're running to escape from something that you never directly confront. Running is a healthy way to relax and put the day's problems in perspective, but it becomes addictive if the goal repeatedly shifts to avoidance.
- You run ever-greater distances simply for the sake of racking up the numbers or as a way of denying age. It's one thing to expand your racing horizons to longer events. You're in riskier territory if you start feeling driven toward such feats as running your "age" in miles (or kilometers, laps, etc.) each time you have a birthday.

If you sense any of these in yourself, make a list of what's most important in your life and ask what sacrifices you really are willing to make for a sport that is, after all, a hobby. You may also need to examine your reasons for running. Are you logging all that mileage because you enjoy it and are pursuing a goal that's important to you? Or is because the rest of your life is facing dead ends or conflicts that you don't want to deal with? If so, you don't necessarily have to quit running, but you do need to deal with the problems directly (possibly with the help of counseling).

There's also something that might be called layoff phobia. Even runners who are by no means running addicts often suffer an irrational fear of getting out of shape by missing workouts. In my case it tended to manifest itself when I'd try to take a week off for an injury. Midway through the planned rest, my resolve would falter and I'd be back on the roads, pretending I was healed. The solution, of course, is having the self-discipline not to run. But that's often easier said than done.

PART 3

THE RACE

T RAINING HAS BEEN compared to putting money in the bank—not for the proverbial rainy day, but to save it up for something special. That "something" is the race.

If you've set a reasonable goal and followed the program outlined in the first half of this book, you should be reasonably prepared to race for your personal record—or whatever other target you might have set.

But to reach your goal, you need more than training: you have to run the race. And the wisdom—or folly—with which you approach it will have a large impact on what you achieve.

This book assumes that you're taking the race seriously enough to be seeking your best possible performance. That's not a foregone conclusion. I only shot for peak performances in about one-quarter of my races. The rest of the time, I was merely out to win; in those races a PR was never in the cards.

In my case, this was generally because I was saving energy for more important races. On occasion you may do the same, fun-running an event simply because you want to be part of it, even though it's not really part of your long-run racing plan. Alternatively there may be days when you're feeling a bit frazzled, under-prepared, or simply not willing to put out a maximum effort. You still want to attend a race, but not to really *race* it, so you run 15 or 20 seconds a mile slower than your maximum, treating the race as a tempo run.

(PHOTODISK/GETTY IMAGES)

There's nothing wrong with running in this manner, particularly if racing ca-maraderie is a piece of your social life. But true *racing* involves a higher degree of commitment. You're out to do your best, and you're willing to put yourself on the line to find out what that best might be. The next four chapters are designed to help you find those last few seconds of speed, so that your "best" is truly that. They will also coach you on what to expect on race day, so that even if you're a first-time racer you can approach the event like a veteran.

Topics are organized chronologically, beginning with your prerace preparations, and carrying you through warm-up, the start, uphill and downhill running, and the finish. The focus will be on races shorter than a marathon, but much of the in-formation applies to races of all distances. Marathon-specific information is pre-sented in chapter 15.

GETTING READY

B Y THE TIME YOU'VE worked through 4 to 6 weeks of speed training, the chances are that you've already chosen your target race. Most likely, you picked the event in advance and arranged your training schedule around it.

If you're undecided, it's unlikely to be due to lack of opportunities. There are thousands of races in the United States alone, with new ones springing up each year. Unless you live in rural Nevada or the Alaskan bush, you're likely to have a plethora of events to choose from within an hour's drive of home. Here in race-happy Oregon, it's possible to race every weekend from St. Patrick's Day through Halloween—and on plenty of occasions in the winter, as well.

CHOOSING YOUR RACE

Most races are well run, but a few are organizational nightmares, with poorly measured courses, inadequate water stops, and badly marked routes or poor traffic control. Here are some tips for finding good races:

- Talk to the clerks at your favorite running store. Ask them to recommend favorite races. They may hesitate to down-talk badly organized events, but they'll be lavish in their praise of good ones. They can also tell you how many runners to expect—a useful indicator of the race director's management experience.
- Look for nicely designed race registration brochures circulated well in advance—a good sign that other aspects of the race are also professionally managed. Races are typically advertised by fliers that double as registration forms.
- Look for announcements in the race calendar section of *Runner's World* or local running publications. These are good ways to fill out your racing sched-

ule, and the presence of races on these lists is another good sign that race directors are thinking in advance, rather than doing everything last-minute.

- Check the Internet. Some races have their own Web sites; others are listed on Internet services such as www.active.com, which maintains a nationwide race calendar. Active.com and similar Internet services can even process applications online for a nominal fee. Seeking information on the Web, however, can be frustrating; even the best-organized races often fail to show up on Internet search engines.
- Think twice about attending inaugural events or one-time charity fund-raisers unless your primary goal is to support the charity.
- Pay special attention to events that advertise courses that have been *certified* by USA Track and Field (USATF). Not only do such courses have to meet exacting measurement specifications, but any race director who is willing to go through the certification process has the determination to put on a quality event. Races that are *sanctioned* (as opposed to *certified*) by USATF undergo lesser scrutiny, but can be equally high-quality events.
- Pay special attention also to events put on by running clubs. These are races planned by runners, for runners. Even small ones can be organizational gems.
- Check the race's Web site (if any), or online race registration services such as active.com, which maintains a nationwide race calendar, for last year's results. This will tell you how many runners participated—and will also let you size up the competition if you have dreams of an age-group award.
- Avoid extremely early starts. You'll run faster (unless midday heat is an issue) later in the day, or even in the early evening.

Finally, pick a race that doesn't conflict with the rest of your life. You'll do a lot better if the race is one of your month's most important activities than if you're trying to squeeze it into an overly busy schedule.

PLANNING YOUR RACE

The best way to achieve your time goal is by running the entire race at precisely the target pace (picked according to your training, race experience, and the table on page 64)—with allowances, of course, for hills and wind. This means there are two things you can do in advance: calculate when you want to arrive at each mile marker, and familiarize yourself with the course.

Some people can compute paces in their heads, even while running at maximum effort. Other perfectly intelligent people couldn't think in base 60 if their lives depended on it. If you're one of the latter, sit down in advance with a calculator (buy a pace calculator if necessary) and figure out your mile-by-mile time targets, memorizing them if necessary. At large races, particularly marathons, you may be able to obtain computer-generated *pace bands* that do this for you. These can be obtained (sometimes as a promotional gift, sometimes for a nominal fee) at the prerace exhibition. They strap to your wrist, with your target times printed where you can't forget them.

RACE-QUALITY CHECKLIST

As you gain racing experience, you'll form your own list of the factors that differentiate great races from also-rans, but here are nine factors that most runners consider to be critical:

- accurately measured course
- well-marked route, with plenty of volunteers making sure you don't go astray
- good traffic control to keep cars from straying onto the route
- each mile marked, with signs you can't easily miss
- enough toilets at the start
- adequate parking (or good access by public transportation)
- lots of well-stocked aid stations
- start time commensurate with the anticipated weather
- accurate timing, with results promptly mailed or posted on the Internet

If the course is flat and "fast," calculate these target times according to the pace you've been training to run. Gently rolling courses are also fast, but hilly or windy courses will slow you down, possibly by quite a bit. You need to account for this in your race plan, so that you don't try to run a faster pace than the course allows.

Doing this takes experience. I usually looked at the best performances other runners had been able to achieve in earlier years. If, for example, a 10K course had generated fast times in the past, then I'd target on a 4:30 pace. If the course record was a minute on the slow side, I'd scale down my own goals accordingly, for instance to a 4:40 pace.

Most people, though, don't have much reason to know a fast winning time from a slightly slow one, and in smaller races, winning times can be highly variable, depending on who shows up. The best solution is to do your first races on fast courses. Then, if you like hills, you can move incrementally toward more challenging courses, adjusting your target pace slightly each time, until you learn your own benchmarks.

In addition to looking at prior finishing times, I always previewed the course, at least by car. Often, I ran part or all of it, particularly to familiarize myself with the last few miles, where knowing the course can easily make the difference between winning and losing. Most recreational racers don't bother to do this, but at a minimum, you should scan the race brochure for descriptors such as "flat" or "rolling," which will help you set your target pace. Many race directors, particularly of larger races, have taken to posting elevation profiles on the Internet. If you have a mathematical mind-set, you can then use the table on page 196 to estimate how much the terrain is likely to slow you down.

Unless you've previewed the course yourself or seen a detailed elevation profile, take all descriptions with a grain of salt. One person's "flat" is another's "rolling," and "downhill from X to the finish" may actually have a few bounces.

Even though I always knew which parts of a course were hilly and which ones were flat, I never tried to fine-tune my race plan to account for their impact on each mile's target time. It was enough to know my intended average pace. On a hilly

THE ART AND SCIENCE OF TIMING

Timing a large race is a sensitive business, and good finish-line crews deserve more acknowledgment than they typically get. Traditionally it's a two-step process. One step involves punching a button or using an electronic triggering device to record the clock reading each time a runner crosses the finish. The second step is to keep track of the order in which runners finish. Classically, that's done by herding people into finishing chutes and begging, pleading, cajoling, or browbeating them to stay in order until their identities can be recorded—typically by pulling off tear-away tabs on their race numbers. (When safety-pinning your race number to your shirt, don't complicate the finish-line workers' job by pinning down the tab.) Finishing times and names are correlated later.

Experienced finish-line crews can produce remarkably accurate results for thousands of runners using the traditional system—quickly enough for printouts of the front-runners' times to be posted before the back half of the pack reaches the line.

Increasingly, large races are shifting to electronic timing, which operates via an electronic chip that straps around your ankle or hooks into your shoelaces. It's not quite a bar code, but it functions similarly. When you cross the start line, you step on an electronic mat that recognizes your chip and records the precise moment when you got there. At the end of the race, you step onto a similar mat, which again scans the chip and clocks your arrival at the finish. A computer tabulates the results, providing an instant printout of race standings. Don't take the chip home as a souvenir; they cost money, and the finish-line officials will want them back for reuse.

Chip-based timing is the wave of the future, but it isn't without drawbacks. It does provide quick, accurate results and greatly reduces finish-line congestion. It also reduces the tendency of runners to cheat forward at the start, since they know their times will be calculated according to when they actually reach the line, regardless of how long it takes them to get moving. It's even possible to be caught in the toilet line at the start of the race and still run a good time, coming out of the back of the pack. But there are lingering questions over whether races should base finishers' competitive standings on the net *chip times* or on the traditional *clock* or *gun* times. Using chip times makes race tactics difficult for runners chasing high places in the standings because they and their competitors may not have the same starting time. That means you can stave off challengers in the final mile and still lose to them due to the difference in start times—an aggravating discovery. Not to use chip times when they're available, however, undercuts the whole purpose of having them.

Realistically, this is only likely to be an issue at the elite level, where it's hard to imagine giving first prize to someone who wasn't first across the line. For age-group awards, most but not all electronically timed races opt for using chip times.

Some races, such as the Boston Marathon, have chip sensors at each mile mark. These are connected to Internet-based computers that allow friends all over the globe to monitor your progress. It's like having a virtual-reality cheering section following you along the course. Such races also allow you to download your mile-by-mile times for later analysis of your race strategy. Your watch can give you the same data, but the chips offer a good backup in case you forget to push the right button on your watch.

course, uphill miles would come in slower than target, flat miles would be fast, and downgrades faster yet. If I set the overall goal correctly, the ups, downs, and flats would average out, and all I needed to do was to track my average rate of progress, without worrying too much about the minutiae of terrain.

TAPERING

As race day draws near, it's time to taper your training so that you're rested for the event itself.

The biggest beginner mistake at this point is to try to use the week before the race to make up for lapses in training. The temptation is obvious: the race is looming, and suddenly you feel terribly inadequate, so you try to squeeze in just one more hard workout. But it's too late. You'll merely tire yourself and do more harm than good. In the week before the event, you can't do much to boost the training that you have (or haven't) been doing for the previous month. What's all too easy, though, is to undercut everything you've been trying to achieve.

How much to taper depends on the race distance. It's possible to turn in a good 5K or 10K even if you're a bit tired on race day, but the more endurance the race calls for the more important it is to be adequately rested.

For events up to about 10K, target on scaling down your mileage by about 25 percent during the week before the race, mostly in the 2 or 3 days before the start. Thus, if you normally run 30 miles a week, you might want to cut back to about

SUGGESTED TAPER FOR RACES OF VARIOUS DISTANCES

Race Distance	Duration of Taper	Description
5K to 10K	3 to 4 days	25 percent reduction in total weekly mileage avoid speed work, long runs, or weight lifting during the 3 days prior to the race
15K to half-marathon	4 to 5 days	33 percent reduction in total weekly mileage avoid speed work, long runs, or weight lifting during the 3 days prior to the race also avoid long intervals during first half of week, prior to your "official" taper
marathon	3 weeks	see chapter 15

22, dropping your mileage in the second half of the week from, say, 15 to 10. You should also avoid hard workouts (including long runs or speed workouts) during the half-week before the race.

For a longer race, such as a half-marathon, cut your week-before mileage by about 33 percent, primarily during the 4 days before the event. Avoid extremely taxing workouts, such as long intervals, during the entire week before the event.

Other useful tips for tapering:

- Take a full rest day 2 days before the race. Since you're probably not running 7 days a week anyway, this is just a matter of arranging your schedule to put a rest day at the proper time.
- Do a light run on the day before race day. Many people are less nervous, and their bodies feel looser, if they jog 2 or 3 miles on the day before they race.
- Don't lift weights, even with the upper body, during the 3 days before the race.

Don't enter the race tired. In the days beforehand, take it easy rather than trying to squeeze in even a small amount of extra training.

REGISTRATION AND PACKET PICKUP

Most races allow either advance or race-day registration. Advance registration is done by mail, in person at cooperating running stores, or by credit card on the Internet. Race-day registration is done on site, starting 90 minutes or so before the race.

Advance registration is cheaper and helps assure that races with participant limits won't fill without you. But the fee is nonrefundable. If you can't run, don't let a friend take your place, especially if the friend isn't in your age group. That messes up the age-group standings, and if your 30-year-old friend posts a good time in your 50-year-old age group, it can deprive someone else of an award. Similarly, make sure to put your correct age on the application form (legibly). Race directors say that it's amazing how many people apparently can't remember their exact ages—a real bane for officials trying to figure out age-group standings.

Even if you register in advance, you still need to pick up your race packet, which contains your race number and sometimes a collection of sample products, coupons, and informational material such as a map of the course. Electronic timing chips, if any, may be included in the packet or distributed separately; make sure you have one before leaving the packet-pickup area.

Most races distribute packets on race day, but really big events may encourage (or require) you to come to a prerace exposition to reduce race-day congestion.

Races that permit race-day registration usually handle it at a separate table from preregistered runners' packet-pickup. Ironically, the race-day registration line is often the short one.

THE NIGHT BEFORE THE RACE

Obviously, the night before a race isn't a great time to take in a midnight movie. Most races start early in the morning, so you want to get to bed early. Hitting a bar is also a bad idea. Just as airline pilots aren't allowed to fly within 10 hours of taking a drink, many experienced runners can feel the performance-damping effects of a single drink the morning after. One beer won't have much impact, but two may leave you feeling sluggish. Alcohol also dehydrates you, so be particularly careful about drinking on the night before a warm-weather race.

The degree to which you want to limit your prerace activities depends on how much you care about the race. That late-night movie or second beer isn't likely to keep you from crossing the finish line, but it may slow you down enough to preclude a PR.

Eating Right

The prerace dinner is a major ritual among many racers, who talk of the importance of *carbohydrate loading* with high-starch, low-fat dinners such as pasta or potatoes. The idea is that you want to boost the muscles' glycogen supply as high as possible so that you have enough fuel for the race.

You're not at risk of completely running out of glycogen in most races; a trained runner's body has enough stored glycogen to go about 20 miles. But even in a 5K your body feels better—and runs faster—when your fuel stores are nicely

> **Carbohydrate loading on the evening before a race needn't mean stuffing yourself with high-starch foods. A modest plate of spaghetti or the equivalent should do the trick nicely.**

topped off. This may have something to do with how fast your body can access that energy.

For that reason, it's possible to run a terrible 5K simply by not watching your nutrition ahead of time. Even if you desperately want to lose weight, it's best to suspend the diet on the night before the race. That doesn't mean you need to pig out—just that you need to eat a reasonably large meal, high in the complex carbohydrates found in such foods as spaghetti, bread, or potatoes. Protein is also OK, but there should be at least 100 grams of carbohydrates (400 calories) in your prerace meal—equivalent to 4 slices of bread, 4 ounces of spaghetti, or one very large potato.

Also important is to eat foods that you're used to; experiments can lead to abdominal woes under the stress of racing. Eat fairly late in the evening or schedule a late-night snack so you don't deplete overnight.

> **Have a race plan firmly in mind before the start.**
> **It needn't be any more complicated, though,**
> **than knowing your target per-mile pace.**

Sleeping Right

As a parent, I'm always preaching to my kids the value of a good night's sleep before any important activity. If you can get it, that's great. But prerace jitters often lead to restlessness, and there are few things more hopeless than attempting to force yourself to sleep when you're not ready.

Go to bed early the night before the race if you actually think it might accomplish something. Otherwise, relax, read a book, talk to your family, or engage in your normal evening routine until you're tired enough to do something other than toss, turn, and fret. Don't try a sleep medication unless you've used it regularly; it might leave you groggy in the morning. If insomnia strikes, remember: it's the sleep you get *two* nights before the race that really matters. As long as you're decently rested going into the 24 hours before the race, losing sleep the night before won't make much difference.

12

RACE DAY

RUNNING YOUR BEST race means knowing exactly what to do on the big day and giving yourself time to do it without panic. To some extent, what you'll need to do on race day depends on how serious you are about the race. We'll talk later about how often you can race at maximum effort. If you're running at less than maximum effort for the pleasure of a good pace or distance workout with lots of company, your race-day preparations needn't be all that meticulous. But if you're after your best-possible performance, your actions should be carefully orchestrated.

(PHOTODISK/GETTY IMAGES)

RISE AND SHINE

Your first race-day decision comes the night before, when you choose what time your alarm should go off. For most races, that decision will be determined by how long it takes to eat breakfast and get to the race start with time to find a parking place, check in, and do an unhurried warm-up. Most runners are last-minute people; if you arrive at the start an hour in advance you'll probably have easy parking, no crowds, and plenty of time to check in without panic.

Don't cut it too close in an attempt to get a few more minutes of sleep. Going a little short on sleep the night before the race won't hurt you as long as you've been well rested during the preceding week. Missing the start *will* hurt you badly—and even if you make it on time, dashing around in a panic trying to get to the race will undercut your performance.

Even if the race starts right outside your door (or you've traveled to a hotel within walking distance of the start), don't sleep in until the last moment. Your body temperature drops while you're asleep, and it takes about an hour and a half to two hours for it to come up to speed in the morning. You don't want to start racing before it does.

Make sure that you've set a reliable alarm to get you up. If you're at home, you know what that is. But if you've spent hundreds of dollars traveling to the start, don't trust the hotel alarm clock or wake-up call. Bring a travel alarm, set your watch alarm, or use the alarm on a cell phone as a backup.

Clothing

Many runners lay out their race-day clothing the night before. You may not know exactly what you're going to wear until you see the morning weather forecast, but you can make sure that you have clothing set aside to cover all possibilities. Some people maintain permanently stocked race bags containing a supply of easy-to-forget items such as sweatbands, sunscreen (for the postrace celebration, when the sun may be high in the sky), moleskin and scissors, petroleum jelly, ibuprofen (hopefully you won't need it!), water, energy gels (see pages 205–6), a fanny pack or race belt (see pages 205–6), and other potential necessities.

Dress for the race at home or your hotel room; very, very few races provide changing rooms. If the morning is chilly, pull a jacket and loose-fitting sweat pants over your running attire. Many races have places to check this gear at the start, typically by putting it in a plastic bag with your registration number written on the outside (make sure the number is legible and correct). Otherwise, you can leave your warm-ups in your car or trust to the honesty of your fellow runners by tossing a gym bag somewhere out of the way.

Running in the pack in large races, Rick has observed another alternative for a chilly start: wear old or otherwise disposable warm-up attire that you wouldn't mind losing. The 45,000-runner Lilac Bloomsday Run, in Spokane, Washington, begins with hundreds of runners tossing sweatshirts onto the sidewalks. Volunteers collect the clothing and donate what's usable to homeless shelters. It's become a Bloomsday tradition. At other races you may need to retrieve throwaway sweats so they don't become just that much more urban litter—but if a street person beats you to them, you've done someone a favor. If you don't have anything raggedy enough to discard, try wearing a plastic garbage bag. Just punch head and arm holes through it and pull it on over your race clothes, ripping it away just before the starter's horn, or even a few minutes into the race. Garbage bags are particularly popular at early-starting fall marathons where dawn temperatures can hover around freezing but sunrise will quickly warm the course into the 50s or 60s. Some runners also find them to be reasonably good protection against cool drizzle.

Breakfast

Some runners are tempted to skip breakfast. They fear that having anything in their stomachs will slow them down, and might produce a catastrophic bellyache or side stitch. I agree that even a bagel would be a mistake 60 minutes before a race. And I wouldn't want to eat a plate of greasy sausage, eggs, and hash browns *anytime* on race day. But think about how your energy dips toward lunchtime if you skip breakfast on a business day. Do you want to feel like that during a race, when you're calling on all the energy you have?

> **Don't skip breakfast the morning of a race, even if all you eat is a packet of carbohydrate gel. But make sure that what you eat is easily digestible before the race starts.**

I usually ate breakfast 2 to 4 hours ahead of an event. How much I ate depended partly on the distance of the race, but mostly on how far in advance I was willing to get up. On the morning of my Boston Marathon win, for example, I ate a substantial stack of pancakes—but did so 4 hours before the start.

To a large extent, what you should do will be governed by the tolerances of your own body, learned by trial and error on training runs. Ideally, you should eat a light meal, no more than 400 to 500 calories, about 3 hours before the start. It should be heavy in complex carbohydrates and light in fat and protein, which digest more slowly. Fruit, oatmeal (without milk), breads—all of these are good. Drink plenty of water, even if it sends you to the toilet several times before the start.

If you absolutely *can't* get yourself up in time to have breakfast 3 hours before the event, eat something anyway but keep it light: a glass of orange juice and/or a banana should be OK 2 hours before the race. Better might be to mix up a drink from one of the many carbohydrate energy powders now on the market or to eat a packet of carbohydrate gel (see pages 205–6). These athletic foods are designed to clear your digestive tract quickly, and should be no problem an hour before the race—in fact, they're intended to be eaten *during* the race. You'll find them at running or triathlon stores.

The longer the race, the more important it is to eat breakfast. Skipping the meal probably won't hurt you much in a 5K, but it could be a major detriment in a marathon. Even in the 5K, if you're not going to have breakfast, make sure you have a late-night snack. But there's really no reason for not getting something into your system on race day, even if it's just a gel or Gatorade.

> **A cup or two of coffee will not only wake you up for the start, but it will also speed you up in the race.**

Caffeine

In addition to breakfast you can also have your morning cup of tea or coffee. These no-calorie beverages don't linger in your digestive tract any longer than water—and you certainly don't want to complicate your race with a debilitating caffeine-withdrawal headache.

Even people who don't normally drink coffee might consider having a couple of cups the morning of the race. Caffeine has been proven to give you extra energy—so much so, in fact, that caffeine pills (about the equivalent of eight cups of coffee) have been banned in top-level competition.

Caffeine does have one major downside. It's a diuretic, forcing you to urinate not only the liquid in your coffee, but additional water as well. Compensate by drinking extra water before you run, and resign yourself to a couple of last-minute trips through the toilet line. Be particularly careful about using caffeine in hot-weather races, where dehydration is a potentially dangerous risk.

Evening Races

The vast majority of races are held in the morning, seldom later than 10 A.M., and generally earlier. But a few are held at dusk, or even on special midnights, such as New Year's Eve.

It's hard to time your eating around such events. Try to arrange your day so you haven't eaten a major meal within 4 hours of the start—and don't eat any enormous meals that will still be with you hours later. You're better off to eat a normal lunch and then snack a few hours before the race than to try to pack it all in at lunch.

Luckily, most evening events are short. That means you probably won't feel unduly weak if you skip dinner, particularly if you eat a prerace banana, glass of juice, bagel, energy powder, or gel—something similar to the light breakfast you'd eat before a similar-length morning event. In evening races it's easier to do yourself harm by eating too much, too close to race start, than by not eating enough.

> **Plan to arrive at your race about an hour before the start.**

WARMING UP

Once you've reached the start and gone through the necessary check-in proce-dures, it's time to begin warming up. For the final 45 minutes before the race start, you should always be stretching or moving—although long toilet lines may interfere with this in some races.

The purpose of warming up is to get your body ready to move at race pace. This reduces the risk of pulling a muscle, keeps you from feeling stiff, sluggish, and un-fit for the first mile, and saves valuable seconds in the opening portion of the race. Most recreational racers do very little warm-up, so you'll also get a step up on your competitors if you're better warmed up than they are. Warm-up may also stave off side stitches at the start; some sports physiologists believe that race-day stitches are often brought on by instantly jumping from a standstill to an all-out effort.

Begin with 5 or 10 minutes of stretching (more if time permits), then take a warm-up run. Most recreational racers who warm up at all (and most do nothing but stretch) run only half to three-quarters of a mile, under the illusion that they shouldn't be spending energy so soon before the race. But the warm-up run is ac-tually more important than the stretching—and if you're properly trained for the race, you're trained to warm up properly, too. I typically ran 3 or 4 miles, but there's not much reason for most runners to go beyond 2 miles.

If you're racing mostly for the challenge of going the distance, of course you can't afford to add even 2 miles to your effort. Instead, you'll have to save the bulk of your warm-up for the first mile of the race. Remember, though, that for opti-mum prerace stretching you need to run enough beforehand to start sweating. If you skimp on the warm-up, you really should go slowly on that first mile of the race.

> **Plan a 2-mile warm-up routine before a race. Stretch, too.
> Then do your best to keep limber and warmed up
> while in line for the start.**

If you're taking a full warm-up, begin with a slow jog, then gradually speed up until, somewhere between three-quarters of a mile and a mile, you reach your normal training pace. That's where most racers who do any warm-up at all quit. But it's only the first part of an optimum routine. Now it's time to add a few gentle bursts of speed, culminating at race pace, so your body's prepared for what's going to be expected of it.

The best way to do this is with a series of 100-yard *strides*. These aren't sprints, and they're not like intervals, either, where you jump out rapidly at a fast pace. Starting from a jog, accelerate smoothly until you hit a target pace, hold it for about 100 yards (about 27 seconds at an 8:00 pace), then drop back to a slow jog for an-other 100 yards. Repeat this at ever-increasing paces until, after 8 or 10 repetitions, your last 100-yard stride is at race pace or slightly faster. Thus, if your goal is to

WALLETS AND CAR KEYS

Elite runners usually don't have much problem with mundane logistical issues such as what to do with their car keys. If nothing else, race officials will generally bend over backward to help. But unless you as a recreational racer have a very supportive nonrunning friend or spouse attending the race as a cheering section, you're going to have to deal with these matters on your own.

In training, you can carry important personal items in a small fanny pack, but in a race, you're not going to want the weight bouncing against your hip. Most racers just leave their wallets in their cars and hope for the best. Hide your valuables out of sight in the car before you reach the start, in case there's an enterprising thief hanging around the parking lot watching what people are hiding.

Rick puts his car key in the pocket of his checked warm-ups. Other runners hide them on or near their cars, possibly in a magnetic key case that secures beneath the vehicle. Beware, though, that car thieves long ago figured out all the good hiding places.

run a 7:00 pace, your first stride might be at an 8:00 pace—not much faster than the pace you reached at the end of your first mile of warm-up. Your next one might be at a 7:50 pace, then 7:40, 7:30, 7:20, 7:10, 7:00, and possibly 6:50. It won't be that precise, of course, unless you have an extremely well-developed sense of pace, but interval training and prior racing experience will give you a sense of what it feels like to do a gradual speedup across the range between your endurance-training pace and race pace. You won't do yourself much harm if your pacing is a bit off; just don't exhaust yourself with a series of all-out sprints.

WARM UP TO SPEED UP

A proper warm-up will not only help you run more comfortably and with less injury risk, but it will also speed you up. The only race that I lost in my senior year of high school came when I nearly missed the start of an indoor track meet. I dashed into the arena only 2 minutes before my 1,000-yard event was due to begin, with barely enough time to strip off my sweats and stuff my feet into my racing shoes. What warm-up I had was limited to the panicked dash from the parking lot to the track. I ran 2:27 and took second place, a major upset for the boy who beat me.

The next week, I got to the start with plenty of time for a warm-up, and ran the same distance in 2:20. The difference may not sound like a lot, but the 2:20 was a new league record, and it's 5 percent faster than 2:27.

In a 10K or even a 5K, failing to warm up is unlikely to slow you down by 5 percent all the way—eventually, the race itself will warm you up. But for the first mile or so, you're either going to be sluggish or working harder than necessary to drive your overly tight muscles. If for you, like me, the difference amounts to about a 5 percent energy loss, the missed warm-up could easily cost you 20 or 30 seconds.

PRERACE CHECKLIST

TIME BEFORE START (HOURS AND MINUTES)	RECOMMENDED ACTIVITY
3:00	Optimum time for 400- to 500-calorie breakfast. Drink water, too.
2:00	Latest wake-up time; latest time for light breakfast (banana, juice); if you've not already done so, start drinking fluids.
1:00	Arrive at race start; check in or register if not already done (allow extra time in large races); visit toilets (no lines this early); optimum time for eating energy gel or powder drink if you skipped a real breakfast; continue drinking fluids.
0:45	Begin prerace stretching.
0:35[1]	Start warm-up jog, followed by strides.
0:20	Return to race start; stretch again; last visit to toilets.
0:10	Shed warm-up clothes; do 2 or 3 more strides.
0:05	Line up for start (in large races, this may have to be done substantially earlier); continue stretching, keep moving.

[1] The optimum time for starting your warm-up run depends on your pace. Slower runners might need to start both this and their stretching a few minutes earlier.

Nor must the distance be all that precise; 75-yard strides probably do you as much good as the 100-yard variety. The goal is simply to get yourself breathing and moving comfortably at race pace, before you have to do it in competition.

Eight 100-yard strides with 100-yard recoveries is about a mile, so your warm-up has now totaled 2 miles. For a long race, you'll do a little less—partly because you're conserving energy for the race, and partly because it takes fewer strides to reach the slower pace of the longer event.

FEEL SLUGGISH?

Don't worry if you feel sluggish during your prerace warm-up. Everyone does. My theory is that the body knows the race is coming and tries to conserve energy. Sometimes I actually felt sleepy during the hour before the start, even though I'd been nervous for days beforehand. You may feel both jittery and sluggish at the same time—but don't worry, the energy will be there when you need it.

Finish your warm-up run back near the race start, for another 5 or 10 minutes of stretching. Then make your final trip through the toilet line, shed your warm-up clothing, and put in two or three more strides just before lining up for the start. Whatever you do, don't finish your warm-up 20 or 30 minutes before race start and then stand around doing nothing. It's a common mistake, and completely counterproductive. All you'll do is cool back down again, winding up worse off after the supposed warm-up than you would have been without it. Keep moving, especially if it's cool, trying to do occasional strides until as close before the race start as is possible (which may not be all that close). Similarly, if it's cold, keep your warm-up clothes on until as close to the start as possible.

THE START

Try to line up for the start about 5 minutes beforehand. Closer to the gun than that and the standing around will make you nervous (and possibly chilled). Later, and you run the risk of being cut off by a crowd, caught in a bathroom line, or otherwise relegated to the back of the pack.

In some races, particularly large ones, you'll have to line up earlier than you'd like or risk losing your place. Even elite athletes are sometimes strictly corralled, far

> **Begin the race at a pace that feels slow, even after you've cleared the herd and found some running room. Even then, you may be going too fast. Adrenaline is deceptive!**

ahead of the start. I've been in track meets where runners were confined to communal waiting rooms 45 minutes ahead of time, to ensure that we'd be on hand the moment our races were called. The first time it happened, a teammate gave me a simple piece of advice that stood me in good stead: "Don't let it get to you," he said. "Nobody likes it, but everyone's in the same boat."

However far in advance you need to line up, continue to keep moving while you're waiting for the race to get under way. Elite runners often jog back and forth along the first few yards of the course, doing low-key strides just to keep loose. In really small races you may be able to join the front runners, but in larger events (anything more than a couple hundred people), you'll lose your place if you go in search of jogging room. And if something blocks you from getting back to your starting place, you've sacrificed more time than the extra warm-up can gain. Stretch, jog in place, or do anything that works to keep yourself warm and loose, but keep near to your planned starting position.

Where to line up is often a difficult question. Theoretically, you want to line up according to your expected finishing position. If you anticipate being in the top 20 percent of the pack, 20 percent of the way back is ideal; if you anticipate being in the back 25 percent, that's where you should start (just make sure you're lining up with runners, rather than with the hundreds of walkers who form the back of the pack at many races). Really big races may give you color-coded race numbers based on information you provided on your entry form. These are your tickets to the proper sections of the start, and the rules are often strictly policed.

Other races will post signs directing you where to stand: 8:00-milers here, 10:00-milers there, etc. If there are no signs, figure that the middle of the pack (neglecting walkers) is about a 9:00 pace in a 5-mile race, a 9:30 pace in a half-marathon. Three-quarters of the way forward is about a 7:30 pace in short events and an 8:00 in a half-marathon, while three-quarters of the way back is a 10:00 to 10:30 pace, depending on race length. If the signs and the number of runners ahead or behind you don't quite jibe, go with the percentages. A lot of people tend to be overoptimistic in their assessments of how fast they'll run. Don't line up too far forward, though. That just makes the race miserable, as a seemingly end-less string of runners goes by you.

Once the horn sounds, resist the temptation to blaze out at a self-destructive speed. By the time the race begins, your adrenaline is running full-bore, then sud-denly (finally!) all that flight-or-fight hormone finds release. Your body knows what it's supposed to do: *run! chase! go!* The trouble is that it won't be giving you very ac-curate feedback for the first few minutes. A pace that feels easy will be way too fast.

Coaching high school runners, I have to drill this into them again and again. If I have a talented boy who's targeting on a 9:20 3,000-meter (a good high-school time), I'll tell him to run that first lap at a 75-second pace—exactly his race pace. But he's unlikely to hold back; instead he'll go out at 70 seconds because he feels so strong and excited. Then he runs out of gas and finishes in 9:30, rather than the 9:20 we both know he can do. The next week, I remind him, over and over: "75 sec-onds, no faster." And then the gun goes off, the adrenaline flows, and he's out again on another 70-second tear.

You'll have to fight the same thing, probably with the same initial lack of success. If the start doesn't feel *slow*, you're going too fast. If you feel like you're running your target pace, you could easily be running a minute a mile too fast. The first sign that you're going too fast may come about a quarter-mile out, when you notice that you're breathing too hard for such an easy-seeming pace. Another sign is if you're too close on the heels of racers who you know are better than you. Pay at-tention to these signals, and ratchet the speed down immediately. An overly fast quarter at the start will hurt you, but it's not as significant in a long race as it is for my high school 3,000-meter runner. If you wait for confirmation at the 1-mile split, you may well have blown the race.

If you're going to err in the first mile, try to err on the side of going too slowly. Most likely you'll still be going too quickly, but at least you'll minimize the dam-age. Keeping that first mile under control will pay enormous dividends later on.

Similarly, there's not much reason for killing yourself to pass people early on in the race. If you lined up properly, you'll be finishing more or less with the people who are near you at the start. Let the rabbits go, and be the one who runs them down later. That not only saves energy, but passing a steady stream of people in the back half of the race because you were smarter in the front half is a wonderful confidence-builder.

Be especially careful if a race starts on a substantial upgrade or downgrade. Starting too fast on an upgrade will suck energy out of you faster than doing so on the level; going too quickly on a downgrade will pound your legs, wearing out your quads. A great many people have this problem at the Boston Marathon, which begins with 10 miles of downgrades, then encounters the first of its infamous hills. A lot of racers go out too fast, pound up their legs on the descents, then tire more rapidly than expected when they hit the hills. With a downhill start, it's a fine line be-

BACK IN THE PACK

Rick has run in a race's main pack many times, sometimes in races so large that there were several thousand people ahead of him, even at his fairly fast pace. Here are his observations:

Back in the pack in a large race, you may not have to worry too much about starting too fast, at least not initially. One of the ironies of these races is that everyone's keyed up for the start, then the horn sounds . . . and not much happens. Everyone around you surges a step forward, then discovers there's nowhere to go until the people ahead begin to move. It's somewhat comical: the race has begun, the elite runners are out there somewhere, streaking ahead, but everyone in your vicinity is standing still.

Try not to fret; only the largest races will keep you standing for more than a few seconds. Soon you'll be moving at a slow walk that gradually evolves into a jog, though it may be several minutes before the pack thins enough to allow you to stretch into your normal stride.

Racing for time is difficult in events like this, but it can be done. In a longer race such as a 20K or half-marathon, in fact, the camaraderie of being part of that sea of humanity may buoy you up substantially, helping you make up a lot of time later on.

The first rule of running such races is not to worry about the time shown by the official clock. Many big races have electronic chip timing, which does not count the time you spend waiting to get to the starting line. But even in races without such advanced methods, time spent waiting for the folks ahead of you to get moving needn't count against your personal mark. Just delay starting your watch until you cross the starting line. What it reads at the finish is what you really ran, regardless of the official results.

These races will give you some difficulties in judging pace, however. Unlike the adrenaline-pumped start of a smaller race, their starts really are slow. But the adrenaline is still there, and it's likely to rear its head once the pack starts to thin. Worse, the time you clock for the first mile may mask the fact that you're speeding up. Thus, you might go through the 1-mile mark in 11:00, but be doing 7:30s by the time you finally get there. Your pace for the second mile will reveal this, but it's now taken 2 miles to get an accurate measure of your speed. In big races, it's critical to keep your speed under control, particularly in the first few minutes after the pack has thinned enough that you've finally gotten room to run.

tween working the descent to maximum benefit and beating yourself up enough to regret it later. The only solution, other than wise pacing, is to run some downgrades in training, so that you've strengthened your downhill muscles enough to prepare them for the strain.

At the elite level, the start functions a bit differently. When I was targeting on a 2:08 marathon, my ideal race would have been run at a steady 4:53 pace. But in the front of a big race, one of my main concerns was to avoid being tripped up at the start by people seeking their moment of glory by running, however briefly, with the front pack. The best defense is to sprint out at full speed—even if it wastes energy—until you've opened a large enough gap on the main body of the pack that you can drop back to your normal pace.

For most people, though, going out at your target pace is critical. Even if you're after an age-group medal, it's usually best to run your own race—and the single best way to do that is to avoid getting sucked out too fast at the start.

AFTER THE GUN

13

DISTANCE RACES, PARTICULARLY those longer than 5K, tend to have fairly well-defined beginnings, middles, and ends. We've already discussed the beginning, when you're feeling fresh and excited, and your biggest goal is to avoid running too fast. That portion of the race lasts from less than a mile (in a 5K) to several miles (in a half-marathon). Then you settle into the middle section, when you're engaged in the serious business of running but not yet approaching the finish.

SPLIT TIMES

Beginning at mile 1, and hopefully every mile thereafter, well-organized races provide *split times*, or *splits*. These are simply announcements of the elapsed time since the start of the race. The name comes from the fact that you're "splitting" the race into mile-long subunits.

Ideally, splits are provided by extroverted people with synchronized stopwatches and loud voices. But don't leave your own watch at home. In some races, splits are read by nervous teenagers with tiny voices, and you'll need your watch to figure out what they said. In other events, all the miles will be well marked, but the only volunteer you'll see will be at mile 1—or there will be volunteers at each mile but the times they're reading won't make sense because someone failed to start his or her watch at the proper time. Often, the best and most reliable way to obtain split times is with your own watch.

Use the splits to keep track not only of your overall pace, but of your mile-to-mile performance. Are you speeding up? Slowing down? Running a steady pace? Is the change in pace explainable by hills or a shift in the wind, or are you straying off your race plan in ways you need to correct before it's too late? These are the types of questions you can answer by paying close attention to split times.

Answering them, of course, requires the ability to remember your splits from one mile to the next, and the mathematical ability to do the arithmetic in your head—all while running hard. It's one reason why you may want to invest in a good racing watch that will do all this for you—but these watches only do their jobs if you can remember how to work them on the run, without accidentally pushing a wrong button. Many runners just do the arithmetic in their heads. If this sounds daunting, practice in training. The math is simplified by the fact that you know approximately what pace you'll be running.

TRACKING SPLITS FROM THE PACK

Here's Rick, with more tips on running with a large herd:

Even if the race brochure promises splits at each mile, always look for the marker at mile 1, so you know what the others will look like if they're unattended. Also, be aware that in racing parlance, "splits" can refer either to the split times or to the mile markers themselves. Unless you know for sure, presume that "marked splits" simply means that the race will have mile markers, but that nobody will be calling out the elapsed time.

In some races, half the runners never see any of the mile marks. This is particularly easy if miles are marked on the pavement rather than with roadside signs. Chalk or paint on pavement doesn't show up well from a distance, and back in the pack there may be enough runners around that you'll barely get a glimpse of each mark before running past it.

If you're having trouble locating the markers, glance at your watch occasionally, so you know when one should be drawing near. It's possible to run a decent race without the feedback of split times, but missing splits makes it very difficult to stick to your target pace.

RACE STRATEGY 101

Whatever you may have heard about tactical surges and efforts to break your competitors, experienced competitors know that you get your best performance by running an evenly paced race. Surges are simply deliberate decisions to wear yourself down a bit in the hope that you'll thereby wear down your rivals even more. If it works, you win, but you don't post quite as good a time as you would if you felt free to concentrate on running your own race.

Recreational racing usually involves racing predominantly against the clock. That means that your midrace strategy is the same as your strategy at the start: settle into your target pace as soon as you can and run the entire race as close to that pace as you can manage. If you do this perfectly, your split times will proceed like clockwork, precisely on the schedule that you worked out beforehand. In racing jargon, you're doing *even splits*. Don't attempt to "put money in the bank" by running the first half of the course more quickly than your goal; that's a formula for breakdown, later on.

If you really do have extra energy, you can speed up as the race proceeds, once you're sure you won't burn out. This is referred to as running *negative* splits (because you're subtracting time from them as you proceed). It's fun, but also a sign that your target pace was too conservative. Set a more challenging goal next time. Your fastest race usually comes at the pace you can just barely sustain. Conversely, the easiest way to achieve any given goal is generally with a constant exertion level. Stick to the goal for which you were training, and trust your training to see you through. Then, if you think you can do better, up the ante by training for a faster pace next time.

Elite runners sometimes run slightly negative splits. I ran the first half of my world record marathon, for example, in 1:04:20, and the second half in 1:03:53. Physiologically, this appears to be slightly more efficient than running the entire distance at precisely the same speed—my body was still warming up ever so slightly in the first 13 miles. But it requires extremely precise pacing—enough to distinguish the very slight (less than 2 seconds per mile) speedup that marked the second half of my race. It also requires the confidence to know that you can speed up slightly in the second half and the willingness to put that into your race plan.

FLAMEOUTS

If your split times gradually lengthen as the race proceeds, you're running positive splits— a strong indication that you either went out too fast at the start or set an unrealistic goal. Positive splits can also result from an incipient illness (such as a cold) or from starting the race unduly tired. Sometimes the slowdown is merely temporary—a bad patch lasting a mile or two—but if you started the race far too fast, the ensuing positive splits can snowball into a true disaster. Running lore is full of stories of people who undermined their races with fast starts, then compounded the error by failing to adjust soon enough. Here's Rick:

The most dramatic flame-and-die I've ever encountered involved a marathon and a friend with enough experience that he should have known better. My friend, no slouch of a road racer, hit the 20-mile mark in precisely 2 hours. But it then took him another 2 hours to finish—meaning that he'd dropped from 6:00s to a not-all-that-brisk walk.

Spectacular collapses are most common in long races, but in the final mile of 5Ks I've sped by people who somehow stayed in front of me for the first two-thirds of the race and were now running 30 to 40 seconds per mile slower than me. So don't jettison the race plan just because you're feeling frisky at the start. That can cost you a lot of time later on.

THE DICTATES OF NATURE

You can only run a constant pace, of course, if conditions are constant along the way. Hills, winds, sharp corners, heat—all of these will affect your pace, sometimes drastically. Rather than cursing, however, you can make these factors work for you, minimizing how much they slow you down, and moving up on competitors who run the course less intelligently. It's even possible to run PRs on courses that on first impression look impossible.

Hills

Many runners dread hills, often because they approach them incorrectly. They try to "attack" hills simply by "sucking it up" and attempting to charge up them like they don't exist. Instead, hills should be tests of patience, race planning, and pacing.

Your goal should be to run uphill at the same level of effort that you're using to run on the level, slowing down as much as necessary to allow this to happen. It's easier to be patient if you bear in mind the ultimate fate of everything that goes up. Except for a few nasty point-to-point courses that press resolutely in one direction, most will reward your hill-climbing efforts with an equal amount of descent; be patient enough to avoid running out of energy before you run out of hill. Practice this type of pacing in training, wearing a heart-rate monitor if you own one. If your heart rate increases more than slightly on the upgrade, you're running too hard. Similarly, you should run downhill at that same, constant level of effort.

Most racers make three major pacing errors on hills. First, they run uphill too fast, treating the hill as though it's a tough interval in a speed workout. The problem with doing this is that it requires a recovery, which slows you down by more than you gained on the surge. Secondly, the moment they can see over the crest, many runners slack off, fooled into thinking they've reached the top, even though they actually have a few feet left to climb. Finally, even experienced racers often run too slowly on the downgrade. In part it's because they went too fast uphill and need to recover. But they're also responding to an illusion caused by the speed of running downhill: they think they're working hard when actually they're just coasting.

The best way to keep from pushing too hard uphill is by slowing down so much it feels as though you're trying to rest. You won't actually rest (unless you carry the slowdown to an extreme), but dealing with the hill this way may keep you from significantly increasing your exertion level, leaving you still feeling fresh at the top.

The top is the place to start pushing. Even if you find that you ran a bit too hard on the upgrade, push through the summit anyway, and take whatever recovery you need on the downgrade. You'll be surprised by how much you can recover in 40 or 50 yards. Then push hard on the remainder of the downgrade, seeking to maintain that constant level of effort (unless the descent is so steep that you can't keep in control at full speed).

I learned all this the hard way in my junior year of high school. I was in the state cross-country championship, when I tried to break my chief rival on a 600-yard hill that started about a half-mile from the finish. Having led for the entire race, I presumed that this, the toughest part of the course, was the best place to administer the coup de grâce. I pushed hard enough that at first I thought I'd succeeded; by the top of the hill, I'd opened a 25-yard lead. But the hill drained so much energy out of me that there was no spring left to my stride. The other boy, who'd let me draw away from him on the upgrade, surged back on me, outkicking me to the finish by about a second.

I lost the race, but won a valuable lesson: namely, that running really hard uphill gives you limited returns. It's a lot like running in sand—the harder you push, the more the hill fights back. Had I used the same energy earlier on the flat, I'd probably have picked up a 50-yard lead and won the race. I see the same effect today, coaching high school kids. When we do hill repeats, the speed difference between "easy," "medium," and "hard" intervals is a lot less than it is on a track.

The best place to try to run away from people is right at the crest of the hill. Most of them, even elite runners, are over their lactic threshold, feeling the resultant "dead" legs. After that one disappointment, my strategy on hilly courses was to surge past my competitors right at the crest, when they're feeling their worst, then push hard and quickly open a gap.

> ### Don't charge the upgrades. Let the hill slow you down as much as necessary, then work the downgrade.

There are courses where other strategies might apply. In our 1982 Boston Marathon duel, Dick Beardsley's race plan, from the start, was to beat me on the hills. But Boston has 4 miles of hills, late in the course. There's a difference between attempting to open up a small gap by killing yourself on a 300-yard upgrade and in systematically burying someone on an extended series of hills. Dick's strategy didn't work—but that was because I was able to hold with him on the hills and outkick him at the finish, not because it was a bad strategy.

In general, though, the basic rule of hill racing is that it's better to go uphill a little too slowly than too fast.

RUNNING THE UPS AND DOWNS

Racing uphill, you should lean slightly into the hill—angling your whole body forward, not simply bending forward at the hips. Proper form will feel pretty natural, so you probably won't have to think much about it. You'll also be running (naturally) more up on your toes than you do on the level.

Running quickly downhill doesn't feel as natural. Your main task is to let the hill carry you forward and to avoid "putting on the brakes" if you possibly can—within the confines, of course, of not going so fast that you trip or run into something. There are hills that are simply too steep for any approach other than cautious braking.

The way to run fast downhill is by leaning forward while consciously lengthening your stride. It's the lean that scares beginners. It's very different from walking, where your instinct is to hold your body upright to keep from falling on your face. Running, you will indeed be falling forward, but as long as you stay in control, you'll be moving your legs fast enough to keep up. You'll also pound your knees and thighs less by running this way than by leaning backward in a braking motion.

For optimum downhill running, your body should be perpendicular to the ground; that is, leaning forward by exactly the slope of the hill. This not only helps gravity give you forward momentum, but it ensures that each stride carries you parallel to the pavement, rather than bouncing you jarringly up and down.

Unless you have extremely fast leg turnover, though, you won't keep up unless you lengthen your stride. As we discussed in chapter 4 on running form, you can't do this on the flats by focusing on your stride length per se. You have to work on increasing the stride's power and frequency; otherwise what you'll usually achieve is overstriding. Running downhill, though, it's not as easy to overstride, and even if it happens, overstriding isn't as bad as leaning backward and braking. On downgrades it's OK to consciously endeavor to increase your stride length.

Downhill racing isn't an art you'll perfect instantly. Practice in training, in small doses to avoid lengthy pounding on your knees. Once you get the knack, there's no real benefit from additional practice unless you need to strengthen your "downhiller" for a truly mountainous race. In hill training (as opposed to racing), you're best off to spare your knees by going gently on the downgrades.

RUNNING YOUR OWN RACE

When I'm coaching high school runners, I constantly remind them not to worry about the folks ahead of them. It's almost a mantra. "Don't worry about them," I say. "Run your own race." Rick applies a variant on the same theme:

In most races, I finish in the top 5 to 10 percent, but at the start, it usually seems as though everyone is running away from me as they surge ahead at a pace that I know I can't sustain. I ward off depression (and the urge to chase) by reminding myself that these runners fall into two groups: those who can hold that pace for the duration of the race, and those who can't. In the first case, these runners are, quite simply, out of my league. In the second case, it will be my turn to pass them later. Either way, they're irrelevant to my present plans. And experience has taught me that by running my own steady pace, I'll catch as many as half of them before the end.

How Hills Affect Speed

How much do hilly courses slow you down?—not as much as you might think.

A 1 percent upgrade (which climbs about 50 feet per mile) will slow you by about 3 percent. In round numbers, that's about 10 seconds per mile of climbing for a 5:00-miler, 15 seconds for an 8:00-miler, and 20 seconds for a 10:00-miler. A 2 percent upgrade will have twice the effect and a 3 percent upgrade will have 3 times as much, and so forth. Thus if a course has a mile of 4 percent upgrade, an 8:00-miler can expect to lose about 60 seconds climbing it. Another way to look at these numbers is in terms of the total elevation change: each 50 feet will cost that 8:00-miler 15 seconds, regardless of whether it's short and steep or long and gradual. Any grade steeper than 4 percent, incidentally, is going to feel like a mountain. The late stages of the Comrades Marathon had a pair of 6 percent upgrades, each about 2 miles long. It felt as though there was no way to slow down enough to make it up them in decent order! But on most courses, few hills are that steep, and few last much longer than a mile.

Descents speed you up, but treadmill studies indicate they give back barely more than half of what the upgrade took away. A hill that robs you of 30 seconds on the climb will speed you up only by 18 seconds on the descent. Nevertheless, rolling courses can work to your advantage because running uphill, downhill, and on the flats uses slightly different muscles. This allows well-trained racers to alternately rest each set of muscles. Several world records were therefore set in the Portland, Oregon, Cascade Runoff (now defunct), despite a 2-mile, 300-foot hill in the first half of the course. The mix of grades apparently gave the racers enough variety in muscle use to let them get better performances than they would have on the flats.

> **Run the entire race at the level of effort corresponding to your target pace. Your best performance comes from maintaining a steady exertion level, or perhaps a very slight speedup. Your worst comes from going out too fast.**

Corners

The fastest possible racecourse would be perfectly straight. Corners slow you down, particularly those 180-degree loops around cones beloved by the designers of out-and-back courses.

ROUGH ESTIMATES OF THE EFFECT OF TERRAIN AND WIND ON RUNNING SPEED

Terrain or Wind	Amount of Time Lost (or Gained)[1]		
	WORLD-CLASS RACERS	8:00-MILERS	10:00-MILERS
100 feet of elevation gain	20 sec.	30 sec.	40 sec.
100 feet of elevation drop	*12 sec.*	*18 sec.*	*24 sec.*
180-degree turn	2–3 sec.	?	?
winding course (running the tangents)	<1 sec./mile	1 sec./mile (approx.)	>1 sec./mile
10 mph headwind	10–15 sec./mile	15–20 sec./mile	20–30 sec./mile
20 mph headwind[2]	30–45 sec./mile	45–60 sec./mile	60–90 sec./mile
30 mph headwind[2]	1:00 to 1:30 per mile	1:30 to 2:00 per mile	2:00 to 3:00 per mile
tailwind	*about half the effect of a comparable headwind*	*about half the effect of a comparable headwind*	*about half the effect of a comparable headwind*

[1] Italics indicate time gained. All numbers are approximate. Individual runners vary.
[2] Calculated from data presented in Tim Noakes's *Lore of Running* (3rd edition).

Twists and turns, however, add interest and prevent the monotony of an endless straightaway. And even the worst pretzel of a course only costs you a few seconds if you run wisely.

The best way to run bends depend on their sharpness. On gentle turns, run the shortest reasonable route (don't run into a gutter or risk getting hit by a car just to save a few feet). If the course runs a series of S-curves, straighten them out by angling from one side to the other. Racers call this *running the tangents*, and it can save several strides per curve. Don't worry; this isn't cheating. Racecourses are measured under the assumption that runners always take the easy route.

Swing a bit wider on sharp turns. Otherwise you have to slow down to make the turn, costing more time and energy than you'd save by running the shortest distance. I've gained as much as 10 or 15 yards on runners who tried to cut corners too tightly. (But slow down anyway on turns with steel grates, railroad tracks, wet pavement, or other slippery-looking surfaces that could take your legs out from under you.)

Swing even wider when doing a 180-degree turn around a cone. How wide depends on your speed; at 4:30s, I usually kept about 8 to 10 feet away. Circling right next to the cone, as most runners do, forces you to slow almost to a walk, then start up again. That costs you time, throws off your sense of pace, and breaks your rhythm. People who try it always lose ground on those who swing wider.

Nobody's really sure how much time you lose circling corners and cones. Based on the finishing times I once observed in an elite mile run on an out-and-back course, it appeared that a 180-degree turnaround cost an elite miler about 2 or 3 seconds. Slower runners might lose more—but that's just a guess.

Not running the tangents probably also costs you 2 or 3 seconds per mile, but again, this is a guess. If you were to swing wide by a full lane-width, for example, you'd lose about 8 yards on a 90-degree bend (2 seconds at an 8:00 pace). Even if there aren't many bends that sharp, sloppy running on gentler curves can add up. When we were writing this book, Rick ran a winding 15K and noted that more than 90 percent of his competitors made no effort to run the tangents on any bend less than 90 degrees. He figures that they *had* to be losing 10 to 20 yards per mile.

In competitive situations, you can work the curves to even greater advantage by passing runners who aren't running them wisely. If you shoot by on the inside,

---

Running the fastest route around bends and corners can easily save you 2 or 3 seconds per mile—maybe more on extremely winding courses.

---

accelerating as you go, it's possible to quickly open a 2-second gap on your competitor. If the other runner's struggling, that may be enough distance to break the psychological "rubber band" that feeds emotional energy between runners in a pack, allowing you to break away as the other runner falls behind, discouraged. Such tactics, of course, are more likely to be of interest to elite runners seeking to demoralize their opponents than to recreational runners seeking PRs, but if surging past fellow runners gives you a psychological boost, this is a good way to do it.

Wind

A 10-mile-per-hour headwind slows you down about as much as a 1 percent upgrade—about 10 to 15 seconds per mile for world-class athletes, more for the average racer. Worse, the effect isn't linear, but goes up exponentially with wind speed. That means that a 20- or 30-mile-per-hour wind feels like it's just about stopped you in your tracks. Tailwinds, on the other hand, can scoot you along fast enough to make it very difficult to decide whether you're going the right pace. At the same time, the benefit of a tailwind is probably no more than half the time-cost of a comparable headwind. Thus, windy out-and-back courses are slow because the two legs don't compensate for each other. Crosswinds can also slow you down, although not as much.

The best way to combat a headwind is to tuck in behind someone else—preferably some big (but fast) bruiser built like a Mack truck. A more sociable solution is to share windbreaking duties with other runners, rotating leads every few hundred yards, like bicyclists riding in a pack. Top runners sometimes do this, although in cutthroat races there can be some nasty verbal exchanges when someone won't take a turn on lead. Following all the way isn't against the rules—just not appreciated by the folks who do the work.

Heat and Cold

Hot weather slows everyone down, although some runners suffer more than others. Anytime the day's over 70 degrees, expect a drop in performance. How much of a drop you'll experience, though, is hard to predict. A day that might slow one runner down by 20 or 30 seconds a mile might have a much smaller effect on another.

Racing, you'll generate more body heat than in training, so the warmer it is, the more careful you need to be to stay hydrated and avoid heat injuries. Feeling chilled on a hot day is a particularly dangerous sign, indicating possible heat stroke. If you feel chilled, forget the race, drink all the water you can find, and seek medical attention immediately.

Cold weather isn't as dangerous unless it's so cold there's a risk of frostbite or hypothermia. But racing in tights or rain gear will slow you down a bit, and chilly conditions increase the risk of pulling a muscle. Warm up carefully, dress appropriately, and remember that the upwind legs of the race will feel a lot chillier than the downwind legs. On the other hand, remember that when racing, you'll feel warmer than when training, so don't wear so much clothing that you're sweltering by mile 1.

FINE-TUNING YOUR PACE

In theory, if you were to race at a perfectly constant exertion level, you'd automatically run as close to even splits as the terrain permits. In practice, you need to use the clock to fine-tune your exertion level whenever you get a chance.

When I was racing on the track, I often ran as many as eight successive laps (3,200 meters) without varying my pace by more than half a second per lap. It helped, of course that I was getting feedback every 400 meters, but this type of precision pacing was possible only because I could read my exertion level well enough to feel the difference between a 66-second lap and a 66.5-second lap. On the roads, I could generally get within 5 seconds of target pace for my first mile, after which I could hit subsequent (flat) miles within 1 second of target.

You're unlikely to be able to fine-tune that exactly, but you should try to be as precise as you can. If your goal is to run a 7:20 pace, don't accept a 7:30 mile as "good enough"—unless, of course, you've been going uphill or upwind and expect to get the lost seconds back, later on. Rather, now is the time to take corrective action, before 10 lost seconds turn into 20, then 30, 40, and more.

If you've lost more than 5 or 10 seconds, don't try to make them all up in a single mile. I've seen elite runners make this mistake in track races where they get tripped up and fall. Those who panic and sprint back into the pack within a lap almost always falter later on. The smart ones catch back up gradually over the course of 2 or 3 laps. The same applies in making up for lost time in road racing. Huge changes in energy expenditure are a mistake. Smaller changes allow you to get back on pace and stay there.

If you attempt to pick up your pace and nothing much happens, don't get discouraged and quit. Maybe there's a reason, such as a very gradual upgrade that you failed to notice. If so, you'll get some or all of the lost time back later, if you're patient.

Reading Your Fatigue Level

As you gain experience, you'll become better at judging whether a level of effort feels sustainable for the remainder of the race. Early in the race, this is rarely an issue. In the first few miles of marathons, for example, racers are always looking at their watches and adjusting their paces if they missed their targets. At that time, everyone feels fresh, and getting off pace simply means that you miscalculated your exertion level and need to either pick it up or slow down—easy to do, early in the race. Later on, though, runners who've dropped off pace may choose not to take corrective action because they're not sure they can speed up and hold the pace all the way to the finish.

Most of the time, you should simply run your chosen pace and trust in your training. But experience will teach you what exertion levels you can or can't hold through the final miles. Your training workouts will also help: if you're working hard, but have sustained equally tough workouts, then you know you can keep going in the race. If you're working as hard as you've ever done in a workout, then trying to pick up the pace is probably a bad idea.

Precision pacing takes practice. Also, it gets easier as you learn to race at ever-higher exertion levels, when even small differences in pace can feel enormous. An experienced, well-prepared racer might be able to run quite comfortably at a 7:00 pace, for example, while a 6:52 might leave her gasping for breath. The closer you push to your body's maximum, the more accurate your sense of pace will become.

And the more experience and training you gain, the closer to maximum effort you'll be racing.

Concentration

Keeping on pace requires concentration. If you "zone out," or deliberately distract yourself with a personal stereo, no matter how inspiring the music, you'll almost certainly slow down as your body tries to settle into a less intense, jogging-

---

WHEN A MILE IS NOT A MILE

You'll undoubtedly run in some large races with prize money and carefully measured courses on which any record will be official; but you may also be drawn to races that are a bit more haphazard in their organization—and sometimes, unfortunately, in the accuracy of their splits. Rick has run more than his share of such events:

Uncertified courses can be very accurately measured—but sometimes they're not. If a split time seems absurdly fast or slow, something's probably wrong with the course, and adjusting your pace will be a mistake. If you're lucky, someone simply placed a mile marker in the wrong place, and the next will be back on schedule. Otherwise, you're best off to pace yourself according to your fatigue level and ignore the splits. The best competitive finish I've ever had came in a race in which remeasurement proved each mile to be nearly 100 yards long. At the first split, other runners tried to adjust to the mile paces they were used to running, and they burned out before the end. I knew I couldn't sustain a faster pace, so I kept going at the same effort level, catching most of the others a few miles later.

Conversely, there are courses on which you know you can't be running that fast. Suspect a short course if everyone runs a PR. I once did a so-called 5K sponsored by some very nice people who obviously weren't runners. When I finished a minute faster than I should have, I asked how they'd measured the course. The answer: with a car odometer—an extremely inaccurate method. (A much better way is with a carefully calibrated bicycle odometer.) The sad thing about such courses is that if you don't figure out what happened, you can spend months vainly trying to replicate or better that false PR.

Another time, a friend and I hit the opposite problem with a course we later dubbed the Twilight Zone run because it felt as though it belonged in the surreal realm of the classic TV show. My buddy and I were in the habit of driving to small towns for races associated with local festivals—lots of fun, but often with no chance to preview the course. This time, we ran what was billed as a 20K (about 12.4 miles) that started in town and circled through woodlands to finish beneath the red-brick steeple of a historic church. At the 12-mile mark, I started to pick up the pace for the finish, only to pop out of the woods, with no church steeple in sight. Ten or 15 minutes later, we crawled to the finish, having run at least 14 miles.

Run enough small-scale races and you'll eventually hit a few like this. Their only redeeming features are that everyone's in the same boat, your finishing time is meaningless but the competitive standings are not, and they make really good stories for your friends.

---

style pace. When you wake up at the next split, you'll be stunned to discover that 10 seconds, 20 seconds, 30 seconds, or more have somehow added themselves to your pace.

Stay focused by thinking about what you need to do in the race. My primary goal was to concentrate on staying relaxed. That sounds self-contradictory, but for me, racing involved focusing on making the effort feel as easy as possible while still keeping up the necessary intensity.

You also need to concentrate on how it feels to be running your target pace, so that you don't inadvertently speed up or slow down. Pay attention to running wisely through hills, corners, and headwinds, and watch for lapses in running form, particularly late in the race when you're getting tired. If you find your pace slipping, review the tips in chapter 4 on running form. Is your arm motion getting erratic? Are you wasting energy by clenching up? Leaning too far forward? Overstriding? Any of these can simultaneously slow you down and increase your fatigue.

HYDRATION

Time was when athletes who drank water during sporting events were considered wimps. High-school football players were told they would cramp up if they drank during the game, and as recently as the 1960s, marathoners weren't allowed to drink before mile 7.

Sports drinks and water are about equally effective in short races.

Times have changed. Today, football players guzzle Gatorade on the sidelines and elite runners seek ever more sophisticated ways to stay hydrated. Even in a 5K race it will often behoove you to snag a cup of water.

Racing performance will start to be affected when dehydration has dropped your weight by as little as 2 percent. At 4 percent, it's more like a train wreck. That means that a 150-pound athlete who loses more than 3 pounds will begin to show the effects—and you can sweat off 3 pounds in as little as half an hour of hot-weather racing.

Nobody can drink enough to keep up with that rate of fluid loss. Racing, your stomach can only absorb about 2 to 4 cups of water per hour. If you drink more, it will just slosh around uncomfortably, waiting to give you a side stitch. That's why people like me, who sweat a lot, are doomed in hot-weather races. In the 1984 Olympic Marathon, on an 80-degree day in Los Angeles, I drank a quart of water within 2 minutes of the start, and drank more during the race than anyone else I knew of. But I still dropped 12 pounds—a full 8 percent of my starting weight. Given what I was drinking, that meant I was losing something better than 3 quarts an hour—far faster than my body could rehydrate.

The only way to combat this problem is to be well-hydrated at the start, particularly if it's a hot day. Don't assume that this will happen automatically. People collapse from dehydration simply by walking around on hot days—something that can only occur if they've been substantially dehydrated for several hours. Drink a lot of water the night before the race. (Beer doesn't count; alcohol is a diuretic that dehydrates you by forcing you to urinate out more liquid than you take in.) Drink more water in the morning. Remember that most Americans don't drink enough and are chronically a bit dehydrated. If that's you, you need to make up for it before the race.

In general, your bladder will provide the best test of whether you're properly hydrated; you've probably done the job if you're needing the bathroom about once an hour before race start and if your urine is so dilute it's nearly colorless. This test won't always work, though, if you're taking diuretic medicines, consuming a lot of caffeine, or have been drinking alcoholic beverages. Cold weather and nervousness are also natural diuretics but they're not as likely to produce dangerous dehydration.

Ultramarathoners, triathletes, and a few elite marathoners sometimes attempt to spike their fluid levels with a new crop of sports drinks containing glycerol. This thick, syrupy substance, when consumed in the day or two before the race, causes you to retain water, boosting your stores by about 2 percent. The extra weight slows you down a bit in the first few miles but pays for itself later, when you start drawing on that extra hydration. As with any food or drink, don't use it without testing it in training; there are reports that it might cause diarrhea in some people.

Racing in hot weather, drink at every opportunity. Even though there's no chance of keeping up with the rate at which you'll be sweating, you can at least stave off the decline. Heat slows everyone down, but some people, like me, are more affected than others. Rick, on the other hand, is a desert rat who runs his competitive best at temperatures that are frankly dangerous for most people. Racing experience will teach you where you lie along this continuum, but here are a few general tips for water consumption:

- Drink before you feel thirsty. Thirst comes on slowly; by the time you feel it, you're already in substantial water deficit.
- Drink even if you're a hot-weather aficionado who's already well heat-acclimated. What keeps such people going when the temperature soars isn't that they can run without water; it's just that their bodies are unusually efficient at using that water. If they get dehydrated, they'll collapse just like the rest of us.
- Plan ahead. It takes about 20 minutes to absorb a drink of water, so the water you drink now is the water you'll be using 2 or 3 miles later.
- Take advantage of water stations even in a short race, a 5K or 8K. Particularly in the 8K, the water you drink early in the race will help you in the second half of the race. Even in the 5K, it may get into your system in time to give you a boost at the end, especially if you weren't perfectly hydrated at the start. At a minimum, it will help speed your recovery after the finish.

That said, I never bothered to drink during cool races of 10K or less (with "cool" defined as anything under 60 degrees). But you should definitely be hitting all the water stations in a half-marathon or marathon, even if the temperature is distinctly chilly.

EACH CUP COUNTS

Dehydration will begin affecting your performance by the time your body weight has dropped 2 percent—about the equivalent of 1½ quarts of water for the average male racer, and as little as a quart for petite women.

Sports Drinks

Many races give you a choice between water and sports drinks. Pick water unless you've tested the sports drink in training. Also, make sure the drink offered by the race is mixed to the right proportion. Sports drinks contain sugar, and if there's too much of it they will draw water into your gut by osmosis. That not only delays the process of hydration, but it can have unpleasant gastric consequences. (The extra sugar is put in some of these drinks to make them more palatable as snack beverages for nonathletes.) Gatorade needs to be diluted with water to half its normal strength for drinking on the run. Drinks designed specifically for runners may not need dilution.

The sugar in sports drinks can be useful in long races where you've dipped deeply into your glycogen reserves. These drinks also contain electrolytes intended to replace chemicals lost in your sweat. But for any race that takes less than an hour, you won't deplete either your glycogen or your electrolytes enough for such drinks to have much effect.

For this reason, relatively few short races provide anything other than water. If they do, there's no reason not to accept it. Just make sure you know how the contents of that cup were prepared before you drink it. Large races are usually careful to mix these drinks to the right proportions, but if in doubt, you can shout your questions to the aid station volunteers, who are usually the people who do the mixing.

Drinking on the Fly

Drinking on the run takes practice. Prior to my first marathon, my coach set up a table next to a track so I could learn to snag a beverage and drink it on the way by. You can do the same with a picnic table, the tailgate of a pickup truck, or the help of a friend. Try it at just slightly faster than race pace; if you can master that, drinking in the race will be easy.

Don't try to drink the whole cup in one big gulp. You'll probably gag and spew it back out. Instead, take small sips, carrying the cup with you until you've finished. That way you never have to try to hold your breath to swallow, which is one of the things that gets you in trouble. Eventually you can learn to sip a full

Drinking on the run is an art. Stop and walk if you haven't mastered it. (VERA JAGENDORF)

8 ounces in 30 seconds or less—about 100 yards. But if you're having trouble, it's better to just cut your pace however much is necessary to get that drink inside you. It'll pay dividends later. When he won his first Boston Marathon, Bill Rodgers shocked everyone by coming to a full stop at several aid stations. It cost him a few seconds each time, but ensured that he always got a good drink.

In Bill's day, even elite runners used paper cups, and sloshing away half of the contents before you could drink it was always a threat if you didn't slow down. Today's elite runners use no-spill squeeze bottles, but you, like Bill, will be drinking from paper cups. Slow down enough to make sure you can handle the cup without spilling. At worst, that might cost you 5 seconds per aid station, in exchange for which you get a full cup of water. Do that 5 times in a half-marathon and you can easily save a lot more than 25 seconds, simply by being better hydrated late in the race.

Sponges and Sprays

Race photographers love dramatic shots of runners dumping water over their heads. There's no harm in doing this with water you never plan to drink. But if you can get it down, the water in that cup will do a lot more good *in* you than *on* you.

Sponges and sprays are equally inferior to drinking. Hot-weather races sometimes provide wet sponges at aid stations or set up mist systems that spray you with cool water as you run beneath them. And local residents may line the course with garden hoses, offering impromptu showers to willing (and sometimes not-so-willing) runners.

These things don't do much real good. The water may feel comfortable, but there's not enough of it to cool you more than skin deep. Your core body temperature, which is what really matters, is unaffected. A few months before the 1984

Olympics, which I knew were likely to be hot, I visited the U.S. Army's Heat Research Institute in Natick, Massachusetts. The army uses this facility to determine optimum training for desert-stationed soldiers, making it one of the world's premier heat-performance laboratories.

> **The water from sprays and hoses may feel good on a hot day, but don't expect it to cool you more than skin deep. You're better off drinking a cup of water than pouring it over your head.**

The army scientists advised me not to run under the water sprays at the Olympics. Not only do those sprays fail to cool your core body temperature, they said, but they may be counterproductive, with the shock of the cold water causing your suddenly chilled skin to shut down its sweat pores. You're still generating heat, but temporarily it can't escape, meaning that a few moments after the water spray, you wind up more overheated than you were beforehand.

Another problem is the risk of getting your shoes wet. Even if that doesn't set you up for blisters, the extra weight on your feet will slow you down. So, run under the hoses and use the sponges if you insist, but do it because it feels good, not because it will make you run faster and cooler. It won't.

GELS

The same carbohydrate sports gel that you might eat before a race can also be consumed during the event, with benefits comparable to what you would obtain from a large cup of properly mixed sports drink.

Gels typically come in 1-ounce packets; simply rip off the top and squeeze out the gel (which has about the consistency of toothpaste). The gel is viscous enough to make this a little awkward, but its consistency is perfect for eating while breathing hard, with minimal risk of inhaling it. Practice helps.

Like sports drinks, you don't have much need for gels in races lasting less than an hour, but in longer events, eat one about every 30 minutes. They usually contain about 100 calories of energy, possibly spiked with about as much caffeine as half a cup of coffee. Both should kick in a nice boost about 20 minutes after you eat them.

Sports gels are designed to be easily digested during heavy exercise, and triathletes (whose events can last upward of 12 hours) seem to fuel entire races on them with no adverse digestive effects. Nevertheless, it's wise to try them first in training, and not to switch to a new brand during the race. Eat the gel shortly before you approach an aid station, so you can wash it down with water. The aid station is also a good place to dump the empty packet without littering.

A small fanny pack will hold enough gels to see you through a marathon. For greater convenience (no zippers) and no pack flapping at your waist, buy an inexpensive race belt. These are simply elasticized nylon straps that clip around your waist. If your running store doesn't carry one, try a store catering to triathletes. Some belts have elastic loops to carry gel packets; on others you staple the packets to the belt, anchoring them carefully so they don't bounce. (Don't create a mess by puncturing a packet's food compartment with a staple.) With a race belt festooned with gel packets, you'll look really professional at the race start—and the gels are there where they're easy to grab when you want one.

GETTING OUT OF THE BOX

If you're racing with the pack, especially in a large event, your tactics will be affected by the fact that it's easy to lose time by being blocked by slower runners (referred to in racing jargon as being boxed out, boxed in, or simply boxed). Rick knows what it's like:

In large races, you may feel like a football player trying to read blocks and dodge tacklers. Some of the people ahead of you will have started so fast that they're reduced to walking by the time you catch them; others will be dashing by you from starts too far back in the pack. It's easy to get tripped up. Play it safe—and avoid big groups of slow runners—by swinging wide on corners. Here are a few other tips for keeping safe, while still picking up a few seconds per mile.

- Stick to the center of the course when possible. If you need to pass, you can then move to whichever side offers more room. Running next to the gutter, you may have to waste energy by jumping a curb onto the sidewalk. You'll also encounter more walkers.
- Beware of people who drop things, such as water bottles, and suddenly veer back to retrieve them. Try not to get too close to other runners, particularly young kids or obvious beginners.
- Plan ahead in search of running room. It's easy to get boxed behind a phalanx of slower runners.
- Glance over your shoulder before moving sideways. That way you won't be the one who causes a crash.
- Watch out for traffic islands and those white knobs sometimes used as lane dividers. If you're not paying attention, the pack can suddenly divide in front of you, like the Red Sea before Moses, as runners veer right and left, leaving you only a step or two in which to react. Some runners refer to the biggest of these knobs as "elephant turds," but even canine-sized ones can twist an ankle.
- Many races, particularly long ones, give walkers and slow runners a head start. Most of these people will be polite and keep as far out of your way as possible, but a few will walk obliviously four abreast down the center of the course. That generates some tension between walkers and runners, but it's not worth the energy to shout at each other. Remember that the walkers paid the same fee you did, and that the race brochure made it clear they would be out there. Concentrate on passing safely, and complain later to the race director if congestion is egregious.

THE FINISH AND BEYOND

OF THE THREE PARTS of a race, the toughest is the final one-third. But don't let that worry you too much. Here, more than anywhere else, is where your training will see you through.

Until the last mile, your strategy should remain unchanged: keep running at a constant effort level, working hills and corners to your advantage, trying to stay relaxed and fluid. You may have to work a bit harder to fight off lapses in concentration, and you may need to pay extra attention to maintaining good form. All of this is normal. If you weren't tiring you'd be jogging, not racing.

> **Run the last mile of a race as a gradual speedup, but save your true finishing kick for the last 200 yards.**

THE FINAL MILE

Strategy changes slightly as the race nears its end. If you've been running hard, you won't have much left for a final-mile speedup, but you will have some, and you can gain a few seconds by spending that energy wisely.

Begin picking up your pace about a mile from the finish, using your watch, if necessary, to gauge approximately how far you have left to go. Speed up gradually, and not by much until the last 200 yards. Most people start their finishing kicks too soon and run out of gas about a quarter-mile from the end. Experience will teach you what you can and can't do, but while you're learning, be conservative.

The race finish is often a big, happy party as you share stories with old acquaintances and make new friends. Here, the runners have been supplied not only with food, but also with foil blankets to keep sweaty bodies warm on a cool day. Blankets are uncommon in races shorter than a marathon.
(VERA JAGENDORF)

Kicking too hard, too soon, can lose you more time than a properly timed kick can gain. Even if you're fresh, it's impossible to hold an all-out sprint for much more than about 200 yards.

If you've run a good race, you won't have enough energy left at the finish for a full sprint. Beginners often like to show off by ending a race with a blazing kick, but what they're actually demonstrating is that they paced the first 95 percent of the race too conservatively. You'll get a better overall performance if you spread that energy more evenly across the entire race. You can still kick, but it won't be as dramatic. I had a good finishing kick, but in 10,000-meter track races, when I was averaging 4:24s, my last mile would only come in at a 4:15 to 4:20, with about half of the extra seconds shaved off in the last lap.

At middle-of-the-pack paces, the same proportionate effort might speed your last mile a bit more, for instance from an 8:48 to an 8:35. But the fundamental point remains: if you have enough energy to speed up by 20 or 30 seconds, you should try running your next race 5 seconds per mile faster, from the start.

AT THE FINISH LINE

At the finish, keep moving all the way across the line; some runners slack off in the final steps, sacrificing one or two hard-won seconds by breaking stride just that little bit too soon. You can also lose a bit of time by paying too much attention to your watch, rather than running strongly through the finish line.

In the finishing chutes, follow instructions and keep moving, both for your own good and to avoid blocking other runners. Even after a hard race, it usually feels good to keep walking as your body adjusts to the sudden drop in exertion. In fact, it's possible, especially in hot weather, to keel over in a faint if you suddenly come to a complete halt. A lot of blood is still flowing to your legs, and you need to keep them moving to help pump it back to your heart. Let your pulse and breathing be your guide, and keep walking until they've returned to something reasonably close to normal.

Other than walking around to keep loose, your next goal is to rehydrate. How important this is obviously depends on the temperature and the length of the race, but even in a cool-weather 5K, you're going to have sweated off some liquid. Drink at least a couple of cups, and keep drinking, off and on, until you find yourself needing to urinate. As with rehydration after a workout, try to get a good postrace drink as soon as possible, and by all means within 15 to 20 minutes.

You also need to follow the race with a warm-down jog. Starting within about 5 minutes of the finish, change to your training shoes (if you've been wearing racing shoes), and jog slowly for about a mile—much as you would at the end of a speed workout. Stretch afterward, at least as thoroughly as you would after a workout.

Somewhere during this process, you should be thinking about food. Research has indicated that you'll recover considerably faster if you get some food into you within 30 to 60 minutes. Ideally you should consume approximately 500 calories, about 25 to 35 percent of which should be protein. The rest should be mostly carbohydrates.

Most races will supply plenty of carbohydrates in the form of bananas or bagels, but don't count on them to supply protein. Stash a nutrition bar with your warm-up clothing or keep one in your car. Another option is a powdered recovery drink such as one of those made by Met-Rx. These beverages contain a mix of carbohydrates and protein that is engineered to reach your muscles as quickly as possible.

POST-FINISH CHECKLIST

Time after Finish	Recommended Activity
0–5 min.	start rehydrating
5 min.	begin slow, 1-mile warm-down jog
20 min.	deadline for your first substantial drink of water or sports drink*
1 hour	deadline for postrace snack

* Keep drinking until your urine runs clear.

RECOVERY

Racing is hard work. That means you need time to recover—more in fact, than you need after your toughest workouts. This doesn't mean you have to take a lot of time off, just that you should take it easy for a few days. The day after the race is an obvious time for a rest day. Then, if you're recovering from a short race (10K or less), you might want to hold back to between 50 and 75 percent of your normal distance for the next couple of days. Don't push the pace; your goal is to relax and recover, so these runs should be fun and gentle.

By the third day, you can return to full training, although you might want to wait a week before putting a truly hard effort into a speed workout. Don't lift weights, at least not with your lower body, on the first 2 days after the race.

A half-marathon is a tougher event, and recovery from it takes longer. If your muscles are distinctly sore, take 2 or even 3 full days off. Also, hold off for at least a week on serious speed work, and consider doing the same for lower-body weight lifting. Let exertion and fatigue be your guide; it takes about 2 weeks to fully recover from races of that distance, although you can be back to perhaps a 75 percent effort by the second week.

> **For optimum performance in your next race, don't return to full training until you're well recovered from your last race.**

Intermediate distances, such as 15K or 10 miles, will take intermediate-duration recoveries. To a large extent you'll learn to gauge your recovery needs by the way you feel. Different runners recover at different rates, partly because they race at different fractions of their all-out effort level. Older runners need more time to recover than younger ones. The fundamental point to remember is that most people don't give themselves enough time to recover, so don't start back into hard workouts simply because that's what your friends are doing. If you don't take enough time to recover, you'll see subpar workouts and a sluggish performance in your next race. You could also tip yourself over the edge into overtraining and injury.

SETTING YOUR NEXT GOAL

Unless the weather's miserable, it's fun to relax at the finish rather than scurrying straight home. After your warm-down jog, sit on the grass and stretch; treat yourself to ice cream; congratulate runners who paced you along the way. Racing is a solo effort but the finish is often a big, low-key party—and race-day acquaintances can easily metamorphose into training partners.

The finish is also a good time to review your effort before details start to fade from memory. Write down as many of your split times as you can remember, so you

SUGGESTED RECOVERY PROGRAMS AFTER RACES

RACE LENGTH	TOTAL RECOVERY PERIOD	RECOVERY ACTIVITIES			
		FIRST DAY	NEXT 2 DAYS	REMAINDER OF WEEK 1	WEEK 2
5K to 10K	4 to 7 days	rest	slow easy runs, 50 to 75 percent of normal training distance no weight lifting with lower body	no hard speed workouts	resume normal routine
15K or 10-mile	1 to 2 weeks	rest	rest or slow, easy runs, about 25 percent of normal distance no weight lifting with lower body	75 percent of normal distance no speed workouts no weight lifting with lower body	return to normal mileage avoid hard speed workouts
20K or half-marathon	2 weeks	rest	rest	slow, easy runs, about half of normal distance no weight lifting with lower body	75 percent of normal distance no hard speed workouts
marathon	6 weeks	see chapter 15			

Note: Individuals will vary depending on age, level of training, and the intensity with which they ran the race.

TRAINING DIARY

```
10

Saturday
    Riverside 15K
    flat, 55°   felt good. No rain, dry pavement
    Warmed up 2 mi, w/ 1 mi strides
    Finishing time: 63:11
    Individual
        miles    1 .... 6:23      8 .... 6:56
                 2 .... 6:57      9 .... 6:46
                 3 .... 6:46
                 4 .... 6:43
                 5 .... 6:54 (curvy)
                 6 .... 6:43
                 7 .... 6:56 (started running
                                    out of gas)
```

Training log entry from a successful race. This is Rick's from a 15K that he viewed as successful but not perfect.

can analyze your pacing. (When you get home, transfer these numbers to your training diary—see above. Your diary might also note the weather, how much sleep you got, what you ate for breakfast, and any other variables that might be useful to recall in months and years to come.)

Did you achieve your goal? Congratulations! Did you fall short? If so, figure out what went wrong. Was the day unexpectedly hot or the course too hilly? If so, the clock didn't reflect your true performance, and you may have done better than you think. Did you mis-pace the hills, or start too quickly? Chalk it up to experience and try to run more wisely next time.

If you're satisfied with your result, you can start thinking about what you want to do next. If your goal was a 25:00 5K and you breezed to it in a seemingly effortless 24:50, you may be able to run a lot faster. But it's best to approach such goals incrementally. Even if you think you could run 23:00, target your next round of training on a 24:30. If you make that, go for 24:00, and so forth. You'll get to that 23:00 in a few months, bolstered by intermediate successes. And if 23:30 proves to be your maximum, you'll feel better sneaking up on it than trying for the faster speed and falling short.

COMPARABLE FINISHING TIMES IN RACES, 5K TO THE MARATHON

Finishing Time ☐   Per-mile Pace ▨

5K		5 mi*		10K		15K		10 mi		20K		Half-Mar.		Marathon	
12:58	4:10	21:35	4:19	27:14	4:23	42:02	4:30	45:19	4:31	57:11	4:36	1:00:33	4:37	2:07:09	4:50
13:37	4:23	22:40	4:32	28:36	4:36	44:08	4:44	47:35	4:45	1:00:03	4:49	1:03:35	4:51	2:13:30	5:05
14:18	4:36	23:48	4:45	30:02	4:50	46:21	4:58	49:58	4:59	1:03:03	5:04	1:06:46	5:05	2:20:11	5:20
15:01	4:50	24:59	4:59	31:32	5:04	48:40	5:13	52:28	5:14	1:06:12	5:19	1:10:06	5:20	2:27:11	5:36
15:46	5:04	26:14	5:14	33:07	5:19	51:06	5:28	55:05	5:30	1:09:31	5:35	1:13:36	5:36	2:34:33	5:53
16:33	5:19	27:33	5:30	34:46	5:35	53:39	5:45	57:51	5:47	1:13:00	5:52	1:17:17	5:53	2:42:16	6:11
17:23	5:35	28:56	5:47	36:30	5:52	56:20	6:02	1:00:44	6:04	1:16:39	6:10	1:21:09	6:11	2:50:23	6:29
18:15	5:52	30:22	6:04	38:20	6:10	59:09	6:20	1:03:47	6:22	1:20:29	6:28	1:25:13	6:30	2:58:54	6:49
19:10	6:10	31:54	6:22	40:15	6:28	1:02:07	6:39	1:06:58	6:41	1:24:30	6:47	1:29:28	6:49	3:07:51	7:09
20:07	6:28	33:29	6:41	42:15	6:48	1:05:13	6:59	1:10:19	7:01	1:28:44	7:08	1:33:57	7:10	3:17:15	7:31
21:08	6:48	35:10	7:02	44:22	7:08	1:08:29	7:20	1:13:50	7:23	1:33:10	7:29	1:38:39	7:31	3:27:06	7:53
22:11	7:08	36:55	7:23	46:35	7:29	1:11:54	7:42	1:17:31	7:45	1:37:49	7:52	1:43:35	7:54	3:37:28	8:17
23:18	7:30	38:46	7:45	48:55	7:52	1:15:30	8:06	1:21:24	8:08	1:42:43	8:15	1:48:45	8:17	3:48:20	8:42
24:28	7:52	40:42	8:08	51:22	8:16	1:19:16	8:30	1:25:28	8:32	1:47:51	8:40	1:54:12	8:42	3:59:45	9:08
25:41	8:16	42:44	8:32	53:56	8:40	1:23:14	8:55	1:29:44	8:58	1:53:15	9:06	1:59:54	9:08	4:11:45	9:36
26:58	8:40	44:53	8:58	56:38	9:06	1:27:24	9:22	1:34:14	9:25	1:58:54	9:34	2:05:54	9:36	4:24:20	10:04
28:19	9:07	47:07	9:25	59:28	9:34	1:31:46	9:50	1:38:56	9:53	2:04:51	10:02	2:12:12	10:05	4:37:33	10:35
29:44	9:34	49:29	9:53	1:02:26	10:02	1:36:21	10:20	1:43:53	10:23	2:11:06	10:32	2:18:48	10:35	4:51:25	11:06
31:13	10:03	51:57	10:23	1:05:34	10:33	1:41:11	10:51	1:49:05	10:54	2:17:39	11:04	2:25:45	11:07	5:06:00	11:40
32:47	10:33	54:33	10:54	1:08:50	11:04	1:46:14	11:23	1:54:32	11:27	2:24:32	11:37	2:33:02	11:40	5:21:18	12:15

* 8K times will be about 10–20 seconds faster. Per-mile paces for 5-mile and 8K are identical.
Copyright www.teamoregon.com. Used with permission.

Read horizontally across the table to use your finishing time in one race to predict an approximate target for a race of a different distance. For distances not in the table, interpolate based on the per-mile paces for the distances shown. For a 12K (about 7.45 miles), for example, your per-mile pace will be about halfway between your pace at 10K and at 15K.

Alternatively, you may find yourself drawn to a longer distance. World-class runners generally race only the distances at which they truly excel, but you'll be a better all-around runner if you do a mix of distances. If nothing else, the variety will keep you fresh by offering new challenges. If you're stagnating at 5K, maybe it's time to attack the 10K. If the relatively high training volume needed for half-marathons is eating into your home life, you can cut your mileage and focus on a shorter race.

If you've only raced at one distance, you may feel at a loss trying to set pace goals for other events. Common rules of thumb help a bit: if you ran 7:30s for a 10K, you can expect to be about 20 seconds per mile faster for a 5K, and the same

> **Don't overrace. Allow at least 2 weeks between races. Three is better.**

amount slower for a 20K. For more precise predictions, Warren Finke, a computer expert and avid ultramarathoner, has compiled a database of the PR performances for more than 10,000 racers of all abilities. Using this, he's created a computer program that allows you to plug in your PR racing time at any distance and obtain reasonable goals for the distance of your choice.

The program is available online at www.teamoregon.com, but simplified output from it is presented in the chart on page 213. Using your recent performance as a benchmark, read horizontally across the chart to find the equivalent performances at other standard distances. For distances not on the chart, convert finishing times to per-mile paces and interpolate the best you can. That should be close enough.

These predictions merely indicate talent and potential. You still have to put in the right training or you'll probably fall short. Also, the predictions are more accurate if you move up and down the scale in small steps. A 25:00 5K might indicate that you're capable of a 4:05 marathon, but if you've never done a race longer than 5K, don't expect to suddenly step up to the marathon and hit that target. You're better off to do a few 10Ks, 15Ks, and half-marathons en route to that marathon goal.

How Often to Race

If you wanted, you could strive to maximize each performance by spending months of training between races, but it's more useful to gain racing experience and obtain frequent feedback.

When I was in college, I ran about 25 races a year. Three-fourths of these were collegiate track and cross-country meets. The rest were road races and meets during the European track season, which runs from June through August. After graduation, I toned that schedule down to about 15 races per year, and except during the whirlwind European track season (in which there can be more than one race per week), I never ran races that were less than 2 weeks apart.

WEIGHTY MATTERS

When runners begin considering ways to improve race performance, their thoughts often turn to issues of pounds and ounces—pounds on the body, and ounces on the feet.

The basic fact is simple: unnecessary weight slows you down. But the key lies in the word *unnecessary*. It's frighteningly easy to turn yourself into an anorexic. Chapter 8 gives some rules of thumb for figuring out what you should weigh, but if in doubt, talk to your doctor. Cutting too much weight won't speed you up, anyway. It will merely make you weak, and it can put women at risk of repeated, career-ending stress fractures (see pages 140–42). Super-lightweight shoes also carry risks. Their limited cushion, arch support, stability, and heel lift can substantially increase the risk of injury.

Nevertheless, *extra* weight can be worth getting rid of. At world-class paces, 7 pounds translates to about 30 to 45 seconds on a 10K. If the effect is proportional to speed (which may or may not be the case), that's equivalent to about 50 to 75 seconds for an 8:00-miler: that is, at middle-of-the-pack paces, each extra pound of fat costs you about 1 to 1½ seconds per mile, give or take a bit.

If you're 25 pounds overweight, that's a lot. Getting rid of the extra will also cut your injury risk by reducing stress on your feet, knees, and hips. But if you're close to your ideal weight, a few pounds one way or the other won't make much difference. Staying healthy is more important than quibbling over minor weight differences.

Getting rid of extra ounces on the feet has spawned a category of lightweight racing shoes (sometimes called *racing flats* to distinguish them from the spiked shoes for extra grip in cross-country and track races). An old rule about hiking boots (which have a lot more weight to be concerned about than do running shoes) says that each extra ounce on your feet saps as much energy as 7 ounces in your backpack. In running, the effect seems to be about the same, which means that an 8:00-miler can shave off a little less than a half-second per mile for each ounce of reduced shoe weight. That compares well to anecdotal evidence from elite runners, who estimate from track workouts that their 10K times would be about 20 or 30 seconds slower in 10-ounce training shoes than in 4-ounce racers. In other words, 6 ounces off each foot (12 ounces, total) speeds them up by about 3 to 5 seconds per mile. Slower runners might see about the same percentage increase in speed (about 1 percent to 2 percent, in the above example).

Featherlight racing shoes are for serious racers. They're designed for speed first, comfort second. They're also less durable than training shoes. Use them in training before committing yourself to racing in them, and think twice before wearing them in a long race, where they can leave your feet feeling like raw meat. A potential compromise is to split the difference between racing shoes and your normal training shoes by racing in the lightest-weight trainers in which you can run comfortably, even if they're not supportive enough for everyday training.

A good rule of thumb is not to race on back-to-back weekends unless you're treating one of the races as a fun run and doing it as a slow-paced trainer or at most a tempo run. Ideally, you should allow at least 3 weeks between serious races.

Racing too often courts injury and never gives you time to improve: recovery from one race will merge into tapering for the next, with no time for real training. Even with races every 3 weeks, you'll have to modify your speed training to function in 3-week segments, rather than the 4- to 6-week blocks described in chapter 5. With less time for training between races, you'll also see less improvement per race: target on speeding up by only 5 seconds per mile.

Many runners like to have an off-season, when they lay off both racing and speed work for as long as 2 or 3 months. You don't *have* to take a break, but you should do so any time you find that you're losing interest in racing or in intense training. Such slumps are good signs that you're overworked, and trying to push through them without reducing your training rarely succeeds. It can also get you hurt. If you *feel* like you need a break, you need one, even if you're still turning in good performances.

Take a sabbatical from running if you're losing incentive or feeling sluggish. Elite runners often take a 2- to 4-week rest at the end of their most intense racing season.

Most elite racers take 2 weeks totally off sometime each year. They then spend another 2 to 4 weeks jogging only 3 to 5 miles a day—a dramatic reduction from the 110-mile weeks many of us averaged during the rest of the year. You don't need to drop your mileage that substantially, but whatever mileage you run should be at an easy pace, never pushing, never even thinking about speed.

At the end of this interlude, allow one week to get back up to steam for each week of limited running, plus another 2 weeks for each week that you took completely off after the first two. In other words, if you took a full month off from running, followed by 4 weeks of easy jogging (a fairly long break), you should allow 6 more weeks to return to full training. Increase gradually during this phase-in period until, by the end, you're doing your normal mileage and interval training without undue effort. You won't be all the way back to peak, but that's OK. You have the entire racing season to regain your edge and, hopefully, to continue improving.

PART 4

THE MARATHON —AND MORE

(PAUL J. SUTTON/DUOMO)

FOR MANY RUNNERS, the marathon is the pinnacle of the sport. Some run one marathon and are satisfied; others run more often, seeking to improve their performances, just as they would in shorter races. But for both groups, the marathon is special—far more so than any shorter distance.

It's a big step from a half-marathon to a marathon, but most marathon runners don't bother with intermediate distances. Races of 25K and 30K are rare, anyway. It's as though the entire racing world realizes that if you're going to run a race longer than a half-marathon, you might as well go the whole way and earn that coveted title of *marathoner*.

Chapter 15 will tell you how to make this transition, if you so desire. (It's also OK *not* to want to run a marathon!) That chapter presumes that you've run at least a few shorter races, and it builds on your familiarity with them to show you how to adjust your training and your race strategy for the longer distance. Although the marathon has some differences from other races, it has important similarities, as well.

The two chapters after that will then address additional challenges, unrelated to the marathon. Chapter 16, for example, will shift the focus from the length of the race to the length of your racing career, discussing how you can keep racing as you age—or how to move into the sport for the first time in your 40s, 50s, 60s, 70s, or above. Chapter 17 will then conclude this book with a mixed bag of other types of racing that offer alternatives to conventional road racing. There will even be a brief discussion of ultramarathoning: the sport of running distances longer than the marathon. Not many Americans ever attempt an ultra, but it's a national passion in South Africa, where in 1994 I concluded my racing career by winning a 54-mile event that draws as many participants as the Boston Marathon.

But first, let's return to the apex of American road racing: the marathon.

15

THE MARATHON

I SPENT MY TEEN YEARS in a Boston suburb, 3 miles from the Boston Marathon course. Growing up under the influence of North America's oldest marathon, I long knew that marathoning would be my ultimate calling. Each year, my brother and I would drive to choice spots along the course. As the best runners in the world whisked by, I'd fantasize that I was out there with them, leading the pack.

As a junior in high school, I started running with the Greater Boston Track Club, which included many former collegiate competitors in their mid-20s. One was Bill Rodgers, who would soon start a multiyear reign as the world's top marathoner—and at age 16, I could almost keep pace with his track workouts. That's when I set the goal: once high school and college had sufficiently matured me as a runner, I would graduate to the roads for the race that had inspired my youth.

Other marathoners are drawn simply by the challenge. That's how Rick came to run his first marathon, although, like many first-timers, he'd barely finished before he was scheming about how to run another marathon, faster.

No other distance has accumulated so much lore. If nothing else, there's the story of Pheidippides, the ancient Greek warrior who, wearing full battle armor, dashed something on the order of 25 miles (now standardized as 26.2 miles) from the Plains of Marathon to the city of Athens, where he barely managed to croak out his message of victory before collapsing, dead. What other race can rival the mystique of an event that killed its first competitor, even if it's likely that Pheidippides (who'd previously covered 120 miles in 2 days) succumbed to heat stroke or dehydration, rather than simply the rigors of the distance?

There are two ways to approach the marathon, and this chapter will help you prepare for either. One is simply to target on completing it, without worrying too much about time. To do that, all you'll need is to log the weekly mileage volumes in the chart below, and to strive not to run too fast, come race day.

Alternatively, your goal may be to truly race a marathon. That means that you have a time goal and are willing to do some speed work to make it happen. For your first marathon, set the goal based on recent performances at other distances (the longer the better) and the chart on page 213. Then, scale down your expectations a bit from the numbers in the chart, which is based on the performance of runners who may have run several marathons.

MARATHON TRAINING

Preparing for a marathon involves the same training principles as preparing for shorter races. The chief difference is that you're going to increase your volume, slow down your speed workouts (if any), and substantially increase the distance of your week's longest run. Each aspect of this has a separate goal.

- Increasing your total weekly mileage will provide the basis for your body to withstand the stress of the marathon.
- Running slower-paced speed workouts will allow you to extend their length (useful for the longer race), while also helping you find your target pace in the marathon, rather than going out too fast.
- The long runs will enable you to go the distance on race day.

Because all of this training is fatiguing—and the race itself requires you to be well rested at the start—you'll need a more extended taper than for shorter events: a full 3 weeks is ideal.

> **Don't start marathon training unless you've been running at least 30 miles per week for the previous 2 months.**

There are programs that will take you from nonrunner to completing a marathon in less than a year—sometimes in as little as 9 months. But I believe that before beginning your marathon training, you should have built up to 30 miles a week using the volume-building guidelines in chapter 3, then run an average of 30 miles a week for at least 2 months. In *Alberto Salazar's Guide to Running*, I recommend that beginners take a full year to advance to 20 miles per week. From there, if you follow the guidelines in chapter 3 of this book, it will take the better part of another year to reach the 30-mile-per week level. Overall, therefore, nonrunners should view their first marathon as at least a 2-year goal—preferably a few months longer. Otherwise, the injury risk is too high.

Starting from that 30-mile base, you should plan on about 3 more months of training. The program in this chapter encompasses 14 weeks, but it could

FOURTEEN-WEEK MARATHON TRAINING SCHEDULE

WEEK	BASELINE MILEAGE	ADDED MILES	TOTAL MILEAGE	LONGEST RUN
0 (BASELINE)	30	0	30	7
1	30	2	32	8
2	30	2	32	8
3	30	4	34	9
4	30	4	34	10
5	30	6	36	11
6	30	6	36	12
7	30	8	38	13
8	30	10	40	15
9	30	12	42	17
10	30	12	42	18
11	30	10	40	20
12	30	7	37	15
13	30	2	32	12
14	n/a*	n/a*	15	race!!

* Not applicable. In this week, your total mileage is less than baseline.

just as easily have been 15 or 13. Anything less than 3 months, though, is too abrupt.

For the first 8 weeks you should gradually increase your mileage to about 42 per week, with a long run of 18 miles. In week 9 you'll run a 20-miler but drop the total mileage to 40. In week 10, you begin to taper. The accompanying table shows the schedule for all 14 weeks. The long runs should be approximately 1 week apart, and the 20-miler should be about 21 days before the marathon. (For proper tapering, the long runs in the following 2 weeks should be about 14 and 7 days ahead of the marathon, respectively.) Most likely, this means that you'll be doing these runs on weekends.

If you're running simply to complete the race, this is all that you need to do. Run 5 days a week, distributing the rest of the mileage with a conventional hard-easy pattern as described in chapter 3. Take one rest day immediately after your long run, and the other whenever is convenient. If you're running for time, you'll also be doing speed work, as described later in this chapter, so schedule the second rest day for the day after an interval workout.

This program assumes that at baseline your longest run is 7 miles. That may not be the case, particularly if you've been racing 20Ks or half-marathons. You still need the full 14-week program to phase in the extra volume, but if you're already doing long runs of 10 or 12 miles, there's no reason to drop back to 8 miles in week 1. Rather, start with what you're accustomed to doing, and revise the schedule of long runs to phase in your 20-miler in week 11. Starting from a baseline that includes a weekly 10-miler, for example, your long runs might increase ac-

---

Build up to a 20-mile training run 3 weeks before marathon day. If you decide to do more than one 20-miler, keep them at least 3 weeks apart.

---

cording to the following pattern: 11, 11, 12, 12, 13, 14, 15, 16, 17, 18, 20. Note that there's still only one 20-miler, and that we're not adding an intermediate 19-miler; doing that and a 20 on back-to-back weeks is unwise.

If this buildup seems too tame, given what you're already used to, you can revise the schedule of long runs to include more than one 20-miler. Just don't do that long run before your weekly total has reached 40 miles, and don't schedule 20-milers closer than 3 weeks apart. Instead, cycle the length of your long runs over several weeks. If you started with a weekly 12-miler, for example, you could try a schedule something like this: 13, 14, 14, 15, 16, 17, 18, 20, *15*, 17, 20 (italics indicate a drop in mileage at the start of a new cycle).

Starting from Higher Baseline Mileage

Obviously, if you can train for a marathon from a baseline of 30 miles a week, you can do so from higher baseline levels. If your goal is merely to survive the marathon, all you'll need to do is build up to 42 miles a week and add the requisite long runs. You could do this fairly quickly if your baseline program already looks like week 7 or 8 of the 14-week program. There are runners, in fact, who do exactly this: taking a 35- or 40-mile base and adding some long runs and a little extra mileage so they can jog through a marathon in reasonable comfort.

But for most people, a marathon is a huge commitment, and you might as well prepare to run your best. That requires a 14-week program that adds about 10 or 12 miles to your weekly schedule.

The program is similar to what you use starting from 30 miles a week, although the extra mileage may make it necessary to run 6 days a week, rather than 5. If you're already doing a long weekly outing, you may want to be even more aggressive in the number of 20-milers you do. Starting from a background of 13-milers and 40 miles per week, for example, your long runs might rotate through the following cycle: 14, 15, 17, 20, *14*, 15, 17, 20, *15*, 17, 20 (italics indicate the start of a new cycle), followed by tapering as in the Fourteen-Week Marathon Training Schedule (see page 221). Design the cycle so there's a 20-miler in week 11, and keep those 20s at least 3 weeks apart.

The Marathon Training Schedule is arranged to make it easy to design schedules for any baseline mileage. Simply plug the appropriate number into the "base-

GREAT RACE 1: BOSTON MARATHON

The Boston Marathon is the oldest and most prestigious in North America. Organized in 1897, one year after the first modern Olympiad, it has grown from a field of 15 to 15,000, and is the only large race in the United States for which participants must secure qualifying times to enter. That in itself adds to the mystique. Qualifying for Boston is a dream of many speedy recreational racers.

The course is fast—with a net downgrade of nearly 500 feet—running point-to-point from the suburb of Hopkinton to downtown Boston. But it's not an easy course, thanks to the challenge of 200-foot-high Heartbreak Hill, which rears its nasty head just after mile 20. The race is held on Patriot's Day (the third Monday in April), a state holiday that commemorates the start of the Revolutionary War.

Boston is the Super Bowl of marathons, drawing a media corps of more than 1,400 reporters from 15 countries. The racing field is likewise international, featuring many of the finest racers in the world. To qualify, runners need to post qualifying times on a certified course in the 16 months preceding the application deadline (typically February 1). These cutoffs are based on age and gender on race day. That means that a 39-year-old trying to qualify for next year's Boston Marathon need only make the 40-year-old qualifying time—a major advantage. If you're marginal for Boston, your best shot at getting in is by running your qualifier just before you move into a new age group. You can also pick up a few minutes by running your qualifier on a downhill course, such as the Las Vegas International Marathon or the St. George Marathon in St. George, Utah.

For additional information, consult www.bostonmarathon.org.

BOSTON MARATHON QUALIFYING TIMES (AS OF 2002)

Age Group	Men	Women
18–34	3:10	3:40
35–39	3:15	3:45
40–44	3:20	3:50
45–49	3:25	3:55
50–54	3:30	4:00
55–59	3:35	4:05
60–64	3:40	4:10
65–69	3:45	4:15
70+	3:50	4:20

line mileage" column and adjust the totals accordingly, until you reach week 12, when you're beginning your taper. Then follow the rules on tapering, discussed later in this chapter.

The schedule can even be used at baseline volumes as high as 70 or 80 miles a week, although now you're getting close to elite training schedules that will benefit from fine-tuning beyond the scope of this book. When I was training for marathons, I sometimes *averaged* 18 miles a day, with grueling speed work, very few rest days, and long runs of 20 miles. People who can train at these levels don't need this table; hopefully they have coaches to help them work out personalized training schedules.

Speed Training

Preparing for a marathon, you'll want your speed work to include the usual mix of short intervals, medium-length intervals, long intervals, and tempo runs (see table, page 225). For shorter races, chapter 5 constructed speed workouts based on recent racing performances. For marathons, that's less practical, so this chapter bases them on your *target* pace instead. Pick the target based on your marathon experience (if any) and the chart on page 213, which projects your probable marathon time from your performance in shorter races. Even if the goal on the chart looks a bit aggressive, you might as well train for it. You might change your mind and decide to go for it anyway; and even if you don't, you'll be well trained for a slightly more conservative pace, come race day.

Not surprisingly, long intervals are the most important. There are two ways to approach them. One is by doing a conventional interval workout, with 5 to 7 repeat miles at about 20 seconds per mile faster than your marathon pace. But a better workout is more of a fartlek-style workout, which involves a more continuous run, often done on roads rather than a track. Technically, this workout is too structured to be a true fartlek (see pages 78–79), but it has somewhat the feel of a fartlek's "speed play." In it, you'll run 5 repeat miles at a slightly slower pace, but with a faster-than-normal recovery pace. These recoveries, however, are extended from their normal 800-meter duration to a full mile.

That's the theory. Here are the details: do the fartlek-style repeats at 10 seconds per mile faster than your target marathon pace, and the recoveries at 20 seconds per mile slower than your goal. This will help teach you how to relax while running for an hour or longer at a fairly substantial effort. In conventional intervals, your focus is generally on getting through the next repeat. It's possible to do so with bad form or by clenching up and gutting your way through. In the marathon, you can't get away with that, and this hotly paced 10-mile workout will exact a similar toll. Those fast-paced recoveries will make it hard to complete if you tighten up in the early going.

The *fartlek* approach is also a great psychological boost. It runs you for 10 miles at a pace that averages 5 seconds per mile slower than your planned marathon pace, but the *fast-slow-fast-slow* alternation means that when you hit the marathon itself, its pace will feel a lot easier than the workout—even though its average pace is actually faster.

The one caveat is that this workout involves a fairly substantial amount of mileage—at least 12 miles, when you add in the warm-up and cooldown. It won't fit easily into a training schedule starting from a baseline of less than about 40 miles a week, and even then it's a fairly long run. If necessary, cut it back to 10 miles total, including warm-up and cooldown, by dropping one of the repeat miles. Even that may be too long for your first weeks of marathon training. As a general rule, don't let your speed workout exceed one-fourth of your total weekly mileage.

The other categories of speed workouts will follow familiar patterns, but they too can stand some fine-tuning.

- For short intervals, don't do 200s. Stick to the longer members of this category: 300s and 400s. Do them at the pace you'd use when training for any race of 10K or longer—that is, 30 to 35 seconds per mile faster than 10K race pace.
- Medium-length intervals should be run at about 25 seconds per mile faster than your target marathon pace. Increase the number of repeats by one or two over what you'd do for a half-marathon.
- Tempo runs should be extended to 6 to 9 miles in length, run at marathon pace. As with shorter races, they can be split in half, with a 1- or 2-mile recovery between the two segments.

SUGGESTED SPEED WORKOUTS FOR MARATHON TRAINING

WORKOUT	DESCRIPTION	PACE
short intervals	5 to 8 x 300 meters 4 to 6 x 400 meters	0:30 to 0:35 per mile faster than 10K race pace
medium intervals*	8 to 12 x 800 meters 11 to 16 x 600 meters	0:25 per mile faster than target marathon pace
long intervals*	5 to 7 x 1 mile	0:20 per mile faster than target marathon pace
fartlek*	8 to 10 miles	alternating fast miles (0:10 per mile faster than target marathon pace) and moderately fast recovery miles (0:20 per mile slower than target marathon pace)
tempo runs*	6 to 9 miles OR 2 x 3 to 4.5 miles	target marathon pace

* Total speed-workout mileage, including warm-up and cooldown, should not exceed 25 percent of weekly total.

Tapering

Tapering is an integral part of marathon training. Shorter races require a week or less of tapering, but the intensity of marathon training and the need to be well-rested for a demanding race mean that you'll run a lot better if you taper longer. It's a point that some runners find hard to grasp, so drill it into your head now, so you won't be tempted to overtrain as the race approaches.

Even though you need 3 weeks of rest before the race, you can't completely halt training or you'd feel hopelessly flat on race day—about the way you'd feel after a 3-week injury layoff. Marathon tapering involves phasing in the rest to avoid detraining. In the first week, drop your long run to 15 miles and cutting your total mileage by 10 percent. Unless you're running more than 50 miles a week, this reduction will all come from the cutback in your long run. In fact, that may produce slightly greater than a 10 percent drop, which is OK. If you're lifting weights, quit doing lower-body workouts. Also, turn down the intensity of your speed workouts by slowing them down by about 15 seconds per mile. In the second week, cut your total mileage by another 10 percent and drop your long run to 12 miles. Slow down your speed work by an additional 5 seconds per mile. Finally, the week before the marathon, do one easy speed workout in the first half of the week (such as seven 300-meter runs at a pace that's 25 seconds per mile slower than normal), and cut your total mileage to half of your original baseline level, running all but the speed workout at the easiest possible pace. Take a full day off 2 days before the marathon, and jog just enough to keep loose and relaxed on the day before the race, just as you would for a shorter race.

Given the intensity of marathon training, it'll take the entire first week of tapering before you begin to feel that you're recovering. By the end of the second week, you ought to be feeling really good. And in the third week, if you've done it right, you're going to start feeling downright antsy, thinking that you're doing too little work. That's the feeling you want to carry into the marathon, because it means you're rested and really, really ready to run. Stay disciplined for just a few more

DO AS I SAY, NOT . . .

The temptation to skimp on your premarathon tapering can be extreme. I succumbed to it prior to the 1984 Olympic Marathon, when I was under a great deal of pressure to win. Knowing that my training had been going badly, I tried to use the last 3 weeks to "catch up" rather than tapering properly. Lots of things went wrong on race day (heat was one of them), but I also had the horrible experience of watching the leaders pull away from me in the first mile, and knowing there was nothing I could do about it.

Carlos Lopes of Portugal had the opposite experience. He got hit by a car a week before the race and was banged up enough that he didn't run at all for 3 or 4 days. He then did a couple of days of light jogging—and won the race.

The moral is clear: it's better to taper a little too strongly than not enough.

TAPERING FOR THE MARATHON

DAYS UNTIL RACE	TRAINING REGIMEN
21	20-mile run
20 to 14	reduce total mileage 10 percent drop long run to 15 miles do speed workouts 0:15/mile slower than normal eliminate lower-body weight lifting
13 to 7	reduce total mileage by another 10 percent reduce long run to 12 miles pace speed workouts at 0:20 slower than normal
6 to 1	reduce total mileage to 50 percent of premarathon- training level do one short speed workout early in week at 0:25/mile slower than normal rest on the next-to-last day before the race, and consider jogging slightly on the last day

days, and don't go speeding out on a high-energy training run that will cause you to lose your hard-won edge.

Carbohydrate Loading

A few days before the marathon, you should start thinking about making sure that your glycogen reserves are fully stocked for the race.

You do this by engaging in some form of *carbohydrate loading*, just as you may have been doing for shorter races. The main difference is that carbohydrate loading is much more important for a marathon. In a 10K, you're unlikely to actually run out of glycogen if you don't eat properly beforehand. In a marathon, that's a very real risk—and a major contributor to hitting the wall, which I describe later in this chapter. At the end of your marathon training, you've probably trained your muscles to store about 18 to 22 miles worth of glycogen. You want to make sure that their supplies are at maximum when the race begins.

Most people do this simply by eating diets rich in complex carbohydrates during the final 3 or 4 days before the race, rather than simply the night-before carbohydrate loading practiced for shorter events. You don't need to eat huge amounts of food. Merely make sure that your meals include high-starch foods such as pasta, bread, or potatoes.

As always before a race, stick to foods you eat regularly, especially as race day draws near; this is a bad time to court abdominal woes by experimenting. Make sure your dinners have at least 400 calories worth of complex carbohydrates—equivalent to four slices of bread, 4 ounces of pasta, or one very large potato. Fruit is also good. You can also jack up the fraction of carbs in your lunches and breakfasts.

There is no reason to stuff yourself with extra food. The goal is simply to ensure that your diet is rich in carbohydrates, rather than to add hundreds of calories per day to your normal consumption. In fact, since you're heavily into your taper at this point, you may actually be eating less than you were at the time of your most intensive training.

On the night before the race, you should eat a moderately large dinner, fairly late in the evening. Or eat earlier and plan a late-night snack so that you don't burn too much of it off overnight. (I talk about breakfast in the next section of this chapter.) On the evening before race day, it's also a good idea to eat a low-fat meal. Protein is OK, but fat digests more slowly, and you don't want it lingering in your gut come morning. And although runners like to point out that beer is high in complex carbohydrates, you really should restrain yourself the night before the race if you want to do your best.

A GROWING, SLOWING SPORT

Marathon running is seeing its share of the racing boom. According to USA Track and Field's Road Running Information Center, marathoning in the United States has grown nearly twentyfold since 1976, adding about 19,000 finishers per year since 1990. The accompanying table shows the number of finishers tabulated in 116 marathons (not all of which have been in existence since 1976).

U.S. MARATHON FINISHERS

YEAR	ESTIMATED NUMBER OF FINISHERS
1976	25,000
1980	120,000
1990	260,000
1995	347,000
2000	451,000
2001	424,000*

* Decline attributed to aftermath of Sept. 11 terrorist attacks.
Source: USA Track and Field, Road Running Information Center. Used with permission.

Simultaneously, the speed of the average finisher has declined fairly substantially, partly due to an increase in the number of walkers (who figure into the statistics as slow runners) and partly because of a trend toward thinking in terms of simply *finishing* a marathon rather than racing it. One could spend a great deal of time wondering about what these trends mean for the future of racing versus fitness running, but the most important message for this book is that you'll have lots of company preparing for and completing your first marathon. The fabled "loneliness of the long-distance runner" is largely a thing of the past.

GREAT RACE 2: NEW YORK CITY MARATHON

The New York City Marathon is huge in all ways. An enormous field of 30,000 runners tours a great city, cheered on by an estimated 2 million spectators, as the front-runners compete for more than $500,000 in prizes. What Boston claims in 106-year tradition, New York makes up for in scale. Furthermore, you don't have to be fast to qualify for entry: only lucky. Runners speedy enough to finish in the top 0.5 percent or so of their age groups are guaranteed entry, but the rest are chosen by lottery from applications received by a cut-off date, traditionally June 1 (and yes, there are substantially more than 30,000 applicants). Domestic and foreign applicants enter separate pools, as the race seeks to obtain a 2:1 ratio of American-to-foreign racers—making it an extraordinarily international event.

Like Boston, the race started small. Only 55 people finished the first race, which ran multiple laps of Central Park in 1970. The explosive growth began in 1976 when the marathon moved onto the roads and was extended to all five boroughs (Staten Island, Brooklyn, Queens, the Bronx, and Manhattan). In 1976, there was considerable skepticism that police could actually keep the streets clear for the runners. Now it's hard to imagine New York City without the marathon that shuts down traffic each year on the first Sunday of November.

The New York City Marathon was good to me, and I have fond memories of it. But even if I'd never run it, I'd hail it as one of the world's finest.

For more information, consult www.nyrrc.org.

THE DEPLETION-REBOUND DIET

There's also a more complicated carbohydrate loading mechanism called the *depletion-rebound* approach. It's not one that you should use for your first marathon. The theory is that if you deplete your glycogen stores for a few days, then suddenly add a lot of carbohydrates to your diet, your body will be so pleased with the sudden bounty that it will temporarily overstock. Timed correctly, the rebound can increase your race-day glycogen supply by perhaps 10 percent—enough to carry you an extra 2 miles before it runs out.

That's the theory. The keys are the timing, and getting sufficiently depleted that your cells are hungry for glycogen when it reappears.

If—with a few marathons under your belt—you choose to attempt this, you should begin your depletion with a gentle, midlength run about a week before the race. If you've not yet done your last "long" run of 12 miles, this is the ideal depletion run; otherwise run 8 or 9 miles. Then, starting immediately after your depletion run, drop all carbohydrates from your diet, fueling yourself with protein and fats. This is great if bacon, eggs, sausage, steak, etc., are your idea of culinary heaven; it's horrible if you're a vegetarian or pasta-lover. It's more-or-less impossible, by the way, to remove *all* carbohydrates from your diet. Just get rid of as much carbohydrate as you can. Moderate amounts (up to about 150 grams per day) will be scavenged up by your brain, which has metabolic first dibs on this type of fuel. You'll also be continuing to do short runs as part of your normal tapering routine; these will help burn up any carbohydrates that do work their way into your diet.

Persist with this regimen for 3 or 4 days (don't worry, you can't clog otherwise healthy arteries that quickly). Then, for the final 3 or 4 days before the marathon, reverse the process, eating lots of carbohydrates and resting as much as possible while your muscles store them up.

The depletion-rebound diet is definitely not for everyone. Try it once in association with a long training run before attempting it for a race; if you get the timing or diet wrong, you can produce a miserable result. There's also a considerable amount of misery that goes with the diet itself. At the peak of the depletion stage, a 5-mile jog may feel almost as bad as a 20-mile run, and you'll start wondering how you can ever be fit in time for the race. Even when you've finally reached the rebound phase, it will take a couple of days before you start feeling really energetic.

Elite marathoners are about evenly split on whether the depletion-rebound diet is worth the psychological cost of feeling so draggy so shortly before the race. You can actually hit the wall in a 5-mile jog. (If that happens, stop and walk home; you're definitely depleted enough!) I only tried the depletion-rebound approach once, when I was trying to make a comeback in 1992. Other factors, most notably a troublesome Achilles tendon, contributed to a bad race, but I decided then that this approach wasn't for me. Whatever you do, don't try this before your first marathon. And there's no reason to attempt it for shorter races.

GREAT RACE 3: TWIN CITIES MARATHON

The Midwest has at least three great marathons, each with a different flavor. Grandma's, in Duluth, runs along the blue waters of Lake Superior in late June (the name comes from Grandma's Restaurant, its first sponsor). The LaSalle Banks Chicago Marathon, in early October, follows an extremely fast, flat course that's the site of the current American record. But if you're going to run only one Midwestern marathon, Rick (a former Midwesterner) votes for the Twin Cities Marathon.

First run in 1982, the race is a relative newcomer. But it's a marathon that was born to be great. Starting with 4,500 entrants (then the largest ever for an inaugural event), it's chosen to remain midsized, with about 5,500 finishers. That means that it quickly fills to capacity.

Part of the race's popularity is due to the strength of the Minnesotan running community, but it also has a well-deserved claim to beauty. The route starts in the urban canyons of downtown Minneapolis but quickly moves onto the city's parkway system, circling a large lake and running through endless trees that, with luck, are just nearing their peak fall colors. After an excursion along the bluffs of the Mississippi, it makes a beeline for the state capitol, on a hill overlooking downtown St. Paul. Extra spice comes from the fact it's a fast course.

For more information, consult www.twincitiesmarathon.org. The race is typically held in late September or early October.

THE BIG DAY

If you've run a lot of races, most of what you'll encounter in a marathon will be familiar. There are a few adjustments, however, that you need to make for the longer event.

Breakfast

We discussed the value of a prerace breakfast in chapter 12, regarding shorter races. For marathons, it's especially important to replace even the small amount of glycogen that you burn off in your sleep.

This doesn't mean you should eat a huge breakfast; you still have to digest it before you begin running, just as you would in a shorter race. Ideally, though, you should eat more than a banana or a carbohydrate gel. For a marathon, I recommend setting your alarm for an early enough wake-up to allow a light but "real" breakfast of up to 400 or 500 calories, about 3 hours before the start. To put that in context, 450 calories is a large deli bagel (without cream cheese) plus a banana or a glass of orange juice. And you should definitely skip the cream cheese! Your prerace breakfast should be composed almost entirely of carbohydrates.

Unfortunately, because marathons often start quite early, eating this meal far enough before the race may mean getting up at 3:30 a.m. If you can't abide the thought of waking up that early, you should still be up and moving at least 2 hours before the start, to give your body time to warm up from its night's rest. Then, snag breakfast immediately, when there's still time to digest something more than a carbohydrate gel—perhaps a banana and some orange juice. Also, remember to start hydrating as soon as you wake up. That's important in any race, but particularly in a marathon, where it's especially easy to become dehydrated.

Warm-Up

Because of its slower pace, the marathon requires less warm-up than a shorter race, but unless the thought of jogging even a few extra paces totally terrifies you, some warm-up is useful.

> **A 1-mile warm-up is useful for a marathon, but don't start jogging too early. Start your warm-up about 30 minutes before the race— or you'll have to run extra distance to keep from cooling back down.**

Try jogging a slow mile, ending with a few strides at marathon pace (which won't be all that much faster than your standard training pace). Yes, that spends energy, but it also gives you a chance to work out any muscular kinks, identify which muscles most need stretching, and test important trivia such as the lacing of your shoes and the absence of wrinkles in your socks. A gentle warm-up is also a good way to relax and focus on doing something useful during the nerve-wracking minutes before the start. I always did about a mile and a half of combined jogging and easy strides before a marathon start, but most recreational runners would do better by not exceeding a mile.

Once the race is under way, be particularly cautious about not going out too fast; if you get carried away at the start, you'll pay a bigger price in a marathon than in a shorter event. Until you've run several marathons, it's often a good idea to build a deliberately slow start into your race plan. If your goal is to break 4 hours (a 9:10 pace), for example, you might start out with a pair of 9:25s, then gradually pick up the pace until you're running your target 9:10s. Doing this, you might plan to go through the halfway point in 2:02, rather than 2:00 even. Your plan would then be to make up the time spent on that slow start by continuing to pick up the pace, running 1:58 in the back half of the race.

This works because you were conservative enough at the start to have leftover energy at the end. The ideal way to run the race, of course, is with nearly even

FASTEST COURSE IN THE WORLD

One marathon that can lay claim to the title of "world's fastest course" is the LaSalle Banks Chicago Marathon. In 1999, Khalid Khannouchi (a Moroccan who subsequently became a U.S. citizen) set a men's world record in 2:05:42; in 2001, Catherine Ndereba of Kenya captured the women's mark, at 2:18:47. In 2002, the American records also stood on this course: the men's record of 2:07:01, by Khalid in 2000; and the women's record of 2:21:21, by Joan Benoit Samuelson in 1985.

pacing, but it's better to start too slowly and speed up later to catch up than to do the reverse. If instead you were to attempt that 4-hour race by running 1:58 in the first half, you'd find it a lot harder to meet your goal, even though you "merely" had to do 2:02 in the second half. Not only is it hard to recover from an overly fast

The scenery is part of the action at Big Sur International Marathon.
(DOUGLAS STEAKLEY)

GREAT RACE 5: BIG SUR INTERNATIONAL MARATHON

For sheer spectacle, few places rival California's Big Sur coastline. Mountains plunge directly into the ocean, sea otters bask in the kelp near hidden beaches, and the road twists a cliff-hugging route between high-spanning bridges.

The road has been a favorite of movies and auto commercials since its construction in 1938. In 1986, marathoners were introduced to it with the inaugural Big Sur International Marathon. It's not an enormous run (about 2,500 finishers) but that's enough to make it the world's largest rural marathon. It's also a memorable outing for anyone who's run it, as it bounces along the coast northward from Pfeiffer Big Sur State Park to the town of Carmel.

But "bounces" is the operative word: don't run this course if your chief goal in life is a PR. Although there is a net 300-foot drop, there is also a brutal 2-mile, 500-foot hill near the midpoint. Substantial headwinds are possible, and several smaller hills add additional challenges to the second half of the race. Even with those obstacles, though, the best times aren't bad for a small marathon: 2:16:39 for the men and 2:41:34 for the women.

Big Sur, however, is not a great course for back-of-the-pack runners and walkers. The state requires the highway to be reopened to traffic within 5½ hours, so make sure you can maintain a 12:30 pace before attempting this race.

For more information, contact www.bsim.org. The race is held in late April, when the average temperature is in the 50s.

start, but once your pace starts to drop, its easy to lose confidence, as you begin wondering how much worse you'll do on each successive mile.

Keeping Motivated as the Miles Mount

Any long race has its psychological ups and downs. In a marathon, there will be times when you'll feel as though you can run forever, and others when you may wonder how you can make it to the next aid station.

Keep focused on the task at hand in the same ways that you would in a shorter race. Concentrate, for example, on staying on pace. Check your form periodically to make sure you're not developing energy-wasting habits. Relax. To the extent you can do so without distracting yourself from running well, take time to enjoy the course, the race-day camaraderie, and the adventure of being in a marathon.

You can also help maintain your motivation by practicing smart running on hills and curves. Not only will that get you to the finish more quickly, but if you've followed the advice in this book, you're going to be much better at these than are most of the people around you.

If you hit a bad patch early in the race, don't despair. Tell yourself it will pass in a mile or two, or that you'll get used to it if it doesn't. Usually, that's right. A mile later, you'll often have moved from the bad patch to a good one.

I learned another important motivational trick during my first marathon, the 1980 New York City Marathon. Like any first-time marathoner, I was intimidated by a race twice as long as any I'd done before. To combat this, my coach, Bill Dellinger of the University of Oregon, told me to divide the race into two pieces. The first was 20 miles, a distance I'd run many times in training. Here, he advised me to avoid taking the lead, so I wouldn't burn out by going too fast. From the 20-mile mark, he noted that it was almost precisely 10K to the finish—a specialty in which I'd previously made the U.S. Olympic team. "You know you can beat any of those guys at that distance," he said.

ARE WE THERE YET?

At the elite level, racers pay attention to pace, running form, and their competitors. Even on scenic courses such as the New York City Marathon, landmarks and ethnic neighborhoods slide by in staccato flashes that barely intrude on your consciousness. For the average racer, scenery is more important. It can help keep you motivated—but it can also distract. Recreational racers must not only use the mile markers and their split times to keep on pace, but they must also learn to gauge their progress this way rather than by the slow parade of scenery. This is particularly important for some courses, whose layout otherwise can be psychologically devastating. Here's Rick:

Some marathons are point-to-point courses in open terrain where you can see your destination, all the way. The Las Vegas Marathon does this as it makes a 26.2-mile beeline for the high-rise hotels of the Las Vegas Strip. Other courses run along lakes or curving bays, where the end is often in sight from the start. These courses can be extraordinarily

Dividing the race into familiar subunits is one of the best ways to deal with it. The same trick works with shorter races, but it's particularly important for the marathon, where it breeds confidence and breaks up the hours by giving you intermediate goals.

It also helps if your surroundings are scenic (or at least pleasant) and the weather comfortable. Nobody can guarantee the latter, but at least you can avoid scheduling your first race at a time and place where misery is the norm. If the weather is bad, nevertheless, comfort yourself with the thought that with the notable exception of heat, poor race-day weather usually doesn't feel as bad on the run as it does standing around at the start.

The Wall

The wall is the great bugaboo of beginning marathoners. It's real, and you hit it when you run low on stored glycogen. For the average person, that comes when you've burned about 2,000 calories: enough to run about 20 miles. At this point, your body shifts more strongly to burning fats, and it feels as though someone radically de-tuned your engine.

This collapse is called *the wall* because it comes on suddenly; one mile you're feeling fine, 800 meters later your stride is shot, your breathing is ragged, and each step is a lot tougher than it was only a few minutes before. When experienced marathoners say that you're only halfway though the race at mile 20, it is the wall that they're talking about (although it's not really *that* bad!).

Not everyone hits the wall the same way, or even hits it at all. Training, carbohydrate loading, eating gel packs every 30 minutes on the run, and having a body that's naturally endowed for longer racing all help to stave it off. I never hit the wall until I started training for the 54-mile Comrades Marathon. Then, I found it the first time I ran beyond 26.2 miles. On my first 30-mile trainer, I felt fine at miles 24, 25, and 26. Then suddenly the roof caved in. That's when I discovered the value of gel packs,

scenic, but the sense of "Oh, my gosh, we're going all the way over there," coupled with the slow apparent progress, drives many midpack racers to distraction.

Worse are races that take you close enough to the finish line to whet your appetite for the celebration that won't be yours for another 20 or 30 minutes, then send you back into the boondocks. I once did a marathon that passed at mile 23 within a block of the finish, then swung out into a large park for the next 2 miles. At mile 25, it passed a block on the other side of the finish before looping off into the park yet again. I ran a PR because I believed that "mile 23" meant "3.2 miles to go," regardless of what my eyes wanted to tell me. But many runners found it hard to keep going when the course seemed to be leading away from the finish.

Such courses seem designed to induce depression, but you can beat them by staying focused and believing in the accuracy of the mile marks and your watch.

The last miles of a marathon can be tough. This water-server is obviously feeling better than most of the marathoners, who have passed mile 20 but have yet to see the finish. (VERA JAGENDORF)

learning to use those extra carbohydrates in my long trainers to delay the wall, first to 30 miles and then to about 35.

You can harness the same trick if you tend to hit the wall earlier than I did. Each gel pack contains enough carbohydrates to run about 1 mile, and you can digest them at the rate of about one every half-hour. If you start 30 minutes into the race, that's 5 gels for a 3:00 marathon, enough to carry you, without the wall, for an extra 5 miles.

If you hit the wall nevertheless, try to get some energy into your system right away, either through a gel or a sports drink, unless you're so close to the end that they won't be absorbed in time to do you any good. Drink water, too; dehydration makes the wall even worse, and it interferes with your ability to digest carbohydrate gels.

Even hitting the wall, you can run a good race. Slow down if necessary, but don't give up and walk. Although I never hit the wall at marathon distances, the last 3 miles were generally the toughest. But these same miles were often my fastest. Many people can adjust and continue running fairly quickly, even after hitting the wall. Ten minutes or so later, you may even start to feel better. What it takes, more than anything else, is renewed concentration and determination—and you won't have gotten far enough to be hitting the wall in the first place if you don't already have lots of both.

KEEPING PACE WITH THE SPORT

If you're interested in tracking the progress of world-class marathon racing, the following are good sources of information:

- *Runner's World* magazine; also at www.runnersworld.com
- The Association of International Marathons and Road Races (AIMS): www.aims-association.org
- The Web site Let's Run: www.letsrun.com
- *Marathon & Beyond*, a bimonthly magazine of marathoning, ultramarathoning, and other endurance sports; also at www.marathonandbeyond.com

MORE GREAT MARATHONS

In addition to the races highlighted in this chapter, there are many other well-organized marathons. Five others that consistently draw rave reviews are

- California International (Sacramento, early December)
- Honolulu Marathon (mid-December)
- Marine Corps Marathon (Washington, D.C., late October)
- Portland (Oregon) Marathon (late September)
- Walt Disney World Marathon (Orlando, Florida, early January)

Additional marathons are among the races listed in the table beginning on page 264.

Cramps

Muscle cramps during a race are usually transient spasms, rather than the catastrophic charley-horse cramps that can wring a muscle tighter and tighter. Because they're most commonly brought on by dehydration, some runners call them heat cramps. The best solution is to keep as well hydrated as possible. Cramps can also be signs that a muscle has been taxed beyond its normal limits. Solve that with better training (or better tapering) next time around.

Race cramps usually spasm and release in less than the duration of a single stride. Each one is over the instant you feel it, but a series of them can disrupt your stride and send you lurching into a drunken-looking stagger. They're usually not painful, but they are disconcerting, partly because you're not sure how much more the muscle can take without totally seizing up.

Respond in the same ways you would to hitting the wall (cramps, in fact, are sometimes a symptom of hitting the wall): take some water or a sports drink, eat a carbohydrate gel, slow down a bit, and wait a few minutes to see what happens. That may be all it takes, particularly if you're able to get a really good drink. If not, try stopping for a few seconds of stretching, but don't stop for long or you'll stiffen up enough to make it hard to get moving again.

JOAN'S COMEBACK

Seventeen days before the 1984 Olympic Trials, U.S. marathoner Joan Benoit Samuelson underwent arthroscopic knee surgery. It looked like the death knell on her quest for Olympic gold; for about 2 weeks she couldn't even jog. Instead, she kept in shape mainly with a cranking apparatus that worked her arms. She may also have done some swimming. Four or five days before the race she was able to do a little jogging, but most people assumed it was too little, too late.

The skeptics were wrong. Joan won the trials and went on to win the first ever women's Olympic Marathon in a triumphant run through the streets of Los Angeles—one of the greatest surgical recoveries in sporting history.

WOMEN'S MARATHONING

Women's marathoning is a recent sport. It gained attention in 1967 when K. V. Switzer entered the Boston Marathon, which like other marathons was open to men only. A race official discovered that K. stood for Kathrine, and he attempted to pull her off the course, but she eluded him and became the first woman to complete (officially or not) the Boston Marathon.

The New York City Marathon, in 1971, was the first to officially allow women to compete. But only four women entered that year. The winner's time, a 2:55:22 by 19-year-old Beth Bonner of New Jersey, became the world record.

By the end of 1979, Grete Waitz of Norway had lowered the world mark to 2:27:33 in the first of a stunning string of eight New York City victories in 10 years. Five years after Grete's first New York City victory, women finally won the right to compete in an Olympic marathon.

Today, the majority of marathon finishers are women. Naoko Takahashi of Japan became the first woman to break 2:20, running a 2:19:46 in the 2001 Berlin Marathon. A week later, Catherine Ndereba of Kenya lowered the mark by another minute to 2:18:47 at Chicago. That meant that in the 22 years since Grete ran her 2:27, the women managed to reduce their times by a stunning 5.5 percent, while the men have managed less than half that much.

More significantly, from 1979 to the present, the women have closed about one-third of the gap between them and the men. And while it's likely that the maturation of women's running means that the big gains are over, you certainly won't see me betting against them!

RECOVERY

Most marathoners don't take enough time for recovery. I must admit that I was among the worst of them. Like many top competitors—and more than a few recreational racers—I was so driven to get back in training that I'd be out running the day after a marathon, even though it hurt so much to walk that I couldn't get downstairs without turning around and descending facing backward.

Don't succumb to this temptation. If necessary, reread the discussion of running addiction in chapter 10. If you gave the race everything you had (or nearly everything), marathon recovery *should* be a 6-week process. Don't run at all for 2 weeks. If you start feeling stale and want some exercise, try swimming, or maybe some light bicycling. *Stroll* around the neighborhood. After all the time you've spent training, your family and nonrunning friends will love you for it.

In the third week you can begin your return to running. Start at one-third of the mileage that you were running before your marathon buildup, and take the next 3 weeks to gradually return to your original baseline volume. Don't even think of doing speed work until you've returned to baseline, and don't race even a 5K until a couple weeks after that.

For those of us with the motivation to train for a marathon, taking time for a proper recovery may require more self-discipline than did the training and the race itself. Partly, that's due to the nagging fear of missed training. View the forced rest simply as part of the commitment involved in running a marathon: you boost your training, run the race, and take 6 weeks to recover—all part of the package. The only exception is if you didn't run the marathon as a serious effort. Some people collect large numbers of marathons with little more exertion than other racers expend in 20-mile training runs. These people may be able to recover much more quickly than do those who gave the race everything they could. But don't delude yourself into thinking you're one of them if you actually ran a hard race.

RECOMMENDED MARATHON RECOVERY SCHEDULE

Week	Permissible Base Training	Permissible Speed Work
1	no running easy cross-training OK	none
2	no running easy cross-training OK	none none
3	up to 33 percent of baseline*	none
4	up to 50 percent of baseline	none
5	up to 75 percent of baseline	none
6	up to 100 percent of baseline	none
7	normal baseline	return to normal

* "Baseline" is the amount of running per week that you were doing before you started marathon training. For most people this will be 30 miles per week.

How often you can run a marathon depends on how hard you run them. If you actually race your marathons (rather than simply trying to finish), it's not a good idea to do more than about two per year.

16

Masters Running

Running is a sport in which age means everything—and nothing. Age is important because athletic potential increases through childhood, peaks in your 20s and 30s, and slowly declines thereafter. But except for elite runners seeking the big prizes, the true competition is with yourself or others in your age group. Just as there's no glory for a mature runner who outsprints a schoolchild into the finishing chute, there's no shame for an older runner who can't quite hold with the college kids (although outlasting one of "them young whippersnappers" can be a source of great glee).

Running is probably the most age-friendly of all major sports. Races almost universally give first, second, and third-place awards in more than a dozen age brackets, male and female, and the esteem is the same for the 45- to 49-year-olds as it is for the 25- to 29-year-olds. In fact, at award ceremonies, the oldest runners often draw the loudest applause.

Some fortunate people accept aging with grace. But many runners, particularly those who were good in their youth, have trouble dealing with the inevitable slowdown. They find it hard not to compare everything they do today to their lifetime PRs—even though that can become a road to depression, despair, and ostracism by people tired of listening to them whine.

The solution lies in masters running.

In athletics, "masters" means "older"—and in running you graduate into the masters division at age 40. For a lot of competitors it's an enormous psychological boost—enough that many a 39-year-old racer has waited with bated breath for that 40th birthday. Even elite athletes can gain a new lease on life. My asthma prevented me from going this route, but others have led quite successful masters careers.

In most races, winning is no longer within the masters runner's reach (except for a few phenomenal runners in their early 40s), but there are plenty of opportunities to excel in your age group. Particularly appealing are masters-only events, but even all-comers races generally have separate masters trophies (for both men and women), making the 40-to-44 age division one of the most intensely competitive on the circuit.

Moving up the scale brings new age divisions where, every few years, you get to start over again as the "baby"—allowing those benchmark birthdays that depress your nonrunning friends to become reasons for rejoicing rather than dismay. It's delightful to hear a 70-year-old revel at no longer having to chase those 65-year-old "kids." As long as your health holds, there's no upper limit to the age at which you can race.

(VERA JAGENDORF)

MASTERS PHYSIOLOGY: BAD NEWS/GOOD NEWS

Despite the popularity of masters running, studies of the effects of age on athletic performance—and conversely, the effects of athletic endeavor on aging—are still in their infancy. The best data are tables of age-related performance declines compiled by World Masters Athletics (WMA; often cited by its prior name, the World Association of Veteran Athletes). These tables reveal that age affects you differently at different race distances. Your ability falls off most quickly at middle distances between 600 meters and 1,000 meters, but more slowly at both sprint distances and in long-distance races. Marathoners and ultramarathoners show the slowest declines.

GRAY POWER

Even when medals aren't involved, running is a sport that honors its elders. Here's Rick:

When I was in my lower 30s, I ran a cross-country race that finished on a track crowded with spectators. The competition was extremely tough, and I was somewhere in the back half of the pack. Nevertheless, as I approached the finish, a tremendous roar went up from the crowd. At first, I thought the spectators were cheering in every finisher in this fashion. Then I realized that the cheers were lagging slightly behind me. I glanced back and saw a man 2 decades my senior bearing down on me hard.

The lesson: the more your hair grays, the more praise and encouragement you'll draw, regardless of where you run in the pack.

What's happening can best be explained by looking at the effect of aging on three variables: endurance, speed, and experience. Endurance appears to fall off more quickly than sprinting speed—explaining why middle-distance runners do not fare as well as sprinters. But in long races, the decline in endurance is offset by improved racing wiles. The longer the race, the more it calls for care in pacing, hill-climbing, hydration, and nutrition. It takes time to master these skills, and the process of learning them helps offset the purely physical decline in endurance that comes with age. Such, at least, is the theory that best appears to explain the WMA age-related performance tables.

As they near masters age, some runners use this "experience effect" to their advantage by shifting to longer distances. But age will eventually catch up with you, no matter how much experience you have. There are at least four major physiological effects.

- **VO_2max declines after age 30.** Conventional medical wisdom pegs the decline in this, the maximum rate at which your muscles can process oxygen, at about 10 mL/kg/min per decade. But runners who keep in training appear to fare better, seeing only about half the average decline. Better yet, taking up running late in life or doing more intensive speed workouts can boost your VO_2max by the same amount that two or three decades of less active life have lowered it. Nevertheless, aging eventually catches up with you, and your VO_2max will again start to decline, no matter how hard you train. This drop in VO_2max may be part of the reason why endurance falls off faster with age than does sprinting speed. Sprint races are carried out in bursts so short that they largely bypass the body's aerobic processes. That means that VO_2max is nearly irrelevant over the brief interval of a sprint. In longer races, of course, VO_2max is much more important.
- **Your maximal heart rate declines by about one beat per minute, each year.** Until recently, it was believed that this was part of the reason for the decline in VO_2max. Fewer beats per minute, it was presumed, translated to less blood pumped by the heart, and less oxygen reaching the muscles. Then in 2001, Drs. Darren McGuire and Benjamin Levine, from the University of Texas Southwestern Medical Center and Presbyterian Hospital, in Dallas, compared X-ray measurements of the amount of blood pumped by the hearts of five 50-year-old men who had also been tested 30 years before. The researchers found that the increase in stroke volume more than compensated for the decline in maximal heart rate. In other words, the middle-aged heart might beat more slowly than it once did, but it has lost none of its ability to supply blood (and oxygen) to the muscles. This means that the decline in maximal heart rate appears to be irrelevant to the decline in VO_2max, and is quite probably irrelevant to the effect of age on racing. That's good—because there's nothing you can do to offset the change in your heart rate, anyway.
- **You experience a gradual decline in muscle mass.** Frank Shorter, winner of the 1972 Olympic gold medal and 1976 silver medal for the marathon,

put this to the test in 1991, at age 43, when he had his body fat remeasured. At the time of the follow-up test, he weighed the same as he had when he won his medals, but when he had his body fat remeasured, he found that it had increased by 4 percentage points. That meant that he had lost a corresponding amount of muscle, even though he'd continued to run competitively. And lost muscle, of course, means less strength for running—or other activities, as well. The way to offset this is to keep active—especially with weight lifting.

- **You recover more slowly from injuries—and also from hard workouts.** This means that there are limits to how much you can attempt to offset the effects of age by ever-more-intense training. At best, that would leave you feeling increasingly beat up between training runs; at worst it would trigger an endless succession of slow-healing injuries.

At the same time, let's remember the good news: keeping fit is good for you—and the older you are the more important it becomes. Doctors haven't decided whether being in shape truly slows the aging process, but in large part that's because there's no good measure of what aging means. To the extent that aging entails a loss of strength and fitness, exercise clearly counteracts it. Running slows the normal age-related decline in VO_2max. And as a runner, you should be able to retain more muscle mass than your sedentary friends, even if you don't engage in supplemental weight lifting.

Whatever positive effect running has on aging per se, it has an even more pronounced effect on the *diseases* of aging. The best-known benefits are to your heart, blood pressure, and cholesterol level. But diabetics also benefit because exercise helps balance their blood sugar levels and counteracts their tendency to put on weight. And the weight-bearing/high-impact exercise of running helps prevent osteoporosis (loss of bone density) in postmenopausal women by stimulating the body to strengthen its bones.

Basically, no matter what ails you—or might as you grow older—exercise is probably good for it. To date, the U.S. surgeon general has found that regular physical activity

- reduces the risk of premature death
- reduces the risk of heart attack
- reduces the risk of developing diabetes
- helps prevent the development of high blood pressure
- reduces blood pressure in those whose pressure is already high
- protects against colon cancer
- helps control weight
- builds strong bones, muscles, and joints
- improves the strength and balance of older adults, reducing bone-breaking falls
- combats depression and anxiety
- promotes overall psychological well-being

MASTERS TRAINING

The key to successful masters running is to design a training schedule that takes the physiological effects of aging into account. It's a job you'll need to do more than once, modifying your routine again and again as you move through the age groups. But if you do it right, you'll gradually advance in the masters standings, simply by training more realistically than your competitors.

The best thing you can do for the decline in VO_2max is to keep your muscles fit without beating yourself up by overtraining. Cross-training can help because it can give you a good aerobic workout while tendons, ligaments, and other connective tissues recover from prior workouts. Try fitting some biking, cross-country skiing, rowing, swimming, or hiking into your schedule as low-impact supplements to running. Don't neglect the speed work, though. Just as interval training is the best way to boost VO_2max for racing, it's probably the best way to minimize the decline of VO_2max with age, as well.

> **As a masters runner, you shouldn't try to compete against your own marks from years before. Start collecting new personal records every time you move into a new age group.**

Offset the reduction in muscle mass by adding weight lifting to your schedule if you're not already doing it. Sedentary people can lose 30 to 40 percent of their muscle mass by age 70. Recent studies at the Human Performance Laboratory at Ball State University in Muncie, Indiana, have found that this comes disproportionately at the expense of fast-twitch muscle fibers—the ones that give you strength and speed for hill-climbing and your finishing kick. Once these fast-twitch cells are gone, the same studies show that it is very difficult to get them back.

Luckily, it's never too late to begin lifting. The Ball State researchers have found that even octogenarians can bulk up, and that people of all ages appear to gain strength equally quickly if put on comparable weight-lifting programs. How much weight lifting is necessary to offset nature's slow decline? The answer probably varies from person to person, but it's easy enough to monitor your progress. If you start seeing a decline in the amount you can lift, you're losing muscle. If your strength is going up, you're building it. For more precise feedback, you can have your body composition measured periodically (see pages 119–25).

To hold your own as you age, you may need to do exercises that would make a younger lifter bulk up, using slightly higher weights and fewer reps than are recommended in chapter 7 on weight training. But I know of no hard-and-fast rules on this subject, so you'll have to let common sense be your guide. My own experience, at a relatively young 44, is that weight lifting has allowed me to gain a substantial amount of muscle since my running days. Whether I'll be able to retain it into my 50s and 60s is an open question.

Unfortunately, there is no simple cure for the worst bugaboo of aging: the slow-down in recovery from intense workouts. As the body's ability to recover from stress declines, rigorous adherence to the hard-easy pattern recommended in chapter 3 becomes increasingly important, and even then, most masters runners eventually discover that they need to tone down their training schedules. Many successful masters runners, including some top competitors, have gone so far as to only run on alternate days, using the easy days for complete rest or for nonimpact cross-training.

Toning down your training schedule, however, does not require reducing the intensity of your speed training (except perhaps for people who are well up the masters age scale). In 1984, Carlos Lopes of Portugal won the Olympic marathon at age

JOHN KESTON

John Keston is a retired British singer and actor who took up running at age 55. Now living and training in Oregon, he's set more speed records than he can easily count. In 1994, at age 69, he became the oldest man ever to run a sub-3:00 marathon. Two years later, at age 71, he came within a minute of doing it again.

In 2001, John had a particularly good year, setting 11 world records at distances ranging from the mile to the marathon. Some of these marks were in the 75–79 age group, others were single-age records for 76-year-olds. Clearly, John is doing something right. Here's Rick, who knows him better than I do:

John's training is based on a combination of intensity and a great deal of rest. When one of his children, a weight lifter, reminded him that weight workouts should only be done every third day, John got to wondering if the same principle applied to masters training. Going a step beyond the every-other-day pattern favored by younger masters racers, John decided to run only every third day. The rest of the time he walks, about 6 miles per outing.

The runs are all long, and most are intense enough to contain embedded speed workouts. The toughest workouts are built around races, which John uses as his primary source of speed training. After a race, he typically runs enough cooldown mileage to bring the day's total to 15 to 17 miles. Three days later, he does another 15 to 17 miles, often with a 3-mile tempo run midway through. For marathons, he'll extend some of the runs to 20 miles. His weekly totals range from 35 to more than 50 miles, depending on whether his schedule fits 2 or 3 runs into any given week.

John, of course, is a gifted athlete who would have been a world-class runner if he'd discovered his talent earlier in life. His 15-mile runs would break down many less-talented seniors; they work for him partly because he's been running such distances for the better part of two decades. But 5K races could be done with a similar schedule using much shorter runs, well within the reach of many senior competitors. And John's basic advice applies to all: "There are days when I want to run," he says, "and I don't." In other words, he's a disciplined enough masters runner to know that he needs to be well-rested between workouts.

John has another tip for senior runners: try taking a couple of ibuprofen tablets the night before a race. When John does that, he wakes up feeling more limber and ready to go.

37, then went on to win the Rotterdam Marathon at age 38, setting a new world record of 2:07:11 (a full minute faster than my own record). Although 38 is a couple years shy of being a masters runner, Carlos was definitely at an age where most elite athletes start having to make adjustments. I asked him what he'd done to perform so well at that age, and he told me that his main adjustment had been to reduce the frequency of his hard workouts. These workouts, he said, still needed to be as intense as ever; he simply allowed more recovery time between them to keep from sliding into overtraining.

There will come a point when the more aggressive workout schedules in chapter 5 simply won't work for you, especially if combined with weekly long runs. At age 48, for example, Rick does best if his speed workouts are 5 days apart. Let your body be your guide; if you're stiff and sore, you need rest, and it may take a day or two longer than it once did to recover from a hard workout. You'll also need to pace your workouts to match your current race performances, not those you ran a decade ago. But don't slack off too far. Rather, take a cue from Carlos and maintain the subjective intensity of your workouts, even as you reduce their frequency. And take heart in the fact that your age-group competitors face the same constraints.

As the decades pass, you may also need to ratchet down the distance you run, even on easy days. As your speed declines, you're spending more time per mile pounding the pavement, and if you insist on running the same mileage you did as a youngster, those extra minutes can add up. Alternatively, you can reduce wear and tear by shifting more of your training to soft surfaces such as trails and treadmills.

AGE-GRADED PERFORMANCE STANDARDS

Once you've accepted the fact that you won't always be 25—or 35, 45, 55, or whatever—you can have a lot of fun with advancing age, using it as an opportunity to wipe the slate clean with each passing birthday. So what if you can't at 55 do what you once did at 50? You're in a new age bracket, and can start collecting PRs all over again!

There is a way, however, to compare those performances at age 55 with those at age 50—or performances at any other pair of ages, as well. It's called *age adjustment* and it works by shifting your past and present performances onto an age-graded performance scale.

The key to making such comparisons lies in adjusting for the normal effects of age. Athletic performance increases rapidly through childhood, then reaches a broad peak somewhere in your 20s and 30s. After that, the top competitors' speeds decline by about 8 to 10 percent per decade—with middle-distance runners declining most rapidly and sprinters and long-distance runners faring the best.

The graph opposite shows this in more detail for two popular road-racing distances: 5K and the marathon. Just for comparison, it also shows the effect of aging on 600-meter runners. Note that the graphs—or aging curves—don't specify a gender. The aging curves for men and women are so similar that if we put them side by side, you'd have trouble telling them apart.

There are, of course, substantial variations among individuals. I ran my world

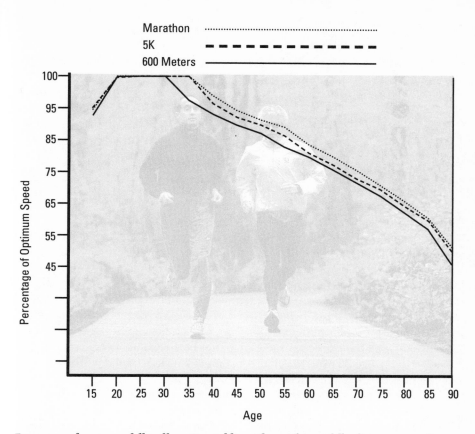

Legend:
- Marathon (dotted line)
- 5K (dashed line)
- 600 Meters (solid line)

Y-axis: Percentage of Optimum Speed (100, 95, 85, 75, 65, 55, 45)

X-axis: Age (15, 20, 25, 30, 35, 40, 45, 50, 55, 60, 65, 70, 75, 80, 85, 90)

Racing performance falls off most quickly with age for middle distances, such as 600 meters, and more slowly for long distances, especially the marathon.
(SOURCE: WORLD MASTERS ATHLETICS. USED WITH PERMISSION)

record at age 23. Carlos Lopes ran his at 38. In part, such variation is due to factors that have little to do with aging—the avoidance of injuries, the ability to peak for an important event, race-day weather, and a host of other contingencies that can contribute to running the race of your life. But in real life the effect of age on athletic performance isn't quite as precise as the curves make it look.

You'll notice that there are no actual times given with the aging curves. Instead, the data is presented in terms of percentages. Thus the age at which the curve crosses 90 percent is the age at which you can expect to be running about nine-tenths the speed you could have at peak. The 85 percent mark represents a 15 percent slowdown, and so on. This allows the same curves to be used for world-class and middle-of-the-pack competitors. Exercise physiologists believe that athletes of all abilities slow down at about the same rate.

If you're new to racing, your first few years of performances won't follow these curves. The aging curves depict the impact of age on your *potential*—which you'll only reach with training and experience. When you first take up racing, even if it's as a senior citizen, you'll probably see several years of steadily improving times, as your racing skills and training strategies mature. In effect, you'll be climbing up onto the curve; only when you reach it will the effects of aging start to become apparent.

> **Older runners need more rest and training volume—but speed workouts should feel as intense as ever.**

Crunching the Numbers

Age-graded performances are calculated by making use of the data underlying the aging curves. Your age-graded performances can then be compared with your own prior age-graded postings or to open-division world records. World Masters Athletics (WMA) encourages masters runners to calculate personal records this way, giving them the opportunity to set new, age-adjusted PRs anytime in their lives. If nothing else, this provides a wonderful psychological boost to racers who can no longer hit their onetime marks. Rick loves it because it tells him that the 32:30 he did in a 5-mile race at age 47 is better on an age-adjusted basis than the 29:30 he did at age 32. And to achieve a comparable age-graded performance on his next birthday he merely needs to beat 32:47.

It's possible to make age adjustments using the curves, though the math can get a bit tedious and it's difficult to read the graph with any precision. The tables on pages 250 and 251 therefore give the same data in terms of numbers called *age-adjustment factors* for a wide range of ages, male and female. Let's use them for a couple of real-world examples.

While we were writing this book, Rick posted a 40:50 in a 10K, on about his 48th birthday. His lifetime best at that distance was 37:44, run when he was in his early 30s. Comparing the two finishes is a matter of multiplying the 40:50 by 0.9121, which is his 10K age-adjustment factor from the men's table on page 250. The 37:44 does not need to be adjusted because it was run at an age for which the adjustment factor is 1.000. The result: Rick's 40:50 is comparable to a youthful 37:15—a new age-adjusted PR.

(To do these calculations, first convert race times into seconds. Rick's 40:50 equals 2,450 seconds. Multiplying that by the age-adjustment factor of 0.9121 for age 48, you get 2,235. To convert back to a usable form of minutes and seconds, divide by 60 to get fractional minutes—37.25—then multiply that fractional .25 by 60 to put it back into seconds. The answer: 37:15.)

You can work the numbers in the opposite direction, as well. Suppose Rick wants to better that age-adjusted PR at age 49. What's the mark he has to beat? This time, the calculation starts with the age-adjusted 37:15 and *divides* by the 49-year-old age factor, shown as 0.9051 in the table. The answer: 41:09.

The tables list adjustment factors for all common racing distances, but they're not limited to those distances. If you've raced a nonstandard distance, you can still adjust your result by using the column of the table applying to the closest standard distance; that will get you within a few seconds of the right answer.

> **Age-adjusting your race results allows you to factor out the effect of age, providing an age-neutral method for comparing past and present performances.**

Age- and Gender-Neutral Competition

Another use for the age-adjustment factors is to design races in which all participants compete directly for the top trophies. Such races are uncommon but they're not hard to set up. The person whose age-adjusted time is the highest fraction of the time for the 20-to-34 age category for their gender is the winner, regardless of age or sex or actual finish time. (The 20-to-34 category is chosen for the basis of comparison because these are ages for which the age-adjustment factors are 1.0000 at all racing distances.)

The computations are similar to those used to calculate an age-adjusted performance, but they can be simplified by using a set of age-adjusted standards compiled by World Masters Athletics. These standards, listed in the tables on pages 252 and 253, are world-class times "slowed down" to the appropriate age by application of the age-adjustment factors. They are simply the performances that age-adjust to approximately the world-record mark for each age and distance.

To use the age standards, first find your age and race-distance in the men's or women's table. Divide the time given there (after converting it to seconds) by your actual race performance (also in seconds). The answer will be your percentage used for comparison with all other runners. For example, a 54-year-old-woman who runs 53:12 for a 10K scores 66 percent. That's a good performance, probably good enough to allow her to win age-group medals in small races. Scoring 100 percent would mean running at or near the world age-group mark. A moderately brisk walk would put you at about the 30 percent level.

WMA has divided runners into several competitive categories according to how they score against the age-graded standards:

- world class (above 90 percent)
- national class (above 80 percent)
- regional class (above 70 percent)
- local class (above 60 percent)

These categories are a bit generous. A runner who can hit only 80 percent of the world record is going to have difficulty competing *(continued on page 254)*

AGE-ADJUSTMENT FACTORS FOR COMMON RACE DISTANCES: MEN
(see explanation on page 248)

Age	5K	5 mile/ 8K	10K	15K	10 mile	20K	Half-Marathon	Marathon
20–34	1.0000	1.0000	1.0000	1.0000	1.0000	1.0000	1.0000	1.0000
35	0.9963	1.0000	1.0000	1.0000	1.0000	1.0000	1.0000	1.0000
36	0.9895	0.9934	0.9953	0.9989	0.9996	1.0000	1.0000	1.0000
37	0.9827	0.9866	0.9884	0.9921	0.9928	0.9951	0.9957	1.0000
38	0.9760	0.9797	0.9816	0.9852	0.9859	0.9882	0.9888	0.9973
39	0.9692	0.9729	0.9747	0.9784	0.9791	0.9814	0.9820	0.9904
40	0.9624	0.9661	0.9679	0.9715	0.9722	0.9745	0.9751	0.9835
41	0.9555	0.9592	0.9610	0.9646	0.9653	0.9676	0.9682	0.9765
42	0.9487	0.9523	0.9541	0.9576	0.9583	0.9606	0.9612	0.9695
43	0.9418	0.9454	0.9471	0.9507	0.9514	0.9537	0.9543	0.9626
44	0.9350	0.9385	0.9402	0.9437	0.9444	0.9467	0.9473	0.9556
45	0.9281	0.9316	0.9333	0.9368	0.9375	0.9398	0.9404	0.9486
46	0.9211	0.9246	0.9262	0.9297	0.9304	0.9327	0.9333	0.9415
47	0.9141	0.9175	0.9192	0.9226	0.9233	0.9256	0.9262	0.9344
48	0.9071	0.9105	0.9121	0.9156	0.9163	0.9186	0.9192	0.9272
49	0.9001	0.9034	0.9051	0.9085	0.9092	0.9115	0.9121	0.9201
50	0.8931	0.8964	0.8980	0.9014	0.9021	0.9044	0.9050	0.9130
51	0.8859	0.8891	0.8907	0.8941	0.8948	0.8971	0.8977	0.9057
52	0.8787	0.8819	0.8834	0.8868	0.8875	0.8898	0.8904	0.8983
53	0.8714	0.8746	0.8762	0.8795	0.8802	0.8825	0.8831	0.8910
54	0.8642	0.8674	0.8689	0.8722	0.8729	0.8752	0.8758	0.8836
55	0.8570	0.8601	0.8616	0.8649	0.8656	0.8679	0.8685	0.8763
56	0.8495	0.8525	0.8540	0.8573	0.8580	0.8603	0.8609	0.8686
57	0.8419	0.8449	0.8464	0.8497	0.8504	0.8527	0.8533	0.8610
58	0.8344	0.8374	0.8388	0.8420	0.8427	0.8450	0.8456	0.8533
59	0.8268	0.8298	0.8312	0.8344	0.8351	0.8374	0.8380	0.8457
60	0.8193	0.8222	0.8236	0.8268	0.8275	0.8298	0.8304	0.8380
61	0.8113	0.8142	0.8156	0.8187	0.8194	0.8217	0.8223	0.8299
62	0.8033	0.8062	0.8075	0.8107	0.8114	0.8137	0.8143	0.8218
63	0.7954	0.7981	0.7995	0.8026	0.8033	0.8056	0.8062	0.8137
64	0.7874	0.7901	0.7914	0.7946	0.7953	0.7976	0.7982	0.8056
65	0.7794	0.7821	0.7834	0.7865	0.7872	0.7895	0.7901	0.7975
66	0.7708	0.7735	0.7748	0.7779	0.7786	0.7809	0.7815	0.7888
67	0.7623	0.7649	0.7662	0.7692	0.7699	0.7722	0.7728	0.7801
68	0.7537	0.7563	0.7575	0.7606	0.7613	0.7636	0.7642	0.7715
69	0.7452	0.7477	0.7489	0.7519	0.7526	0.7549	0.7555	0.7628
70	0.7366	0.7391	0.7403	0.7433	0.7440	0.7463	0.7469	0.7541
71	0.7273	0.7298	0.7309	0.7339	0.7346	0.7369	0.7375	0.7447
72	0.7180	0.7204	0.7216	0.7245	0.7252	0.7275	0.7281	0.7353
73	0.7087	0.7111	0.7122	0.7152	0.7159	0.7182	0.7188	0.7258
74	0.6994	0.7017	0.7029	0.7058	0.7065	0.7088	0.7094	0.7164
75	0.6901	0.6924	0.6935	0.6964	0.6971	0.6994	0.7000	0.7070
76	0.6798	0.6821	0.6832	0.6861	0.6868	0.6891	0.6897	0.6966
77	0.6696	0.6718	0.6729	0.6757	0.6764	0.6787	0.6793	0.6862
78	0.6593	0.6615	0.6625	0.6654	0.6661	0.6684	0.6690	0.6759
79	0.6491	0.6512	0.6522	0.6550	0.6557	0.6580	0.6586	0.6655
80	0.6388	0.6409	0.6419	0.6447	0.6454	0.6477	0.6483	0.6551

Source: World Masters Athletics. Reprinted with permission.

AGE-ADJUSTMENT FACTORS FOR COMMON RACE DISTANCES: WOMEN
(see explanation on page 248)

AGE	5K	5 MILE/ 8K	10K	15K	10 MILE	20K	HALF- MARATHON	MARATHON
20–34	1.0000	1.0000	1.0000	1.0000	1.0000	1.0000	1.0000	1.0000
35	0.9913	0.9954	0.9974	1.0000	1.0000	1.0000	1.0000	1.0000
36	0.9835	0.9876	0.9896	0.9934	0.9941	0.9963	0.9969	1.0000
37	0.9758	0.9798	0.9818	0.9856	0.9863	0.9885	0.9891	0.9979
38	0.9680	0.9721	0.9741	0.9779	0.9786	0.9807	0.9813	0.9901
39	0.9603	0.9643	0.9663	0.9701	0.9708	0.9729	0.9735	0.9823
40	0.9525	0.9565	0.9585	0.9623	0.9630	0.9651	0.9657	0.9745
41	0.9447	0.9486	0.9506	0.9544	0.9551	0.9572	0.9578	0.9666
42	0.9368	0.9408	0.9428	0.9466	0.9473	0.9493	0.9499	0.9587
43	0.9290	0.9329	0.9349	0.9387	0.9394	0.9415	0.9421	0.9509
44	0.9211	0.9251	0.9271	0.9309	0.9316	0.9336	0.9342	0.9430
45	0.9133	0.9172	0.9192	0.9230	0.9237	0.9257	0.9263	0.9351
46	0.9053	0.9092	0.9112	0.9150	0.9157	0.9177	0.9183	0.9271
47	0.8973	0.9012	0.9032	0.9070	0.9077	0.9097	0.9103	0.9191
48	0.8894	0.8932	0.8952	0.8990	0.8997	0.9016	0.9022	0.9110
49	0.8814	0.8852	0.8872	0.8910	0.8917	0.8936	0.8942	0.9030
50	0.8734	0.8772	0.8792	0.8830	0.8837	0.8856	0.8862	0.8950
51	0.8652	0.8690	0.8710	0.8748	0.8755	0.8774	0.8780	0.8868
52	0.8570	0.8608	0.8628	0.8666	0.8673	0.8691	0.8697	0.8785
53	0.8488	0.8525	0.8545	0.8583	0.8590	0.8609	0.8615	0.8703
54	0.8406	0.8443	0.8463	0.8501	0.8508	0.8526	0.8532	0.8620
55	0.8324	0.8361	0.8381	0.8419	0.8426	0.8444	0.8450	0.8538
56	0.8239	0.8276	0.8296	0.8334	0.8341	0.8358	0.8364	0.8452
57	0.8154	0.8190	0.8210	0.8248	0.8255	0.8273	0.8279	0.8367
58	0.8068	0.8105	0.8125	0.8163	0.8170	0.8187	0.8193	0.8281
59	0.7983	0.8019	0.8039	0.8077	0.8048	0.8102	0.8108	0.8196
60	0.7898	0.7934	0.7954	0.7992	0.7999	0.8016	0.8022	0.8110
61	0.7808	0.7844	0.7864	0.7902	0.7909	0.7926	0.7932	0.8020
62	0.7719	0.7754	0.7774	0.7812	0.7819	0.7836	0.7842	0.7930
63	0.7629	0.7665	0.7685	0.7723	0.7730	0.7746	0.7752	0.7840
64	0.7540	0.7575	0.7595	0.7633	0.7640	0.7656	0.7662	0.7750
65	0.7450	0.7485	0.7505	0.7543	0.7550	0.7566	0.7572	0.7660
66	0.7355	0.7389	0.7409	0.7447	0.7454	0.7470	0.7476	0.7564
67	0.7259	0.7294	0.7314	0.7352	0.7359	0.7374	0.7380	0.7468
68	0.7164	0.7198	0.7218	0.7256	0.7263	0.7279	0.7285	0.7373
69	0.7068	0.7103	0.7123	0.7161	0.7168	0.7183	0.7189	0.7277
70	0.6973	0.7007	0.7027	0.7065	0.7072	0.7087	0.7093	0.7181
71	0.6870	0.6904	0.6924	0.6962	0.6969	0.6984	0.6990	0.7078
72	0.6767	0.6801	0.6821	0.6859	0.6866	0.6881	0.6887	0.6975
73	0.6665	0.6698	0.6718	0.6756	0.6763	0.6777	0.6783	0.6871
74	0.6562	0.6595	0.6615	0.6653	0.6660	0.6674	0.6680	0.6768
75	0.6459	0.6492	0.6512	0.6550	0.6557	0.6571	0.6577	0.6665
76	0.6347	0.6379	0.6399	0.6437	0.6444	0.6458	0.6464	0.6552
77	0.6234	0.6267	0.6287	0.6325	0.6332	0.6345	0.6351	0.6439
78	0.6122	0.6154	0.6174	0.6212	0.6219	0.6233	0.6239	0.6327
79	0.6009	0.6042	0.6062	0.6100	0.6107	0.6120	0.6126	0.6214
80	0.5897	0.5929	0.5949	0.5987	0.5994	0.6007	0.6013	0.6101

Source: World Masters Athletics. Reprinted with permission.

AGE-ADJUSTED PERFORMANCE STANDARDS: MEN
(see explanation on page 249)

Age	5K	5 MILE/ 8K	10K	15K	10 MILE	20K	HALF-MARATHON	MARATHON
20–34	0:12:58	0:21:19	0:26:58	0:41:26	0:44:40	0:56:20	0:59:03	2:06:50
35	0:13:01	0:21:19	0:26:58	0:41:26	0:44:40	0:56:20	0:59:03	2:06:50
36	0:13:06	0:21:27	0:27:06	0:41:29	0:44:41	0:56:20	0:59:03	2:06:50
37	0:13:12	0:21:36	0:27:17	0:41:46	0:44:59	0:56:37	0:59:18	2:06:50
38	0:13:17	0:21:46	0:27:28	0:42:03	0:45:18	0:57:00	0:59:43	2:07:11
39	0:13:23	0:21:55	0:27:40	0:42:21	0:45:37	0:57:24	1:00:08	2:08:04
40	0:13:28	0:22:04	0:27:52	0:42:39	0:45:57	0:57:48	1:00:33	2:08:58
41	0:13:34	0:22:13	0:28:04	0:42:57	0:46:16	0:58:13	1:00:59	2:09:53
42	0:13:40	0:22:23	0:28:16	0:43:16	0:46:37	0:58:39	1:01:26	2:10:49
43	0:13:46	0:22:33	0:28:28	0:43:35	0:46:57	0:59:04	1:01:53	2:11:46
44	0:13:52	0:22:43	0:28:41	0:43:54	0:47:18	0:59:30	1:02:20	2:12:44
45	0:13:58	0:22:53	0:28:54	0:44:14	0:47:39	0:59:57	1:02:48	2:13:42
46	0:14:05	0:23:03	0:29:07	0:44:34	0:48:00	1:00:24	1:03:16	2:14:43
47	0:14:11	0:23:14	0:29:20	0:44:55	0:48:23	1:00:52	1:03:45	2:15:44
48	0:14:18	0:23:25	0:29:34	0:45:15	0:48:45	1:01:20	1:04:14	2:16:48
49	0:14:24	0:23:36	0:29:48	0:45:36	0:49:08	1:01:48	1:04:44	2:17:51
50	0:14:31	0:23:47	0:30:02	0:45:58	0:49:31	1:02:17	1:05:15	2:18:55
51	0:14:38	0:23:59	0:30:17	0:46:20	0:49:55	1:02:48	1:05:47	2:20:02
52	0:14:45	0:24:10	0:30:32	0:46:43	0:50:20	1:03:19	1:06:19	2:21:12
53	0:14:53	0:24:22	0:30:47	0:47:07	0:50:45	1:03:50	1:06:52	2:22:21
54	0:15:00	0:24:35	0:31:02	0:47:30	0:51:10	1:04:22	1:07:25	2:23:32
55	0:15:08	0:24:47	0:31:18	0:47:54	0:51:36	1:04:54	1:07:59	2:24:44
56	0:15:16	0:25:00	0:31:35	0:48:20	0:52:04	1:05:29	1:08:35	2:26:01
57	0:15:24	0:25:14	0:31:52	0:48:46	0:52:31	1:06:04	1:09:12	2:27:19
58	0:15:32	0:25:27	0:32:09	0:49:12	0:53:00	1:06:40	1:09:50	2:28:38
59	0:15:41	0:25:41	0:32:27	0:49:39	0:53:29	1:07:16	1:10:28	2:29:58
60	0:15:50	0:25:56	0:32:45	0:50:07	0:53:59	1:07:53	1:11:07	2:31:21
61	0:15:59	0:26:11	0:33:04	0:50:37	0:54:31	1:08:33	1:11:49	2:32:50
62	0:16:09	0:26:26	0:33:24	0:51:06	0:55:03	1:09:14	1:12:31	2:34:20
63	0:16:18	0:26:43	0:33:44	0:51:37	0:55:36	1:09:56	1:13:15	2:35:52
64	0:16:28	0:26:59	0:34:04	0:52:09	0:56:10	1:10:38	1:13:59	2:37:26
65	0:16:38	0:27:15	0:34:25	0:52:41	0:56:44	1:11:21	1:14:44	2:39:02
66	0:16:49	0:27:34	0:34:48	0:53:16	0:57:22	1:12:08	1:15:34	2:40:48
67	0:17:01	0:27:52	0:35:12	0:53:52	0:58:01	1:12:57	1:16:25	2:42:35
68	0:17:12	0:28:11	0:35:36	0:54:28	0:58:40	1:13:46	1:17:16	2:44:24
69	0:17:24	0:28:31	0:36:01	0:55:06	0:59:21	1:14:37	1:18:10	2:46:16
70	0:17:36	0:28:50	0:36:26	0:55:45	1:00:02	1:15:29	1:19:04	2:48:11
71	0:17:50	0:29:13	0:36:54	0:56:27	1:00:48	1:16:27	1:20:04	2:50:19
72	0:18:04	0:29:35	0:37:22	0:57:11	1:01:36	1:17:26	1:21:06	2:52:30
73	0:18:18	0:29:59	0:37:52	0:57:56	1:02:24	1:18:26	1:22:09	2:54:45
74	0:18:32	0:30:23	0:38:22	0:58:42	1:03:13	1:19:29	1:23:14	2:57:03
75	0:18:47	0:30:47	0:38:53	0:59:30	1:04:04	1:20:33	1:24:21	2:59:24
76	0:19:04	0:31:15	0:39:28	1:00:23	1:05:02	1:21:45	1:25:37	3:02:04
77	0:19:22	0:31:44	0:40:05	1:01:19	1:06:02	1:23:00	1:26:56	3:04:50
78	0:19:40	0:32:13	0:40:42	1:02:16	1:07:03	1:24:17	1:28:16	3:07:39
79	0:19:59	0:32:44	0:41:21	1:03:15	1:08:07	1:25:37	1:29:40	3:10:35
80	0:20:18	0:33:16	0:42:01	1:04:16	1:09:12	1:26:58	1:31:05	3:13:37

Source: World Masters Athletics and calculations based on the table of age-adjustment factors for men. Reprinted with permission.

AGE-ADJUSTED PERFORMANCE STANDARDS: WOMEN
(see explanation on page 249)

AGE	5K	5 MILE/ 8K	10K	15K	10 MILE	20K	HALF- MARATHON	MARATHON
20–34	0:14:24	0:23:39	0:29:55	0:45:51	0:49:23	1:02:10	1:05:48	2:18:51
35	0:14:32	0:23:46	0:30:00	0:45:51	0:49:23	1:02:10	1:05:48	2:18:51
36	0:14:38	0:23:57	0:30:14	0:46:09	0:49:41	1:02:24	1:06:00	2:18:51
37	0:14:45	0:24:08	0:30:28	0:46:31	0:50:04	1:02:53	1:06:32	2:19:09
38	0:14:53	0:24:20	0:30:43	0:46:53	0:50:28	1:03:23	1:07:03	2:20:14
39	0:15:00	0:24:32	0:30:58	0:47:16	0:50:52	1:03:54	1:07:35	2:21:21
40	0:15:07	0:24:44	0:31:13	0:47:39	0:51:17	1:04:25	1:08:08	2:22:29
41	0:15:15	0:24:56	0:31:28	0:48:02	0:51:42	1:04:57	1:08:42	2:23:39
42	0:15:22	0:25:08	0:31:44	0:48:26	0:52:08	1:05:29	1:09:16	2:24:50
43	0:15:30	0:25:21	0:32:00	0:48:51	0:52:34	1:06:02	1:09:51	2:26:01
44	0:15:38	0:25:34	0:32:16	0:49:15	0:53:01	1:06:35	1:10:26	2:27:15
45	0:15:46	0:25:47	0:32:33	0:49:40	0:53:28	1:07:09	1:11:02	2:28:29
46	0:15:54	0:26:01	0:32:50	0:50:07	0:53:56	1:07:45	1:11:39	2:29:46
47	0:16:03	0:26:15	0:33:07	0:50:33	0:54:24	1:08:20	1:12:17	2:31:04
48	0:16:11	0:26:29	0:33:25	0:51:00	0:54:53	1:08:57	1:12:56	2:32:25
49	0:16:20	0:26:43	0:33:43	0:51:28	0:55:23	1:09:34	1:13:35	2:33:46
50	0:16:29	0:26:58	0:34:02	0:51:56	0:55:53	1:10:12	1:14:15	2:35:08
51	0:16:39	0:27:13	0:34:21	0:52:25	0:56:24	1:10:51	1:14:57	2:36:34
52	0:16:48	0:27:28	0:34:40	0:52:54	0:56:56	1:11:32	1:15:39	2:38:03
53	0:16:58	0:27:45	0:35:01	0:53:25	0:57:29	1:12:13	1:16:23	2:39:33
54	0:17:08	0:28:01	0:35:21	0:53:56	0:58:03	1:12:55	1:17:07	2:41:05
55	0:17:18	0:28:17	0:35:42	0:54:28	0:58:36	1:13:37	1:17:52	2:42:38
56	0:17:29	0:28:35	0:36:04	0:55:01	0:59:12	1:14:23	1:18:40	2:44:17
57	0:17:40	0:28:53	0:36:26	0:55:35	0:59:49	1:15:09	1:19:29	2:45:57
58	0:17:51	0:29:11	0:36:49	0:56:10	1:00:27	1:15:56	1:20:19	2:47:40
59	0:18:02	0:29:30	0:37:13	0:56:46	1:01:22	1:16:44	1:21:09	2:49:25
60	0:18:14	0:29:49	0:37:37	0:57:22	1:01:44	1:17:33	1:22:01	2:51:13
61	0:18:27	0:30:09	0:38:03	0:58:01	1:02:26	1:18:26	1:22:57	2:53:08
62	0:18:39	0:30:30	0:38:29	0:58:42	1:03:09	1:19:20	1:23:54	2:55:06
63	0:18:53	0:30:51	0:38:56	0:59:22	1:03:53	1:20:15	1:24:53	2:57:06
64	0:19:06	0:31:13	0:39:23	1:00:04	1:04:38	1:21:12	1:25:53	2:59:10
65	0:19:20	0:31:36	0:39:52	1:00:47	1:05:25	1:22:10	1:26:54	3:01:16
66	0:19:35	0:32:00	0:40:23	1:01:34	1:06:15	1:23:13	1:28:01	3:03:34
67	0:19:50	0:32:25	0:40:54	1:02:22	1:07:06	1:24:18	1:29:10	3:05:56
68	0:20:06	0:32:51	0:41:27	1:03:11	1:08:00	1:25:24	1:30:19	3:08:19
69	0:20:22	0:33:18	0:42:00	1:04:02	1:08:54	1:26:33	1:31:32	3:10:48
70	0:20:39	0:33:45	0:42:34	1:04:54	1:09:50	1:27:43	1:32:46	3:13:21
71	0:20:58	0:34:15	0:43:12	1:05:51	1:10:52	1:29:01	1:34:08	3:16:10
72	0:21:17	0:34:46	0:43:52	1:06:51	1:11:55	1:30:21	1:35:33	3:19:04
73	0:21:36	0:35:19	0:44:32	1:07:52	1:13:01	1:31:44	1:37:00	3:22:05
74	0:21:57	0:35:52	0:45:14	1:08:55	1:14:09	1:33:09	1:38:30	3:25:09
75	0:22:18	0:36:26	0:45:56	1:10:00	1:15:19	1:34:36	1:40:03	3:28:20
76	0:22:41	0:37:04	0:46:45	1:11:14	1:16:38	1:36:16	1:41:48	3:31:55
77	0:23:06	0:37:44	0:47:35	1:12:29	1:17:59	1:37:59	1:43:36	3:35:38
78	0:23:31	0:38:26	0:48:27	1:13:49	1:19:24	1:39:44	1:45:28	3:39:27
79	0:23:58	0:39:09	0:49:21	1:15:10	1:20:52	1:41:35	1:47:25	3:43:27
80	0:24:25	0:39:53	0:50:17	1:16:35	1:22:23	1:43:29	1:49:26	3:47:35

Source: World Masters Athletics and calculations based on the table of age-adjustment factors for women. Reprinted with permission.

(continued from page 249) at the national level, and someone who scores 60 percent is going to have to search hard to find winnable local races. But the numbers have the virtue of being easy to remember, and any such divisions are inherently arbitrary.

Where you fall in these categories is largely dictated by native talent. Beginning racers might be able to move up by 10 points or more, but experienced ones will find even a 2- or 3-point improvement to be a major challenge. It's a goal, however, that you can pursue even as you age: by beating the aging slowdown, even slightly, you can gradually move up—allowing you to truthfully boast that you are indeed getting better as you get older.

Age adjustment is also possible for sprinters, hurdlers, high jumpers, ultramarathoners, and participants in other racing events. If you want more details, you can obtain an inexpensive booklet containing dozens of pages of additional tables. The booklet is available from *National Masters News*, a monthly publication that covers all aspects of masters running. You can contact the publication at 818-760-8983 or www.nationalmastersnews.com.

Advanced Challenges

17

AFTER RACING FOR a few years, some runners start looking for new realms to conquer. Some are drawn to race over increasingly difficult terrain; others turn to multisport events in which running is only part of the package. Some seek out team events, such as relay races, while others (such as masters runners who notice reduced competition in their age groups) shift their focus from beating the clock to beating their competitors.

RACE STRATEGY 102: RACING PEOPLE RATHER THAN THE CLOCK

Most of this book assumes that your goals are time-based. If you're after a personal record, it doesn't matter how many people beat you, so long as you get the PR. But that's not the only way to race. At the elite level, the goal often is to *win*, and time is secondary.

In the pack, there are also times when you might want to apply elite tactics. Perhaps club bragging rights are on the line, or perhaps you're fast enough to be in the hunt for an age-group medal, and know exactly who you have to beat. In big races, these situations may not call for advanced tactics—if the pack is large enough, you may not be able to *see* your rival and all the elite tactics in the world won't do you any good. But in smaller events, you and your rival may find yourselves racing directly against each other in much the same manner as the frontrunners.

The most straightforward way to win, of course, is by running as fast as possible. That only works, though, if you're confident of being able to run your target pace, and reasonably certain that nobody else can run faster. If you're unsure of either of these, you'll start looking for ways to wear down your competitors so they can't obtain their own best performances—even if doing so slows you down, too.

The most obvious tactical question involves who takes the lead. Psychologically and physically, it's easier to follow. Even in calm weather, you can catch a draft as far as 5 or 6 feet behind another runner—like cyclists riding in a pack. Following is also mentally easier; the leader is the one who has to worry about whether the pace is too fast and who wonders how well those behind are handling it, while you just sit back and bide your time. In elite racing, early leaders rarely win.

Back in the pack you may have similar experiences. Taking the lead in a small group may leave you feeling unpleasantly pushed. Nevertheless, you rarely want to drop below your target pace simply to have company—unless, again, you are racing against specific individuals, rather than the clock.

Surges

Other tactics are designed to break a rival's spirit. This involves more than just out-psyching them. The mind-body connection is so strong that once you believe you're beaten you usually are, unable to run as fast as you otherwise could.

The most common way of breaking a competitor is by taking the lead and *surging* at a critical time, such as when you think your opponent is barely hanging on. A surge involves picking up the pace dramatically (maybe by 20 seconds per mile), for perhaps 200 to 800 meters. The pace is unsustainable, and your rival probably knows it as well as you do. In theory, the other runner could just ignore you and reel you back in when your surge has spent itself, but in practice, your competitor has to try to match you. There's an almost palpable bond of psychological and emotional energy between closely spaced runners—the same bond that makes it easier to follow than to lead. If you stretch that bond far enough, it snaps. The trailing runner begins to feel lost, lonely, slow, and—most importantly—beaten. Once that happens, it's very, very hard to make a comeback.

> **Surging works by opening up enough of a gap
> to break the psychological contact that makes it
> easier for the runner behind you to follow than to lead.
> A few yards' gap is all it takes to turn the inspiring
> feeling of chasing into the energy-draining
> one of being beaten.**

This psychological bond is something you'll feel as strongly as I did, regardless of your pace, even if you're not racing against a specific rival. The difference is that back in the pack, you'll usually feel it either as discouragement from being continually passed, or as extra energy from chasing down other runners, one at a time. Even if you're running solely against the clock, you can work this to your advantage. If you run smart in the first mile, you'll be the one doing most of the passing, later on.

SURGING TO VICTORY—AUSTRALIAN STYLE

Surging tactics first reached prominence in the 1960s when Ron Clarke, one of a long line of famous Australian distance runners, found himself in a 5K track race against Kip Keino, one of the earliest of the great Kenyans.

Clarke knew that Keino had the faster finishing kick so he tried to wear Keino down by surging for half of each of the race's 12½ laps.

Once Keino figured out what Clarke was doing, he countered by letting Clarke press slightly ahead on his surges then reeling him back in when the Australian slowed down to recover. But as the end neared, Clarke changed his pattern. He surged for half a lap—then instead of dropping back, pushed even harder for the rest of the lap. That broke the race wide open. With 1½ laps to go, Keino was out of contention.

I remembered this story and applied it in my third New York City Marathon, when my chief challenger was Rodolfo Gomez of Mexico, who had a good kick. Within a few miles it became obvious that he was pacing off me, biding his time. When he was still with me at mile 24, I began surging. I would run hard for about a minute, take 30 or 40 seconds to recover, then surge again. For the first 2 or 3 surges, he continued to shadow me, then for the next 2 or 3 he would let me pull about 10 yards in front, then catch back up—a sign that he was getting at least a little tired.

Finally with about half a mile to go, I applied Clarke's change of rhythm. I surged, then picked up the pace again, earning a 4- or 5-second lead. Rodolfo could only make up 1 or 2 seconds of it by the time we reached the finish.

At the elite level, surges can also be used to tire your competitors, even if you fail to break them. In my first two New York City Marathons, I was fairly confident that I had the strongest finish, but anything can happen in the last 200 meters, especially if everyone is fresh. My race plan therefore included taking the lead well before the end and surging as hard as necessary to make sure that anyone who was still with me at mile 25 was tiring.

Passing People

Elite racers are taught that if you pass someone in a race, you should do so quickly and decisively, with a brief burst of unsustainable speed. It costs energy, but it discourages them from tucking in behind you and getting the physical and psychological benefits of following *you*. It also exudes confidence, which may contribute to breaking them.

Normally, there's no reason to do this when running in the pack, especially in large races, where you're passing and being passed all the time. If you surge, even briefly with each change of position, you'll quickly wear yourself out, and it's best just to run your own race. On the other hand, if you're battling for an age-group prize with someone you know is in your age group, it pays to pass decisively. That's also useful if there's some friendly (or not so friendly) rival to whom you really want to show your heels.

Looking Back

If there's one fundamental rule to competitive racing, it's *never look back*. Doing so tells whoever's back there that you're worried; you might as well send up a flare saying that you're starting to run out of gas. Rick notes that he's never failed to catch a runner who hears his footsteps and throws a panicked look over his shoulder; I'd guess that his experience is pretty typical.

> **Following is easier than leading. But don't step on the leader's heels—there's no excuse for being that close.**

If you're running solely for a PR, of course, what's going on behind you should be a matter of complete indifference. There's really no reason to break stride or risk tripping by looking back. If you really *must* know who's behind you, take inventory when the course makes a 180-degree bend around a cone. Alternatively, you may be able to use a sharp corner to take a surreptitious backward glance. But beware, anyone who sees it will interpret it as the sign of weakness it is.

CHERRY-PICKING AGE-GROUP AWARDS

Many recreational racers never expect to win awards. But Rick believes that running enough of the right types of races will eventually give you a shot at one. Here's his advice on cherry-picking an age-group award—a term that conjures up images of lazily reaching into low-hanging branches to snag sweet morsels of fruit:

The first time I won an age-group award, I was simply going for a PR until I realized to my surprise that, a mile from the finish, I was far enough forward to be in medal contention. Since then, I've done a lot of thinking about what made for such easy pickings.

Your best chance of placing in the top three, I've concluded, comes from finding small, lightly publicized races in outlying communities. Start-up events are particularly good bets because optimistic planners may hope for more participants than actually show up. The result: medal-rich races with low turnouts. My second age-group award came in one of these, a race so tiny that I was the only one in my division. Most races offer only first-, second- and third-place awards, but some go 5, 10, or even 15 deep. Catch a race like that on a low-turnout day, and virtually everyone wins something.

Other cherry-picking tips:

- Start by recalling how you finished in a typical large race. Divide the total number of finishers by your standing in your age group, then multiply by 3. That's the largest race in which you have a reasonable hope of finding yourself in the medal hunt. For example, in a half-marathon with 3,600 finishers, I recently placed 25th in my age group—way out of award contention. But when I carry out the arithmetic it shows that there were about 150 racers overall for each person who beat me in my age group. In a race of 450 or fewer participants, I would have had a reasonable chance of placing in the top three in my division.

- Look for races with distance medleys, and enter the shortest distance. If there's a 5K and a 10K, for example, the 10K will siphon off most of the fastest runners.
- Avoid races with 10-year age brackets; 5-year brackets offer twice as many awards. Also, shun races with cash prizes or gift certificates for the winners. The competition for even the smallest such prize is intense.
- Look up last year's standings on the Internet and compare your PR to those of the age-group winners. You'd think everyone would do this and flock to the low-competition races, but that rarely happens.
- Go into cherry-picking mode on weekends with lots of races. The people who normally beat you can't be everywhere at once, so the competition may be thinly spread.
- Target the spring racing season. Most people relax during the winter, and are still building stamina in spring. The result: weaker competition.
- Enter a 5-mile or 10K race in the first 3 weeks after a big local marathon. Most of the marathoners won't show up; those who do won't run well.
- Don't give up. If you can't beat your age-group competitors any other way, outlive them! The number of participants drops sharply above age 50, but the number of awards per age group remains the same.

The only semilegitimate reason for looking behind you is if you're running solely to win, don't care about the time, and are wondering if you have a big enough lead to coast to the finish. But woe to you if you discover there's someone close behind and give them an unwanted boost!

> **Looking behind you will only encourage whoever's back there to pass you.**

CROSS-COUNTRY AND TRAIL RUNNING

Racing more competitively is an advanced challenge whose appeal will depend largely on how fast you are within your age group. Other challenges can be taken on by runners of all paces. Two of these are cross-country running and trail running.

For thousands of high school and collegiate runners, cross-country racing is a staple of the annual racing cycle, occupying the same niche in the fall that track does in the spring. All-comers cross-country meets are more rare, but if you search diligently enough through your local race directories, you can probably find a few, not too far from home. Alternatively, you might try a trail run. They have a similar flavor, and are a good deal more common, with hundreds listed each year in *Trail Runner* magazine.

The principal difference between trail and cross-country events is in ambiance. Cross-country races are generally held in open spaces such as parks or golf courses, where spectators can easily watch. Trail races are usually held in more isolated places where the lure is adventure, scenery, and nature. There are also important differences in the terrain. Cross-country races have no formal footpath. Trail runs do, but roots, sticks, and rocks may make for worse footing than on many cross-country courses. Not surprisingly, cross-country races tend to be hotly contested, while trail runs have more of a fun-run atmosphere. Most runners will be interested in trail runs only for variety, but these events also have a small, dedicated following that specializes in them.

Training for either type of race requires getting used to uneven terrain by training on it at least three times a week, starting at least 2 weeks before the race. Better is to start running on soft surfaces 4 weeks prior to the race, and to do some of your speed training on them. Since few such training routes have distances marked in quarter-mile increments, or even at the miles, you'll probably have to do fartleks on them, rather than track-style interval workouts. Gauge your performance by level of effort, trying to mimic the feel of the type of track workout you're trying to duplicate. If distances are marked, expect to be at least 10 to 15 seconds per mile slower than on the roads; soft, uneven surfaces are inherently more tiring. Trail races can be slower yet. On rocky, mountainous terrain, your normal pace expectations are pretty much meaningless. There are off-road races where the winners have trouble posting 8:00s.

Sprained ankles, scratched legs, tick bites, poison ivy, and finishing up looking like you've been mud wrestling are standard risks of trail running. All are reasons why this is likely to remain a specialty sport. Perhaps that's good; it's hard to imagine cramming 1,000 runners onto a narrow forest path. Even in smaller races, passing people can be a bit of a problem, reminiscent of being trapped behind a big RV on the highway. If it happens, take a recovery break and surge when you get a chance to pass. You usually won't have to wait long. Most trail runners won't deliberately block you—and even if they do, you can usually get around.

If you're one of those people to whom all of this sounds like great fun, you're not going to want to run many events without investing in trail shoes. Slightly sturdier than normal running shoes, they're built to give greater stability and to protect your foot from bruising collisions with rocks. They're also built of materials that won't wear out quickly from scrapes against rocks or sticks.

RELAY RACES

In the Olympics, relays are usually sprints or middle distances, such as the 4x100 meter, or the 4x400 meter. But for recreational racers, the most popular relays are longer-distance events, run on the roads. They're booming in popularity, particularly in the Pacific Northwest, where the granddaddy of them all, the 196-mile Hood to Coast Relay, draws 12,000 runners (1,000 teams) for a full-day trek from the flanks of 11,200-foot Mount Hood to the Pacific Ocean.

Registration information on this and other relays can be found the same way you'd find it for any other race: in the back of *Runner's World* or by searching the Internet. I've done the Hood to Coast three times, twice on the winning men's team (at the elite level, this is a highly competitive event), and once just for fun on a mixed male-female team.

Part of the relay-race appeal is simply that these are team events with a lot of camaraderie—something that's hard to find in postcollegiate racing. One approach to participating in them is to put together your own team; another is to ask the organizers to recommend Web sites that match runners with teams faced with last-minute dropouts. Speedy women are always in demand, but men can also find teams this way. Rick once landed a Hood to Coast berth on less than 48 hours' notice.

The primary differences between relays and conventional races is that typically you have to run more than one leg—and that your teammates have to keep pace with you in a van. Keeping the van on schedule involves its own logistical challenges, including a good deal of lost sleep.

On the Hood to Coast, everyone runs three times, with individual legs ranging from 3 to 8 miles. Other races have only two 5-mile legs. Starts are usually staggered to reduce congestion on the course, and individual legs can have challenges you'd never see in an ordinary race. On the Hood to Coast, for example, the first leg drops a pounding 2,000 feet in 5 miles, pretty much wiping out your leadoff runner's quads for the rest of the event. Idaho's Sawtooth Relay, on the other hand, has a leg that climbs nearly as relentlessly: 1,200 feet in 5 miles. Personally, I'd rather go up than down. Part of the team captain's challenge is in figuring out which runners will do best on which legs.

Training for a relay is similar to training for a conventional race that's slightly shorter than the total distance of your relay legs. On the Hood to Coast, for example, each runner does about 16.5 miles, but it feels about like a half-marathon. Unless your goal is simply to fun-run the event, you need to do training comparable to what you would do for a half-marathon. You can specialize that training for the relay by testing yourself a couple of times beforehand with three-times-a-day time trials. Try running 3 miles in the morning, 3 more miles in the early afternoon, and 3 more in the early evening, just to get a feel for what's going to be expected of you. Don't run all-out, but do run quickly—perhaps 15 to 20 seconds a mile slower than your target relay pace. Physically that won't do much for you that you're not getting from your ordinary training, but psychologically it will reassure you that you're indeed up for the task.

In the race, you'll feel fairly tired at the start of the second and third legs (particularly because it's hard not to stiffen up in the van), but you'll be surprised by how well you can move once you force yourself to get going. Most Hood to Coast racers average no more than 10 to 15 seconds per mile slower than their normal 10K or 5-mile marks.

Marathon Relays

The boom in relays has spilled over to the marathon circuit. An increasing number of races have relay divisions in which teams of two complete the marathon, trading off at the halfway mark. The race may provide shuttle buses, making the logistics simple. Training, obviously, is the same as for a half-marathon. Some marathons may divide the race up into 4 or 5 shorter segments.

Multisport Relays

Many multisport relays are triathlon-style events in which teams field a swimmer, a cyclist, and a runner, often in conjunction with a solo "ironman" division. Other relays are more exotic. The central Oregon town of Bend, for instance, hosts the annual Pole, Pedal, Paddle, in which teams descend 9,000-foot Mount Bachelor by downhill ski, cross-country ski, bike, kayak, and foot. It's easy to create similar events, limited only by the organizers' inventiveness and the local climate and terrain. Being the runner in such an event requires no specialized training—simply a collection of suitably skilled (or crazy) friends.

ALTERNATIVE-FORMAT RACES

In most races, the people to cross the finish line are the winners. But there are two types of races that even the slowest can win: predicted-time races, and handicap races.

Predicted-Time Races

A predicted-time run, sometimes called simply a *predict*, is a race in which you estimate your finishing time in advance, then leave your watch at home. Victory goes to the person with the best sense of pace (or luckiest guess). In theory, anyone can win, but racing experience is helpful in finding and maintaining your target pace.

Neither Rick nor I have ever run one of these events. They're not very common, although large running clubs will host them occasionally. If you try such a race, my advice would be to run at a level of effort about comparable to a tempo run. That's the easiest exertion level for most people to find and maintain, and if you've been doing regular tempo runs you have a reasonable feel for it. Also, if you've been clocking those tempo runs on well-measured courses, you should have a reasonable estimate of the pace at which you run them. Another advantage of running a predicted-time run at this pace is that, win or lose, it substitutes for a speed workout.

Handicap Races

Handicap races give slower runners a head start. I've run a few of these events, where the participants are equalized based on their best prior times at the distance. This means that if everyone were to run exactly at PR, they would all cross the finish together. That never happens, but needless to say, these are extremely intense races. You don't need to be fast to win, but you do need to be willing to pour on the effort so that the rest of the pack won't eat you up at the end.

The logistics dictate that handicap races have to be small; most will be club events with limited publicity. If you want to do one, seek information at running stores or check the Web pages of local running clubs. In registering, runners' PRs are typically collected on the honor system, but there's not much glory in winning such a race by sandbagging, so everyone should be pretty honest.

Another type of handicap race gives runners head starts according to age-adjustment factors. At age 70, John Keston ran a marathon that was handicapped in this manner, in Barcelona, Spain. John had the thrill of leading the pack for the first 25 miles until a 41-year-old Russian finally caught him. Masters runners love such races, but they're extremely rare.

MEGA-RACES

There's no official definition of a mega-race, but any event with 10,000 or more people is going to have a very different feel from an ordinary road race. Unless you're fast enough to get seeded in a special starting division, you'll spend the entire race caught in an enormous pack, but for a lot of people, that's half the fun. With turnouts that can exceed 50,000 runners, these events are vast celebrations of

The New York City Marathon draws nearly 30,000 finishers. (LEW BEACH/ALAMY)

fitness—running carnivals that worm their way through town to enormous finish-line parties. Expect a larger-than-usual fraction of slow runners and walkers; there may also be runners in costumes or in "centipede" teams of up to a dozen, linked by ropes (don't trip trying to pass them!).

The most famous mega-race is San Francisco's 12K Bay to Breakers, which has had more than 70,000 participants. Also enormous are several of the Race for the Cure events (which draw large crowds in support of breast cancer research) and the Lilac Bloomsday Run in Spokane, Washington, which pulls off the astonishing feat of clocking nearly 50,000 finishers (the largest event to provide finishing times for everyone). These and other large races are listed in the accompanying table. The rankings vary somewhat from year to year, as do the dates.

THE 101 LARGEST RACES IN THE UNITED STATES

RANK	FINISHERS	RACE (DISTANCE)	LOCATION	TIME OF YEAR
1	52,474	Examiner Bay 12th to Breakers (12K)	San Francisco, CA	mid-May
2	47,428	Race for the Cure (5K)	Washington, DC	early June
3	45,537	Lilac Bloomsday Run (12K)	Spokane, WA	early May
4	40,462	Celestial Seasonings Bolder Boulder (10K)	Boulder, CO	late May
5	35,974	Revlon Run for Women (5K)	Los Angeles, CA	mid-May
6	29,375	New York City Marathon	New York, NY	early November
7	27,889	LaSalle Banks Chicago Marathon	Chicago, IL	mid-October
8	22,652	Honolulu Marathon	Honolulu, HI	early December
9	21,256	Race for the Cure (5K)	Pittsburgh, PA	mid-May
10	18,289	Indianapolis Life 500 Festival Half-Marathon	Indianapolis, IN	early May
11	17,610	Race for the Cure: Orange County 5K (coed + women)	Newport Beach, CA	late September
12	17,192	City of Los Angeles Marathon	Los Angeles, CA	early March
13	17,048	Marine Corps Marathon	Washington, DC	late October
14	15,918	Suzuki Rock 'n' Roll Marathon	San Diego, CA	early June

THE 101 LARGEST RACES IN THE UNITED STATES (cont'd)

RANK	FINISHERS	RACE (DISTANCE)	LOCATION	TIME OF YEAR
15	15,668	Boston Marathon	Boston, MA	mid-April
16	14,144	Cooper River Bridge Run (10K)	Charleston, SC	early April
17	11,883	Quad-City Times Bix (7 mi.)	Davenport, IA	mid-July
18	11,876	Army Ten-Miler	Washington, DC	mid-October
19	11,844	Nationwide Direct Hood to Coast Relay (195 mi.)*	Mt. Hood– Seaside, OR	early August
20	11,445	Manchester Road Race (4.75 mi.)	Manchester, CT	late November
21	11,036	LaSalle Bank Shamrock Shuffle (8K)	Chicago, IL	late March
22	10,526	Race for the Cure (5K)	San Diego, CA	early November
23	9,472	Weinhard's Ale/ St. Patrick's Day Dash (3.5 mi.)	Seattle, WA	mid-March
24	8,003	Michael Forbes Trolley Run (4 mi.)	Kansas City, MO	late April
25	7,891	Utica Boilermaker 2nd (15K)	Utica, NY	early July
26	7,883	Race for the Cure (5K)	San Francisco, CA	mid-October
27	7,751	Portland Marathon	Portland, OR	late September
28	7,660	Walt Disney World Marathon	Orlando, FL	early January
29	7,400	Falmouth Road Race (7.1 mi.)	Falmouth, MA	late August
30	7,089	Spring Lake (5 mi.)	Spring Lake, NJ	late May
31	6,989	Race for the Cure (5K)	Sacramento, CA	mid-May
32	6,875	Junior Bloomsday (2 mi.)	Spokane, WA	mid-April
33	6,798	Race for the Cure (5K)	Ft. Worth, TX	early April
34	6,764	Gasparilla Distance Classic (5K)	Tampa, FL	mid-February
35	6,723	Jingle Bell Run (5K)	Seattle, WA	early December
36	6,703	Broad Street Run (10 mi.)	Philadelphia, PA	early May
37	6,650	Gate River Run (15K)	Jacksonville, FL	early March
38	6,605	Carlsbad 5000 (5K)	Carlsbad, CA	late March

* This is a relay with 1,000 teams of 12 runners each.

(continued next page)

RANK	FINISHERS	RACE (DISTANCE)	LOCATION	TIME OF YEAR
39	6,471	Jefferson Hospital Philadelphia Half-Marathon	Philadelphia, PA	mid-September
40	6,349	Country Music Marathon	Nashville, TN	late April
41	6,342	Kentucky Derby Festival Half-Marathon	Louisville, KY	late April
42	6,312	Race for the Cure: Quad Cities (5K)	Rock Island, IL	early June
43	6,254	Atlanta Half-Marathon	Atlanta, GA	late November
44	6,247	Race for the Cure (5K)	Des Moines, IA	mid-October
45	6,074	Grandma's Marathon	Duluth, MN	mid-June
46	5,991	Run to Feed the Hungry (5K)	Sacramento, CA	late November
47	5,907	Twin Cities Marathon	Minneapolis, MN	early October
48	5,867	Gasparilla Distance Classic (15K)	Tampa, FL	mid-February
49	5,731	Arena Club (5K)	Minneapolis, MN	late November
50	5,596	Cherry Creek Sneak (5 mi.)	Denver, CO	late April
51	5,564	Richard S. Caliguiri Great Race (10K)	Pittsburgh, PA	late September
52	5,548	Crim Festival of Races (10 mi.)	Flint, MI	late August
53	5,528	KNBR Bridge to Bridge (12K)	San Francisco, CA	early October
54	5,514	Omaha Corporate Cup (10K)	Omaha, NE	mid-September
55	5,413	Times Turkey Trot (5K)	Clearwater, FL	late November
56	5,388	Omaha Corporate Cup (2 mi.)	Omaha, NE	mid-September
57	5,355	Race for the Cure (5K)	Portland, OR	mid-September
58	5,182	Nortel Cherry Blossom (10 mi.)	Washington, DC	early April
59	5,178	Tufts Health Plan for Women (10K)	Boston, MA	early October
60	5,061	Running Spot Thanksgiving Day Run (10K)	Cincinnati, OH	late November
61	5,007	Rodes City Run (10K)	Louisville, KY	late March

Rank	Finishers	Race (distance)	Location	Time of year
62	4,977	Chicago Half-Marathon	Chicago, IL	mid-September
63	4,901	Get in Gear (10K)	Minneapolis, MN	late April
64	4,897	Union-Trib Dr. Seuss Race for Literacy (8K)	San Diego, CA	early May
65	4,881	Manhattan Half-Marathon	New York, NY	early August
66	4,811	Cigna HealthCare Corporate Road Race (5K)	Manchester, NH	early August
67	4,809	Charbo's Run (5 mi.)	Dorchester, MA	late March
68	4,743	Run to the Far Side (5K)	San Francisco, CA	late November
69	4,699	Compaq Houston Marathon	Houston, TX	mid-January
70	4,685	Cowtown (5K)	Fort Worth, TX	late February
71	4,680	Race for the Cure: Los Angeles County (5K)	Pasadena, CA	early November
72	4,640	Nationwide Direct Portland to Coast (125 mi.)	Portland– Seaside, OR	early August
73	4,530	New Times Phoenix (10K)	Phoenix, AZ	mid-November
74	4,508	Walt Disney World Half-Marathon	Orlando, FL	early January
75	4,457	America's Finest City Half-Marathon	San Diego, CA	mid-August
76	4,364	Nation's Bank River Run (2 mi.)	Wichita, KS	late May
77	4,266	Philadelphia Marathon	Philadelphia, PA	mid-November
78	4,265	Race for the Cure (5K)	Oklahoma City, OK	late September
79	4,243	Race for the Cure: Twin Cities (5K)	Edina, MN	mid-May
80	4,233	Suzuki Seattle Half-Marathon	Seattle, WA	late November
81	4,161	St. George Marathon	St. George, UT	early October
82	4,158	Canon Long Island Half-Marathon	East Meadow, NY	early May
83	4,157	Cowtown (10K)	Fort Worth, TX	late February
84	4,143	La Jolla Half-Marathon	La Jolla, CA	late April
85	4,099	Annapolis (10 mi.)	Annapolis, MD	late August

(continued next page)

THE 101 LARGEST RACES IN THE UNITED STATES (cont'd)

Rank	Finishers	Race (distance)	Location	Time of year
86	4,074	Motorola Austin Marathon	Austin, TX	late February
87	4,000	Bridge to Bridge (7K)	San Francisco, CA	early October
88	3,988	Bally Total Fitness B-Fit (5K)	Chicago, IL	late October
89	3,976	Old Kent River Bank Run (25K)	Grand Rapids, MI	mid-May
90	3,938	Great Cow Harbor (10K)	Northport, NY	mid-September
91	3,922	Nordstrom Beat the Bridge (8K)	Seattle, WA	mid-May
92	3,833	CVS-Cleveland (10K)	Cleveland, OH	late April
93	3,831	Manhattan Beach Old Hometown (10K)	Manhattan Beach, CA	early October
94	3,821	Cincinnati Flying Pig Marathon	Cincinnati, OH	mid-May
95	3,818	California International Marathon	Sacramento, CA	early December
96	3,815	Zoo Run for Life (10K)	Philadelphia, PA	early November
97	3,795	Cincinnati Heart Mini-Marathon (15K)	Cincinnati, OH	late March
98	3,723	Tommy's Surf City Run (5K)	Huntington Beach, CA	July 4
99	3,714	Redondo Beach Super Bowl (10K)	Redondo Beach, CA	late January
100 (tie)	3,636	Not Quite the NYC Marathon (5K)	New York City, NY	late October
100 (tie)	3,636	Gil Clark Memorial Run (15K)	Louisville, KY	early April

Source: USA Track and Field and the Road Running Information Center. Used with permission. Data is from 2000. For registration information, look for race listings in *Runner's World* or search for the race's home page on the Internet.

TRIATHLONS

Triathlons mix three sports—usually running, swimming, and bicycling, although the world's oldest, Eppie's Great Race in Sacramento, California, substitutes kayaking for swimming. And Rick once participated in a winter triathlon that mixed running, biking, and cross-country skiing.

Being competitive in a triathlon requires more than simply being good in all three sports; their merger creates a new sport with its own training regimens, skills, and strategies. Outstanding triathletes will be very good in each event but needn't excel in any of them.

Although I've done enough biking and swimming to be able to survive a triathlon, I've never felt the desire to enter one. The training would have been counterproductive, bulking up swimming and bicycling muscles that would have cost me valuable seconds in my specialty. Rick, however, has done about a dozen triathlons, including a couple of Hawaii Ironman look-alikes (2.4-mile swim, 112-mile bike, 26.2-mile run). Serious triathlon training is beyond the scope of this book, but here are his suggestions for runners wanting to give the triathlon a try:

- Rely on your normal running training to see you through the running leg. If necessary, slack off a bit to make time for biking and swimming.
- Train your weaknesses. You can lose more time by being undertrained in your poorest event than you can make up by being superbly fit in your best one.
- Try to build up your weekly cycling and swimming to at least twice the race distances, with at least one long swim and one long bike ride per week. If this is impractical, swim and cycle as much as you can. If you're trying to be competitive, of course, you need to do speed work in these sports as well as in running.
- Because cycling and swimming are nonimpact sports, you can probably build up your training more quickly for them than for running. But try not to exceed a 10 percent increase per week—less if your knees or Achilles tendons start to bother you on the bike or if your shoulders are weak points in swimming.
- Apply the usual hard-easy training pattern to these sports, just as you do for running. And make sure that you're not simply alternating hard running days with hard biking or swimming days. Your body needs real rest for optimum recovery.
- Practice the bike-run transition during training by bicycling a few miles before running, at least once a week. Bicycling tires the quads, which are your shock absorbers for running. Practice won't eliminate this, but it will let you know what to expect.
- Swimming in a pack is a good way to get kicked in the face. Be careful in the race, and don't be too aggressive until you've gained experience. On your first triathlon, your greatest difficulty swimming will be steering a straight

line across open water. Use the angle of the sun to help maintain your bearings, and don't be embarrassed to raise your head occasionally to look around. Learn to breathe on both sides so you can keep track of landmarks to left and right. Unless you're extremely fit, swim mostly with your arms, and save your legs for biking and running. Kick fairly vigorously in the last few yards, though, to restore circulation to your legs; otherwise you won't be able to stand up when you leave the water.

- Be organized but not panicked during the transitions. Think through in advance exactly what you'll do, and don't try too hard to save seconds in the actual race; it's too easy to make major mistakes.
- If you're on the course for more than a couple of hours, you're going to need to eat to stave off what cyclists call "the bonk"—which is kind of like hitting the wall during a marathon, but not quite as devastating. Practice eating on training outings to see what you can and cannot eat without getting a side stitch or a bellyache. It's easier to eat on the bike leg than it is while running.
- Have fun during the race! If you like the sport, consult *Triathlete* magazine for additional information.

Duathlons are events that involve only two of the triathlon sports. (Sometimes they're also called biathlons, but technically, that term should be reserved for an Olympic sport that combines cross-country skiing and target shooting.) Most duathlons are bike/run events, often mixing mountain biking and trail running. They seem to be gaining in popularity, especially in parts of the country where the water is too cold for comfortable swimming. Duathlon training is similar to triathlon training, except, of course, that you only need to train for two sports.

ULTRAMARATHONS

Any race longer than a marathon is an ultramarathon. It's an extremely diverse category. Traditional ultramarathoning distances range from 50 miles through 100K (62 miles), but there are also extremely long events such as 100 miles and 24-hour runs. At the short end of the spectrum—if an ultra could ever be called "short"— are 50K races (31 miles), which are basically extended marathons.

Don't attempt any ultra until you've run several marathons fairly comfortably, on enough training that you're not struggling just to make it through 26.2 miles. A short ultra might not sound all that much longer than a marathon, but the extra miles are tough ones.

That said, training for a 50K isn't all that different from training for a marathon. Increase your weekly mileage by about 10 percent, add the same increment to your long runs, and do the same speed work you would do for a marathon. The race will be more challenging than what you're used to, but you should be able to handle it.

For a 50-miler or 100K, you need at least 70 miles a week unless you plan to do a lot of walking. You're also going to need to get in some really long runs. In an

8-week interval before the 54-mile Comrades Marathon, I did two 25-milers, two 30-milers, two 35-milers, and two 40-milers, then tapered as I would for a marathon. (Needless to say, I didn't do the 40-milers on back-to-back weeks; I took 4 weeks to build from 25 to 40 miles, then dropped back to 25 miles and repeated the sequence.)

Pace these long runs and your easy days at your target ultramarathon pace, which you can expect to be about 1:00 to 1:15 per mile slower than your marathon pace. My pace in Comrades, for example, proved to be 6:15s. My best marathon was at 4:54s. Even at this slow pace, these long training runs are tough, and recovery takes more than a day. That forced me to cut back from three to two speed workouts per week; you may need to cut back to one every 5 days. Do six to eight mile-repeats, at 1:00 per mile faster than your expected pace in the ultra.

Training for really long ultras is similar but even more slowly paced. The world records for 100 miles and 24 hours, for example, are 12:05:43 and 290.2 kilometers (180 miles) for men; 13:47:42 and 243.6 kilometers (151 miles) for women. Impressive as those figures are, they represent fairly slow paces: 7:15s and 8:00s for 100 miles and 24 hours, respectively, for the men and 8:17s and 9:32s for the women.

Running an ultra, be extremely careful to keep your pace slow, and to run at a steady, efficient energy level. Also, plan to eat along the way. In the Comrades, I'd expected the race to provide frequent food, but the aid-station procedures changed and that didn't happen. As a backup, I'd taped a gel pack to the water bottles that were waiting for me at each aid station (every 4 miles). That helped, but it wasn't as much nutrition as I'd have preferred—I hit the wall so hard at mile 27 that I dropped nearly to a walk, and barely recovered at all. But recover I did, and went on to win the race by a tidy margin, the first American ever to do so. After years of struggling with my asthma, that 1994 win was also an enormous personal victory and a great note on which to bow out of competitive running to take up my current role as a coach. Today I count it as one of the most gratifying races of my career.

PACE CHART OF COMMON WORKOUT AND RACING DISTANCES

T HE FOLLOWING CHART can function in lieu of a pace calculator to help you calculate per-mile paces from your race performances, or to structure interval workouts based on per-mile paces. Find your pace in the first column and then read across the row.

(PAUL JOHNSTON/ALAMY)

Mile Pace	Duration of Interval						
	200 m	300 m	400 m	600 m	800 m	1,000 m	1,200 m
4:30	0:34	0:51	1:08	1:41	2:15	2:49	3:23
4:35	0:34	0:52	1:09	1:43	2:18	2:52	3:26
4:40	0:35	0:53	1:10	1:45	2:20	2:55	3:30
4:45	0:36	0:53	1:11	1:47	2:23	2:58	3:34
4:50	0:36	0:54	1:13	1:49	2:25	3:01	3:38
4:55	0:37	0:55	1:14	1:51	2:28	3:04	3:41
5:00	0:38	0:56	1:15	1:53	2:30	3:08	3:45
5:05	0:38	0:57	1:16	1:54	2:33	3:11	3:49
5:10	0:39	0:58	1:18	1:56	2:35	3:14	3:53
5:15	0:39	0:59	1:19	1:58	2:38	3:17	3:56
5:20	0:40	1:00	1:20	2:00	2:40	3:20	4:00
5:25	0:41	1:01	1:21	2:02	2:43	3:23	4:04
5:30	0:41	1:02	1:23	2:04	2:45	3:26	4:08
5:35	0:42	1:03	1:24	2:06	2:48	3:29	4:11
5:40	0:43	1:04	1:25	2:08	2:50	3:33	4:15
5:45	0:43	1:05	1:26	2:09	2:53	3:36	4:19
5:50	0:44	1:06	1:28	2:11	2:55	3:39	4:23
5:55	0:44	1:07	1:29	2:13	2:58	3:42	4:26
6:00	0:45	1:08	1:30	2:15	3:00	3:45	4:30
6:05	0:46	1:08	1:31	2:17	3:03	3:48	4:34
6:10	0:46	1:09	1:33	2:19	3:05	3:51	4:38
6:15	0:47	1:10	1:34	2:21	3:08	3:54	4:41
6:20	0:48	1:11	1:35	2:23	3:10	3:58	4:45
6:25	0:48	1:12	1:36	2:24	3:13	4:01	4:49
6:30	0:49	1:13	1:38	2:26	3:15	4:04	4:53
6:35	0:49	1:14	1:39	2:28	3:18	4:07	4:56
6:40	0:50	1:15	1:40	2:30	3:20	4:10	5:00
6:45	0:51	1:16	1:41	2:32	3:23	4:13	5:04
6:50	0:51	1:17	1:43	2:34	3:25	4:16	5:08
6:55	0:52	1:18	1:44	2:36	3:28	4:19	5:11
7:00	0:53	1:19	1:45	2:38	3:30	4:23	5:15
7:05	0:53	1:20	1:46	2:39	3:33	4:26	5:19
7:10	0:54	1:21	1:48	2:41	3:35	4:29	5:23
7:15	0:54	1:22	1:49	2:43	3:38	4:32	5:26
7:20	0:55	1:23	1:50	2:45	3:40	4:35	5:30
7:25	0:56	1:23	1:51	2:47	3:43	4:38	5:34
7:30	0:56	1:24	1:53	2:49	3:45	4:41	5:38
7:35	0:57	1:25	1:54	2:51	3:48	4:44	5:41
7:40	0:58	1:26	1:55	2:53	3:50	4:48	5:45
7:45	0:58	1:27	1:56	2:54	3:53	4:51	5:49
7:50	0:59	1:28	1:58	2:56	3:55	4:54	5:53
7:55	0:59	1:29	1:59	2:58	3:58	4:57	5:56
8:00	1:00	1:30	2:00	3:00	4:00	5:00	6:00
8:05	1:01	1:31	2:01	3:02	4:03	5:03	6:04
8:10	1:01	1:32	2:03	3:04	4:05	5:06	6:08
8:15	1:02	1:33	2:04	3:06	4:08	5:09	6:11
8:20	1:03	1:34	2:05	3:08	4:10	5:13	6:15
8:25	1:03	1:35	2:06	3:09	4:13	5:16	6:19
8:30	1:04	1:36	2:08	3:11	4:15	5:19	6:23
8:35	1:04	1:37	2:09	3:13	4:18	5:22	6:26
8:40	1:05	1:38	2:10	3:15	4:20	5:25	6:30
8:45	1:06	1:38	2:11	3:17	4:23	5:28	6:34
8:50	1:06	1:39	2:13	3:19	4:25	5:31	6:38
8:55	1:07	1:40	2:14	3:21	4:28	5:34	6:41
9:00	1:08	1:41	2:15	3:23	4:30	5:38	6:45

(continued page 276)

Pace per Mile		5K	5 mile	10K	15K	10 mile	20K	Half-Marathon	Marathon
	4:30	13:58	22:30	27:57	41:55	45:00	55:53	58:57	1:57:54
	4:35	14:14	22:55	28:28	42:42	45:50	56:56	1:00:03	2:00:05
	4:40	14:29	23:20	28:59	43:28	46:40	57:58	1:01:08	2:02:16
	4:45	14:45	23:45	29:30	44:15	47:30	59:00	1:02:14	2:04:27
	4:50	15:00	24:10	30:01	45:01	48:20	1:00:02	1:03:19	2:06:38
	4:55	15:16	24:35	30:32	45:48	49:10	1:01:04	1:04:25	2:08:49
	5:00	15:32	25:00	31:03	46:35	50:00	1:02:06	1:05:30	2:11:00
	5:05	15:47	25:25	31:34	47:21	50:50	1:03:08	1:06:36	2:13:11
	5:10	16:03	25:50	32:05	48:08	51:40	1:04:10	1:07:41	2:15:22
	5:15	16:18	26:15	32:36	48:54	52:30	1:05:12	1:08:47	2:17:33
	5:20	16:34	26:40	33:07	49:41	53:20	1:06:14	1:09:52	2:19:44
	5:25	16:49	27:05	33:38	50:27	54:10	1:07:17	1:10:58	2:21:55
	5:30	17:05	27:30	34:09	51:14	55:00	1:08:19	1:12:03	2:24:06
	5:35	17:20	27:55	34:40	52:01	55:50	1:09:21	1:13:09	2:26:17
	5:40	17:36	28:20	35:11	52:47	56:40	1:10:23	1:14:14	2:28:28
	5:45	17:51	28:45	35:42	53:34	57:30	1:11:25	1:15:20	2:30:39
	5:50	18:07	29:10	36:14	54:20	58:20	1:12:27	1:16:25	2:32:50
	5:55	18:22	29:35	36:45	55:07	59:10	1:13:29	1:17:31	2:35:01
	6:00	18:38	30:00	37:16	55:53	1:00:00	1:14:31	1:18:36	2:37:12
	6:05	18:53	30:25	37:47	56:40	1:00:50	1:15:33	1:19:42	2:39:23
	6:10	19:09	30:50	38:18	57:27	1:01:40	1:16:35	1:20:47	2:41:34
	6:15	19:24	31:15	38:49	58:13	1:02:30	1:17:38	1:21:53	2:43:45
	6:20	19:40	31:40	39:20	59:00	1:03:20	1:18:40	1:22:58	2:45:56
	6:25	19:55	32:05	39:51	59:46	1:04:10	1:19:42	1:24:04	2:48:07
	6:30	20:11	32:30	40:22	1:00:33	1:05:00	1:20:44	1:25:09	2:50:18
	6:35	20:26	32:55	40:53	1:01:19	1:05:50	1:21:46	1:26:15	2:52:29
	6:40	20:42	33:20	41:24	1:02:06	1:06:40	1:22:48	1:27:20	2:54:40
	6:45	20:58	33:45	41:55	1:02:53	1:07:30	1:23:50	1:28:26	2:56:51
	6:50	21:13	34:10	42:26	1:03:39	1:08:20	1:24:52	1:29:31	2:59:02
	6:55	21:29	34:35	42:57	1:04:26	1:09:10	1:25:54	1:30:37	3:01:13
	7:00	21:44	35:00	43:28	1:05:12	1:10:00	1:26:56	1:31:42	3:03:24
	7:05	22:00	35:25	43:59	1:05:59	1:10:50	1:27:59	1:32:48	3:05:35
	7:10	22:15	35:50	44:30	1:06:45	1:11:40	1:29:01	1:33:53	3:07:46
	7:15	22:31	36:15	45:01	1:07:32	1:12:30	1:30:03	1:34:59	3:09:57
	7:20	22:46	36:40	45:32	1:08:19	1:13:20	1:31:05	1:36:04	3:12:08
	7:25	23:02	37:05	46:03	1:09:05	1:14:10	1:32:07	1:37:10	3:14:19
	7:30	23:17	37:30	46:35	1:09:52	1:15:00	1:33:09	1:38:15	3:16:30
	7:35	23:33	37:55	47:06	1:10:38	1:15:50	1:34:11	1:39:21	3:18:41
	7:40	23:48	38:20	47:37	1:11:25	1:16:40	1:35:13	1:40:26	3:20:52
	7:45	24:04	38:45	48:08	1:12:11	1:17:30	1:36:15	1:41:32	3:23:03
	7:50	24:19	39:10	48:39	1:12:58	1:18:20	1:37:17	1:42:37	3:25:14
	7:55	24:35	39:35	49:10	1:13:45	1:19:10	1:38:20	1:43:43	3:27:25
	8:00	24:50	40:00	49:41	1:14:31	1:20:00	1:39:22	1:44:48	3:29:36
	8:05	25:06	40:25	50:12	1:15:18	1:20:50	1:40:24	1:45:54	3:31:47
	8:10	25:21	40:50	50:43	1:16:04	1:21:40	1:41:26	1:46:59	3:33:58
	8:15	25:37	41:15	51:14	1:16:51	1:22:30	1:42:28	1:48:05	3:36:09
	8:20	25:53	41:40	51:45	1:17:38	1:23:20	1:43:30	1:49:10	3:38:20
	8:25	26:08	42:05	52:16	1:18:24	1:24:10	1:44:32	1:50:16	3:40:31
	8:30	26:24	42:30	52:47	1:19:11	1:25:00	1:45:34	1:51:21	3:42:42
	8:35	26:39	42:55	53:18	1:19:57	1:25:50	1:46:36	1:52:27	3:44:53
	8:40	26:55	43:20	53:49	1:20:44	1:26:40	1:47:38	1:53:32	3:47:04
	8:45	27:10	43:45	54:20	1:21:30	1:27:30	1:48:41	1:54:38	3:49:15
	8:50	27:26	44:10	54:51	1:22:17	1:28:20	1:49:43	1:55:43	3:51:26
	8:55	27:41	44:35	55:22	1:23:04	1:29:10	1:50:45	1:56:49	3:53:37
	9:00	27:57	45:00	55:53	1:23:50	1:30:00	1:51:47	1:57:54	3:55:48

(continued page 277)

Mile Pace	Duration of Interval						
	200 m	300 m	400 m	600 m	800 m	1,000 m	1,200 m
9:05	1:08	1:42	2:16	3:24	4:33	5:41	6:49
9:10	1:09	1:43	2:18	3:26	4:35	5:44	6:53
9:15	1:09	1:44	2:19	3:28	4:38	5:47	6:56
9:20	1:10	1:45	2:20	3:30	4:40	5:50	7:00
9:25	1:11	1:46	2:21	3:32	4:43	5:53	7:04
9:30	1:11	1:47	2:23	3:34	4:45	5:56	7:08
9:35	1:12	1:48	2:24	3:36	4:48	5:59	7:11
9:40	1:13	1:49	2:25	3:38	4:50	6:03	7:15
9:45	1:13	1:50	2:26	3:39	4:53	6:06	7:19
9:50	1:14	1:51	2:28	3:41	4:55	6:09	7:23
9:55	1:14	1:52	2:29	3:43	4:58	6:12	7:26
10:00	1:15	1:53	2:30	3:45	5:00	6:15	7:30
10:05	1:16	1:53	2:31	3:47	5:03	6:18	7:34
10:10	1:16	1:54	2:33	3:49	5:05	6:21	7:38
10:15	1:17	1:55	2:34	3:51	5:08	6:24	7:41
10:20	1:18	1:56	2:35	3:53	5:10	6:28	7:45
10:25	1:18	1:57	2:36	3:54	5:13	6:31	7:49
10:30	1:19	1:58	2:38	3:56	5:15	6:34	7:53
10:35	1:19	1:59	2:39	3:58	5:18	6:37	7:56
10:40	1:20	2:00	2:40	4:00	5:20	6:40	8:00
10:45	1:21	2:01	2:41	4:02	5:23	6:43	8:04
10:50	1:21	2:02	2:43	4:04	5:25	6:46	8:08
10:55	1:22	2:03	2:44	4:06	5:28	6:49	8:11
11:00	1:23	2:04	2:45	4:08	5:30	6:53	8:15
11:05	1:23	2:05	2:46	4:09	5:33	6:56	8:19
11:10	1:24	2:06	2:48	4:11	5:35	6:59	8:23
11:15	1:24	2:07	2:49	4:13	5:38	7:02	8:26
11:20	1:25	2:08	2:50	4:15	5:40	7:05	8:30
11:25	1:26	2:08	2:51	4:17	5:43	7:08	8:34
11:30	1:26	2:09	2:53	4:19	5:45	7:11	8:38
11:35	1:27	2:10	2:54	4:21	5:48	7:14	8:41
11:40	1:28	2:11	2:55	4:23	5:50	7:18	8:45
11:45	1:28	2:12	2:56	4:24	5:53	7:21	8:49
11:50	1:29	2:13	2:58	4:26	5:55	7:24	8:53
11:55	1:29	2:14	2:59	4:28	5:58	7:27	8:56
12:00	1:30	2:15	3:00	4:30	6:00	7:30	9:00
12:05	1:31	2:16	3:01	4:32	6:02	7:33	9:04
12:10	1:31	2:17	3:02	4:34	6:05	7:36	9:07
12:15	1:32	2:18	3:04	4:36	6:07	7:39	9:11
12:20	1:32	2:19	3:05	4:37	6:10	7:42	9:15
12:25	1:33	2:20	3:06	4:39	6:12	7:46	9:19
12:30	1:34	2:21	3:07	4:41	6:15	7:49	9:22
12:35	1:34	2:22	3:09	4:43	6:17	7:52	9:26
12:40	1:35	2:22	3:10	4:45	6:20	7:55	9:30
12:45	1:36	2:23	3:11	4:47	6:22	7:58	9:34
12:50	1:36	2:24	3:12	4:49	6:25	8:01	9:37
12:55	1:37	2:25	3:14	4:51	6:27	8:04	9:41
13:00	1:37	2:26	3:15	4:52	6:30	8:07	9:45
13:05	1:38	2:27	3:16	4:54	6:32	8:11	9:49
13:10	1:39	2:28	3:17	4:56	6:35	8:14	9:52
13:15	1:39	2:29	3:19	4:58	6:37	8:17	9:56
13:20	1:40	2:30	3:20	5:00	6:40	8:20	10:10
13:25	1:41	2:31	3:21	5:02	6:42	8:23	10:14
13:30	1:41	2:32	3:22	5:04	6:45	8:26	10:17

Pace per Mile		Finishing Time in Race							
		5K	5 mile	10K	15K	10 mile	20K	Half-Marathon	Marathon
	9:05	28:12	45:25	56:24	1:24:37	1:30:50	1:52:49	1:59:00	3:57:59
	9:10	28:28	45:50	56:56	1:25:23	1:31:40	1:53:51	2:00:05	4:00:10
	9:15	28:43	46:15	57:27	1:26:10	1:32:30	1:54:53	2:01:11	4:02:21
	9:20	28:59	46:40	57:58	1:26:56	1:33:20	1:55:55	2:02:16	4:04:32
	9:25	29:14	47:05	58:29	1:27:43	1:34:10	1:56:57	2:03:22	4:06:43
	9:30	29:30	47:30	59:00	1:28:30	1:35:00	1:57:59	2:04:27	4:08:54
	9:35	29:45	47:55	59:31	1:29:16	1:35:50	1:59:02	2:05:33	4:11:05
	9:40	30:01	48:20	1:00:02	1:30:03	1:36:40	2:00:04	2:06:38	4:13:16
	9:45	30:16	48:45	1:00:33	1:30:49	1:37:30	2:01:06	2:07:44	4:15:27
	9:50	30:32	49:10	1:01:04	1:31:36	1:38:20	2:02:08	2:08:49	4:17:38
	9:55	30:47	49:35	1:01:35	1:32:22	1:39:10	2:03:10	2:09:55	4:19:49
	10:00	31:03	50:00	1:02:06	1:33:09	1:40:00	2:04:12	2:11:00	4:22:00
	10:05	31:19	50:25	1:02:37	1:33:56	1:40:50	2:05:14	2:12:06	4:24:11
	10:10	31:34	50:50	1:03:08	1:34:42	1:41:40	2:06:16	2:13:11	4:26:22
	10:15	31:50	51:15	1:03:39	1:35:29	1:42:30	2:07:18	2:14:17	4:28:33
	10:20	32:05	51:40	1:04:10	1:36:15	1:43:20	2:08:20	2:15:22	4:30:44
	10:25	32:21	52:05	1:04:41	1:37:02	1:44:10	2:09:23	2:16:28	4:32:55
	10:30	32:36	52:30	1:05:12	1:37:48	1:45:00	2:10:25	2:17:33	4:35:06
	10:35	32:52	52:55	1:05:43	1:38:35	1:45:50	2:11:27	2:18:39	4:37:17
	10:40	33:07	53:20	1:06:14	1:39:22	1:46:40	2:12:29	2:19:44	4:39:28
	10:45	33:23	53:45	1:06:45	1:40:08	1:47:30	2:13:31	2:20:50	4:41:39
	10:50	33:38	54:10	1:07:17	1:40:55	1:48:20	2:14:33	2:21:55	4:43:50
	10:55	33:54	54:35	1:07:48	1:41:41	1:49:10	2:15:35	2:23:01	4:46:01
	11:00	34:09	55:00	1:08:19	1:42:28	1:50:00	2:16:37	2:24:06	4:48:12
	11:05	34:25	55:25	1:08:50	1:43:14	1:50:50	2:17:39	2:25:12	4:50:23
	11:10	34:40	55:50	1:09:21	1:44:01	1:51:40	2:18:41	2:26:17	4:52:34
	11:15	34:56	56:15	1:09:52	1:44:48	1:52:30	2:19:44	2:27:23	4:54:45
	11:20	35:11	56:40	1:10:23	1:45:34	1:53:20	2:20:46	2:28:28	4:56:56
	11:25	35:27	57:05	1:10:54	1:46:21	1:54:10	2:21:48	2:29:34	4:59:07
	11:30	35:42	57:30	1:11:25	1:47:07	1:55:00	2:22:50	2:30:39	5:01:18
	11:35	35:58	57:55	1:11:56	1:47:54	1:55:50	2:23:52	2:31:45	5:03:29
	11:40	36:14	58:20	1:12:27	1:48:41	1:56:40	2:24:54	2:32:50	5:05:40
	11:45	36:29	58:45	1:12:58	1:49:27	1:57:30	2:25:56	2:33:56	5:07:51
	11:50	36:45	59:10	1:13:29	1:50:14	1:58:20	2:26:58	2:35:01	5:10:02
	11:55	37:00	59:35	1:14:00	1:51:00	1:59:10	2:28:00	2:36:07	5:12:13
	12:00	37:16	1:00:00	1:14:31	1:51:47	2:00:00	2:29:02	2:37:12	5:14:24
	12:05	37:31	1:00:25	1:15:02	1:52:33	2:00:50	2:30:04	2:38:17	5:16:35
	12:10	37:47	1:00:50	1:15:33	1:53:20	2:01:40	2:31:07	2:39:23	5:18:46
	12:15	38:02	1:01:15	1:16:04	1:54:07	2:02:30	2:32:09	2:40:28	5:20:57
	12:20	38:18	1:01:40	1:16:35	1:54:53	2:03:20	2:33:11	2:41:34	5:23:08
	12:25	38:33	1:02:05	1:17:06	1:55:40	2:04:10	2:34:13	2:42:39	5:25:19
	12:30	38:49	1:02:30	1:17:37	1:56:26	2:05:00	2:35:15	2:43:45	5:27:30
	12:35	39:04	1:02:55	1:18:09	1:57:13	2:05:50	2:36:17	2:44:50	5:29:41
	12:40	39:20	1:03:20	1:18:40	1:57:59	2:06:40	2:37:19	2:45:56	5:31:52
	12:45	39:35	1:03:45	1:19:11	1:58:46	2:07:30	2:38:21	2:47:01	5:34:03
	12:50	39:51	1:04:10	1:19:42	1:59:33	2:08:20	2:39:23	2:48:07	5:36:14
	12:55	40:06	1:04:35	1:20:13	2:00:19	2:09:10	2:40:25	2:49:12	5:38:25
	13:00	40:22	1:05:00	1:20:44	2:01:06	2:10:00	2:41:28	2:50:18	5:40:36
	13:05	40:37	1:05:25	1:21:15	2:01:52	2:10:50	2:42:30	2:51:23	5:42:47
	13:10	40:53	1:05:50	1:21:46	2:02:39	2:11:40	2:43:32	2:52:29	5:44:58
	13:15	41:08	1:06:15	1:22:17	2:03:25	2:12:30	2:44:34	2:53:34	5:47:09
	13:20	41:24	1:06:40	1:22:48	2:04:12	2:13:20	2:45:36	2:54:40	5:49:20
	13:25	41:40	1:07:05	1:23:19	2:04:59	2:14:10	2:46:38	2:55:45	5:51:31
	13:30	41:55	1:07:30	1:23:50	2:05:45	2:15:00	2:47:40	2:56:51	5:53:42

INDEX

concentric contractions, versus eccentric, 97, **98**
confidence, building, 158–60
cooldowns, 45, 47
corners, and racing pace, 196–98
cross-country running, 259–60
cross-training, 110–11
crunches, 104, **105**

D
Daniels' Running Formula (Daniels), 65
dead lifts, **103**–4
dead zones, 34–35
dehydration. *See* hydration
depletion-rebound diet, 229–30
diaries. *See* training diaries/ logs
diet. *See also* eating; meals; nutrition
  depletion-rebound, 229–30
  of elite athlete versus average, 115
dieting, 123–25
digestive upsets, 150, 154
dinners, prerace, 177–78
distance categories, of races, 10
  training volume and, 40
DMSO (dimethyl sulfoxide), 147–48
double-leg reverse crunches, **108**
doubts, fighting, 160–61
duathlons, 270

E
eating. *See also* diet; meals; nutrition
  after the race, 209
  before evening races, 182
  gel packs, 205–6, 235–36

eccentric contractions, versus concentric, 97, **98**
endurance training. *See* base training
equipment. *See also* shoes, about; shoes, types of
  pace calculator, **15**, 18
  race clothing, 180–81
  running watch, 15, 18
  training diaries/logs, 14–15, **16–17**, 160, **212**
evening races, 182
even splits, 191
excess pronation, 58, 143, 144–**46**
excess supination, 58, 143, 144–**46**
exercises. *See* lower-body exercises; stretches, types of; upper-body exercises

F
failure, accepting, 162–63
fartlek-style workouts, 78–79, 224–25
fast-twitch muscles, 27
fat, 117, 124
fatigue
  fighting, 164–65
  reading level of, 199
figure-four stretches, 90–**91**
finishing the race. *See also* race day; running the race; starting the race
  crossing the finish line, 208–9
  kicks, 207–8
  keeping moving, 209
  post-finish checklist, 209
  rehydrating and eating, 209
flats (shoes), 13, 215
following, versus leading, 256
food. *See* diet; eating; meals; nutrition

food allergies and intolerances, 117
foot alignment, 58–59
form, running, 50–51, 59–60
  belly breathing versus chest breathing, **54**
  leg motion, 55–59, **56**, **57**
  upper-body, **50**, **51**–53, 55
  using speed workouts to improve, 65, 66

G
Gebresailesse, Haile, 59–60
gels, 205–6, 235–36
glycogen, 26–27
goal-setting, 2–3, 63–65, 66, 158–59. *See also* mental attitude; personal records (PRs)
Gomez, Rodolfo, 257
groin stretches, **90**
group workouts, 78

H
hamstring curls, **100**
hamstring stretches, 88–**89**
handicap races, 262–63
hard-easy training patterns, 41
heart conditions, 20
heart rate
  checking, 43–45
  target-heart-rate speed workouts, 76–77
heart-rate monitors, 43–45, 76–77
heat stroke, 155, 156
heat, for injuries, 128
heel bruises, 148–49, 151
high blood pressure, 21
High-Powered Plyometrics (Radcliffe and Farentinos), 110

P

pace
  benchmark, 67–68
  computing, 18–19
  conditions affecting,
    192–98
  expressing, 12
  fine-tuning, 198–200
  going out at your target,
    187–89
  LSD, 42–43
  per mile, and finishing
    times, 213, 214
  training and, 34–35
pace bands, 172
pace calculators, **15**, 18
pace chart, of common
    workout and racing
    distances, 273–77
passing, 257
patellar straps, 143, **145**
personal records (PRs),
    11, 64, 65, 166–67,
    169–70. *See also* goal-
    setting; mental atti-
    tude
phosphocreatine, 24–26
plantar fasciitis, 133,
    137–38
"plods." *See* overtraining
plyometrics, 109–10
positive splits, 192
postrace recovery and
    planning. *See also* race
    day
  deciding how often to
    race, 214–16
  marathons, 238–39
  planning your next race,
    212–14
  programs for various dis-
    tances, 210, 211
  reviewing your perform-
    ance, 210, 212
  taking time off, 215–16
predicted-time races,
    262
pregnancy, 19–20

prerace preparations. *See
    also* race day
  going to bed early, 177,
    178
  picking up your packet,
    176–77
  prerace dinners, 177–78
  previewing the course,
    173, 175
  registering, 176
  rest, 176, 177, 178
  setting mile-marker tar-
    get times, 172–73
  tapering your training,
    175–76, 226–27
pronation, excess, 58, 143,
    144–**46**
protein, 116–17
purses, safeguarding, 184
pyramid workouts, 75–76

Q

quadriceps extensions, **100**
quadriceps stretches, **89**–90

R

race day, 179. *See also* finish-
    ing the race; postrace
    recovery and planning;
    prerace preparations;
    running the race; start-
    ing the race
  checklist for, 185
  clothing and supplies,
    180–81
  eating before evening
    races, 182
  eating breakfast, 181–82,
    231–32
  feeling sluggish on, 185
  getting up, 180
  lining up, 186–87
  safeguarding wallets and
    car keys, 184
  using caffeine, 182
  warming up, 183–86, 232
race plans, and speed work-
    outs, 65, 70–75

races, choosing, 171–72,
    173, 200
races, types of, 10. *See also*
    marathon racing,
    about; marathon
    racing, training for;
    marathons, specific;
    masters running
  cross-country, 259–60
  duathlons, 270
  evening, 182
  handicap, 262–63
  mega-, 263–68
  predicted-time, 262
  relay, 260–62
  speed workouts and, 65,
    70–75, 79
  trail, 259–60
  triathlons, 269–70
  ultramarathons, 270–71
race timing, 174
racing. *See also* mental
    attitude
  becoming a runner first,
    12
  distance categories, 10,
    40
  knowing your reasons for,
    9
  picking a distance, 7
  popularity of, 1
  weight divisions, 122
racing shoes, 13
reaching out/overstriding,
    55–58, **56, 57**
recovery. *See* postrace
    recovery and planning
recovery breaks, in interval
    workouts, 61, 69–70
relaxation, prerace, 163–64
relay races, 260–62
repeats, interval workouts,
    61, 69
rest. *See also* postrace re-
    covery and planning;
    prerace preparations
  base training rest days,
    42